The Making of Criminal Justice Policy

This new textbook will provide students of criminology with a better understanding of criminal justice policy and, in doing so, offers a framework for analysing the social, economic and political processes that shape its creation. The book adopts a policy-oriented approach to criminal justice, connecting the study of criminology to the wider study of British government, public administration and politics.

Throughout the book, the focus is on key debates and competing perspectives on how policy decisions are made. Recognising that contemporary criminal justice policy-makers operate in a highly politicised, public arena under the gaze of an ever-increasing variety of groups, organisations and individuals who have a stake in a particular policy issue, the book explores how and why these people seek to influence policy-making. It also recognises that criminal policy differs from other areas of public policy, as policy decisions affect the liberty and freedoms of citizens. Throughout the book, key ideas and debates are linked to wider sociology, criminology and social policy theory.

Key features include:

- a foreword by Tim Newburn, leading criminologist and author of *Criminology* (2nd edn, 2013);
- a critical and informed analysis of the concepts, ideas and institutional practices that shape criminal justice policy-making;
- an exploration of the relationship between criminal justice and wider social policy;
- a critical analysis of the debate about how and why behaviour becomes defined as requiring a criminal justice solution;
- a range of case studies, critical thinking discussion topics, seminar tasks and recommended further reading to keep the student engaged.

This text is perfect for students taking modules in criminology, criminal justice, and social and public policy, as well as those taking courses on criminal and administrative law.

Sue Hobbs is a Senior Research Officer in the Home Office. She is currently part of a research team investigating criminal justice policy and practice in the 1980s.

Christopher Hamerton is currently Senior Lecturer specialising in Socio-Legal Studies and Criminology at Kingston University, where he leads the MA Cybercrime degree.

'How does criminal justice policy get made? More importantly, who has the greatest influence? . . . and how? . . . and why? This book critically explores the making and breaking of criminal justice policy, showing just how political criminal justice policy making can be. In a number of striking case studies the book explores who pulls the strings, who holds the purse, who shouts the loudest and whether this is what really makes the difference. The book is a particularly useful addition to criminal justice studies and criminology, drawing upon the insights of policy studies to explain how laws get made, while comprising plenty of useful activities to develop in the classroom.'

– Peter Squires, Professor of Criminology & Public Policy,
University of Brighton, UK

'A fresh, original and highly stimulating approach to the study of criminal justice policy.'

– Professor Emeritus David Downes, Mannheim Centre, LSE, UK

'Many practising and academic criminal lawyers complain frequently about the never-ending stream of criminal justice legislation, as they would complain about the weather. *The Making of Criminal Justice Policy* goes far beyond a critique of the final form and content of legislation. It explains in social, economic and political terms how the policies emerge which ultimately cash out in terms of the legislation that we have. Lawyers, as well as criminologists, should read this book and be educated by it in the fullest sense of that term.'

– Bob Sullivan, Professor of Criminal Law, University of Sussex; Emeritus
Professor of Law, University College, London, UK

'This is a stand-out read among the current criminal justice textbooks on the international market. It does not overly simplify its subject matter, but with detailed real-world examples it gives a lucid account of the complexities of policy-making in contemporary criminal justice.'

– Professor Stephen Tomsen, Sociology and Criminology,
University of Western Sydney, Australia

The Making of Criminal Justice Policy

Sue Hobbs and Christopher Hamerton

Routledge
Taylor & Francis Group

LONDON AND NEW YORK

First published 2014
by Routledge
2 Park Square, Milton Park, Abingdon, Oxon, OX14 4RN

and by Routledge
711 Third Avenue, New York, NY 10017

Routledge is an imprint of the Taylor & Francis Group, an informa business

© 2014 Sue Hobbs and Christopher Hamerton

British Library Cataloguing in Publication Data
A catalogue record for this book is available from the British Library

Library of Congress Cataloging-in-Publication Data
  Hobbs, Sue.
  The making of criminal justice policy / Sue Hobbs and Christopher
  Hamerton.
    pages cm.
  Includes bibliographical references.
1. Criminal justice, Administration of--Great Britain. 2. Crime—
Government policy—Great Britain. I. Hamerton, Christopher. II. Title.
  HV9960.G7H63 2014
  364.941—dc23

                                                      2013041325

ISBN: 978–0–415–67695–3 (hbk)
ISBN: 978–0–415–67696–0 (pbk)
ISBN: 978–1–315–79808–0 (ebk)

Typeset in Times New Roman
by RefineCatch Limited, Bungay, Suffolk

MIX
Paper from
responsible sources
FSC   FSC® C013604
www.fsc.org

Printed and bound by CPI Group (UK) Ltd, Croydon, CR0 4YY

Contents

Notes on authors

Sue Hobbs

Sue Hobbs is currently part of a Home Office-funded research team carrying out an independent investigation into criminal justice policy and practice in the 1980s.

She holds degrees in English Literature and Economic and Social History and Sociology and Social Policy from Manchester Polytechnic and Durham University. She has wide practice experience in the area of criminal justice, and is a former Senior Probation Officer. She worked for eight years as a Senior Lecturer in Community Justice (Probation), delivering teaching on the Home Office-approved degree programme that leads to qualification as a Probation Officer, before joining Kingston University as a Senior Lecturer in Criminology in 2006. She retired from teaching in 2012. She retains an active interest in probation practice and policy development. She recently undertook research for the National Offender Management Service into the transition of young adult offenders from the youth to the adult offending services, and has acted as an academic advisor to Her Majesty's Inspectorate of Probation.

Christopher Hamerton

Christopher Hamerton is currently Senior Lecturer specialising in Socio-Legal Studies and Criminology at Kingston University, where he leads the MA Cybercrime degree. He is also Director of Legal Studies in the Departmental Research Centre, where his role encompasses direction and leadership in socio-legal research. Christopher holds degrees in Law (LLB (Hons), BCL) and Criminal Justice (MA) as a graduate of the Universities of Oxford and Southampton. In addition, he is a Barrister of the Honourable Society of the Middle Temple, and was elected a Fellow of the Royal Anthropological Institute in 2008. He is co-author with Julia Davidson of *International Perspectives on Child Victimisation*, also published by Routledge. His criminal justice policy research interests include theoretical perspectives on the criminal justice process, legal pluralism and international responses to globalised crime.

Foreword

The study of criminology and criminal justice has expanded very markedly in the last decade or so. In parallel, academic publishing in this field has also grown like Topsy. Not only is it impossible to keep up with all the latest literature in criminology, but it is also hard to keep abreast even of sub-fields within the subject. Nowhere has the expansion in publishing in this field been more evident than in relation to textbooks and other materials aimed at the student market. Given this, one might be forgiven for asking 'why another textbook?' The only serious answer to this question involves the filling of some extant gap and/or approaching the subject in a novel way. I am pleased to say that *The Making of Criminal Justice Policy* does both of these things – and does them admirably. Let me explain how.

First, as the title implies, it deals with 'policy'. Now, there is no shortage of texts that talk about policy, and in some cases may even offer some analysis of policy. However, that is where they generally stop. The study of *policy-making* is almost always absent. The tendency is usually to assume that policy documents and legislation – the end result of policy – are all that needs to be studied. Not so. The end results are usually a compromise – a serendipitous and sometimes pragmatic outcome of conflicting demands and necessary trade-offs. That this is the case should give the analyst of policy pause for thought before reading into policy grand designs and rational calculation on the part of political leaders. In short, what our governments end up doing is almost always different – sometimes very different – from what they set out intending to achieve. One of this book's great contributions, therefore, is to introduce students to some of the realities of policy-making and politics.

This leads me neatly to the second point, for again it concerns politics. While criminological texts often discuss the politics of criminal justice, they tend to do so with little reference to political science literature. This reflects an interesting, although odd, dysjuncture between criminology and political science. On the one hand, criminology tends not to engage with political science literature. On the other hand, political science tends to have little or no interest in crime and criminal justice. Here again, *The Making of Criminal Justice Policy* seeks to break the mould, and students will benefit hugely from being introduced to some of the central ideas and key concepts in political science, for these are important tools of which all criminologists should be aware.

Third, *The Making of Criminal Justice Policy* locates criminal justice within the broader sweep of social and public policy. This is vital, for the context of policy – whether it is criminal justice or penal policy – is central to understanding its aetiology, its wider importance and its impact. It is also important because it puts criminal justice and penal policy into perspective. Part of this simply involves the realisation that it is not necessarily *the* most important part of government business (even though criminologists may appear to think it is). Although the Home Office, for example, has long been thought of as one of the 'great offices of state', and for a period of time in the 1980s and 1990s the crime issue really did seem to be important electorally, the reality is that crime policy has more usually been a low agenda item for governments, and taking responsibility for policy in this area has rarely been seen as a good career move. Keeping criminal justice in perspective is therefore an important and significant contribution.

Finally, while the subject is necessarily complex, the authors have written a text that explains straightforwardly without oversimplifying, which uses case studies to allow a somewhat more in-depth coverage and analysis of particular issues, and which links to electronic media in order that students can keep up to date with the fast-moving worlds of policy and politics. *The Making of Criminal Justice Policy* is consequently broad-ranging, accessible, up to date, practical, provocative and innovative. It is sure to become a staple not only for criminology/criminal justice students and teachers, but also for many studying social policy and administration, public law and political science, and to the lay reader wishing a thorough grounding in contemporary criminal justice policy and law-making.

Tim Newburn
London School of Economics

Acknowledgements

Sue would like to thank Dr Stephanie Eaton and Dr Carlie Goldsmith of Kingston University for their invaluable contributions to the project. Their enthusiastic support for the project from its inception, their willingness to provide material and their helpful feedback during the writing stage meant that all the cups of coffee in Picton weren't a waste of time.

Chris would like to thank his fellow directors at the Centre for Abuse and Trauma Studies, Julia Davidson and Toni Bifulco, for providing friendship and intellectual stimulus over the past six years. Thanks are also due to Ramiro Sagarduy for the invitation to contribute to his Controversies in Criminal Justice course at the University of Westminster, and the frequent criminal policy conferences thereafter at the Cock Tavern in Great Portland Street.

Both authors would like to express their gratitude to Tim Newburn of the London School of Economics for providing the foreword, and the editorial team at Routledge, Nicola Hartley, Tom Sutton, and Heidi Lee, for their continuing enthusiasm and unwavering support for this project.

Dedicated to our 'kids' – Patrick and Nik, and Laura and Henry.

List of abbreviations

ACMD	Advisory Council on the Misuse of Drugs
ASB	Anti-social behaviour
ASBO	Anti Social Behaviour Order
BMA	British Medical Association
CA	Countryside Alliance
CCA	Corrections Corporation of America
CDRP	Crime and Disorder Reduction Partnerships
CJA	Criminal Justice Alliance
CPS	Centre for Policy Studies
CRP	Crime reduction programme
EBP	Evidence-based policy-making
ECHR	European Convention on Human Rights
EctHR	European Court of Human Rights
EU	European Union
GDP	Gross domestic product
HO	Home Office
LACS	League Against Cruel Sports
MoJ	Ministry of Justice
MP	Member of parliament
NACRO	National Association for the Care and Rehabilitation of Offenders
PFI	Private Finance Initiative
RDS	Research, Development and Statistics
RSPCA	Royal Society for the Prevention of Cruelty to Animals
SCP	Situational crime prevention
SDP	Strategic Development Projects
SIAC	Special Immigration Appeals Commission
UDHR	Universal Declaration of Human Rights
UKDS	UK Detention Services Ltd
UN	United Nations

1 Introduction

Outrage, frustration, curiosity and surprise have led many people into the study of crime and justice. It might be a newspaper article describing a punishment that seems unduly lenient, or a statement about the mental health of prisoners, or a rise in the number of children in detention. Something, though, triggers a concern that will not go away. Consternation at the apparent lack of 'common sense' in justice is as good a reason as any to stimulate inquiry.

Once the process of asking questions begins, critical analysis of the system follows, and this inevitably leads to views about what is wrong and how to change the system, to improve it or at the very least refine the way it does what it does. It might even lead to a conclusion that something is as good as it can be. This book adopts a policy-oriented approach to criminal justice that connects the study of criminology to the wider study of British government, public administration and politics. Throughout, we focus on key debates and competing perspectives on how policy decisions are made. With this in mind, we will be asking you to consider the groups, organisations and individuals who have a stake in a particular policy issue, and will explore how different stakeholders in criminal justice and punishment mobilise power to influence policy. Inevitably, we will be encouraging you to think about how some groups emerge as 'winners' and others as 'losers' in relation to a specific policy area.

If the rationale for trying to understand a system is to make the system better, then studying criminal justice policy-making is a direct way in which we can explore how the ideas and knowledge of criminologists help us to make sense of why the system operates in the way that it does. Policy-making that drives change in legislation, procedures, definitions and organisational culture offers scope for reducing the harms of crime and enhancing the efficacy or fairness of punishment. While criminologists offer us a range of views on where our attention should be focused, that urge to understand should ultimately lead us to want to *do something* – to correct an injustice, to better manage resources, to expose discrimination. With this in mind, the book describes the process by which criminal justice policy is adopted or created, and explores the frequently messy and contradictory realities of the process.

Who has a stake in criminal justice policy-making?

The view adopted in this book is that the criminal justice policy-making process is a complex and multifaceted process that involves the interplay of numerous individuals and interest groups, alternately competing and collaborating to influence policy-makers to act in a particular way. The authors argue throughout that while the decision to act (or not) is essentially a political one (with the balance of power always retained by the government), modern policy-makers share the political sphere with a proliferation of different interest and pressure groups that have a stake in criminal justice policy, and want to shape the policy process in favour of their vision and preferred outcomes. Although his depiction of politicians may be controversial, Naylor's (2004) description of criminal justice policy as the outcome of the process by which stakeholders (he highlights bureaucrats and police officials) with 'the benefits of co-operative elements of the media, mass market a problem, provide a diagnosis, then connive a prescription that naive or opportunistic politicians co-operate to pass into law' (p. xvi), provides a useful starting point for an analysis that recognises the centrality of interest group politics in criminal justice policy-making.

Policy-making, as Downes and Morgan (2002) remind us, is no longer the preserve of a small elite government 'inner circle' of civil servants and government officials. Rather, contemporary criminal justice policy-makers operate in a highly politicised, public arena under the gaze of an ever-increasing variety of actors with different levels of knowledge, power and influence, all of whom have a stake in the process and its outcomes. Some of these actors (such as commercial organisations and trade unions) are primarily concerned with promoting their own material welfare, whereas others (such as penal reformers) are cause-oriented. The differing levels of power and influence that these individuals and groups wield, and the closeness (or otherwise) of their relationship to the government, have led some to talk about 'insiders' and 'outsiders'.

The insider/outsider pressure group thesis

The insider/outsider thesis differentiates between groups that have considerable political influence and maintain close consultative relationships with the senior echelons of government and senior civil servants, and those which operate at the margins of the body politic. While insider groups have the 'ear of the government', are trusted by the departments and 'play by' the formal rules of policy-making, outsider groups, some of whom are opposed to the political system, exert pressure by less formal means. They seek to mobilise public opinion to their cause by activities such as rallies, protests and demonstrations. They rely heavily on the media coverage that activities such as these attract. On occasions, they resort to direct action to draw public attention to their cause. A recent example of direct action was the environmental group Greenpeace's attempts to occupy a Russian oil platform in protest against drilling in the Arctic, which resulted in 30 arrests on charges of piracy. The event attracted international press coverage (Vidal, 2013).

When identifying the distinguishing characteristics of insider groups, Page makes the following observations:

> First, we would expect insider groups to have frequent contacts with at least one ministry. Their frequent contacts would allow them to learn what proposals are likely to be decided on in the near future, give informal views on their merits and make sure that they are on the list for formal consultations. Second, we would expect insider groups to be consulted on virtually everything in their field; as insiders they should never be the last to know what is on the department's mind on matters that affect them and, indeed, they would have already had a chance to influence something before it is ever made public. Third, we would expect insider groups to be able to influence policy. To be 'on the list' for consultation by the department is of little importance if what the group has to say in the consultation process is routinely ignored . . . Although we would not expect groups to be able to influence decisions all the time, we might expect them to have a chance of influencing policy at least occasionally.
>
> (Page, 1999: 208)

Notwithstanding the argument that there is effectively a policy-making elite with stakeholders occupying different positions in the hierarchy of influence, all stakeholders, in principle, have at their disposal a range of both formal and informal means of influencing the policy-making process. Furthermore, while it is clearly the case that differential access to the government means that some groups for strategic or ideological reasons may favour the informal rather than the formal, the polarisation of groups into distinct groups as suggested by the insider/outsider thesis creates a false dichotomy of binary opposites. In reality, few groups conform to the ideal types and their characteristics place them on a continuum between the two poles (Page, 1999).

The formal processes available to policy-making stakeholders include: making policy submissions in response to public consultations, and giving evidence (by invitation) at select committees and statutory inquiries (such as Lord Scarman's inquiry after the Brixton disturbances in 1981). The informal processes include: lobbying (which has become increasingly prolific with the rise of the commercial lobbying firm), media campaigning, participating in demonstrations and petitioning.

Typology of stakeholders

The typology shown in the following box is indicative of the volume and range of criminal justice policy stakeholders.

Political parties: since the mid-1970s law and order has formed part of all political party manifestos, has featured in party conferences and has become an increasingly important electoral issue. Although political parties shape their policy agenda to fit with their ideological preferences and their electoral ambitions, some argue that a new 'punitive consensus' has been created, with parties trying to out-tough each other on law and order.

Public officials: such as the Home Office and Ministry of Justice civil servants and special policy advisors. They operate within the formal spheres of policy-making, turning the political visions of ministers into policy. They take evidence from policy entrepreneurs and 'experts' at select committees and through public consultations. They present policy proposals in official papers, and draft legislation. They issue policy directives to criminal justice professionals.

Criminal justice professionals and their representative organisations: such as judges, police, probation officers, prison officers, youth offender workers and crime and disorder enforcement officers. As practitioners they implement policy, and as trade unionists they lobby the government through their professional organisations (e.g. the National Association of Probation Officers). They provide formal submissions to public consultations, public inquiries and the Home Affairs Select Committee. As trade unionists, they can withdraw their labour and participate in demonstrations to promote their sectional interests, for example the probation officers' decision to 'walk out' in response to the outsourcing to the private and/or voluntary sector of all but high-risk cases.

Penal reform groups: such as the Howard League for Penal Reform, National Association for the Care and Rehabilitation of Offenders, Penal Reform Trust, Inquest and Women in Prison are cause-oriented groups. They tend to adopt a critical approach to government law and order policy. Many of these groups are well established, highly organised, operate with considerable professionalism and enjoy insider status. Those that have acquired insider status are invited to make formal submissions on policy issues and have their views taken into account. Although they have significant differences in terms of their ideological perspectives, constitutions and credibility with policy-makers, they share a broadly left of centre approach. They use a range of informal and formal tactics including lobbying ministers and conducting media campaigns on specific issues (such as the Howard League for Penal Reform on the detention of children in adult prisons).

Single-issue campaign groups: such as the Ben Kinsella Trust, which was established to tackle the single issue of knife crime following the murder of Ben Kinsella. Although some groups (such as Women in Prison) have longevity, others tend to come and go as the issue that has sparked their formation 'waxes and wanes'. Despite some cause groups (such as Sarah's

Law campaign group) attaining insider status, they tend to supplement engagement with formal policy-making processes with the adoption of tactics associated with outsider groups, seeking to publicise their causes through activities that will attract media attention.

Victims and those that lobby on their behalf: such as Victim Support, are cause groups that both provide practical and emotional assistance to victims of crime, and campaign on behalf of victims. They use formal and informal means to promote their cause. As the victim has moved from the margins of the criminal justice system, victims' organisations have increasingly become insider pressure groups, enjoying privileged access to ministers and their officials. They are central figures in formal consultation processes and tend to be on the list of groups that receive invitations to give evidence to the Home Affairs Select Committee and to make submissions to public consultations.

The general public: can express their preferences through the traditional means of the ballot box, as well as engaging in new forms of communication such as signing an e-petition to force a parliamentary debate, completing government online questionnaires on specific policy proposals, tweeting or emailing a member of parliament, taking part in opinion polls and focus groups, and giving feedback on talk-radio.

Media: whose voices increasingly serve as a 'proxy for public opinion'. They can act as important sources to publicise the interests of pressure groups, and mobilise public support behind specific campaigns such as Sarah's Law. As commercial enterprises, they tend to promote the policy preferences of their owners and readership. With the decline of the traditional elite, they are an important source of law and order knowledge, and play a role in public opinion formation.

Traditional and new experts: such as academics, commercial research companies and think tanks. The marketisation of research has created a wide pool of experts that governments can both consult and use to legitimate their policy decisions. Experts provide evidence to special advisors and ministers, through both formal and informal channels. In recent years, politicians have tended to prefer to consult think tanks rather than academics. However, think tanks are not politically neutral. They provide research and disseminate their data in order to promote the ideological or sectional interests of their members.

Multinational private firms that provide penal services: such as G4S and Serco. They use their close personal connections (the 'old boy' network) and the power of their financial contributions to political party coffers to gain the ear of politicians. Operating to promote the sectional interests of their members, they seek to influence governments to enact policies that will maximise their profit through the provision of penal services. They have a vested interest in global penal expansion.

International institutions and conventions of governance: such as the European Parliament, the North Atlantic Treaty Organization and the United Nations.

They issue international policy directives. The European Parliament passes judgments on the actions of member states (e.g. in relation to human rights) that they expect members to enact. The European Union sets the conditions for successor states to meet in terms of penal policy (such as the abolition of capital punishment) prior to gaining membership.

Sources: Downes and Morgan (2002),
Jones and Newburn (2002), Muncie (2005), Pratt (2007)

Although the authors acknowledge that politicians are faced with a wide array of policy stakeholders offering different policy options, we recognise that politics is both an ideological and a pragmatic business. As a consequence of this, we highlight the way in which politicians invariably favour those groups or organisations who offer pragmatic policy solutions that are broadly in line with their party political ideological preferences, and/or whom they perceive as bringing electoral advantage. Throughout, we recognise that, in the world of practical politics, politicians are in the business of staying in (or gaining) office, and are unlikely to pursue a policy agenda that will attract negative press coverage and/or will play badly at the ballot box. Indeed, we are conscious that there are examples of policy U turns that can be attributed to concerns that criminal justice policies have been contaminated in the eyes of the public by the press. The recent example of Ken Clarke (the Minister of Justice) being replaced by Chris Grayling can be interpreted as the Coalition government seeking to distance itself from a minister ridiculed as 'a teletubby living in la-la land' whose reformist penal policy proposals were the subject of a negative press campaign by the *Sun*, who denounced him as 'going soft on crime' (Baxter, 2011).

We accept that although the 1980s and early 1990s stand out as periods when reforming penal groups were successfully able to lobby for policies that reduced custody (particularly for juvenile offenders) (Downes and Morgan, 2002), the punitive consensus that gained momentum from the mid-1990s has meant that, while most ministers would agree with the need to reduce offending, successive governments have maintained a political reluctance to be seen to yield to the pressure exerted by 'official' stakeholders within central or local government or external interest groups who claim that there is evidence to demonstrate that the most effective way to do this is to de-criminalise some behaviours, and/or to support, encourage, incentivise and help offenders. As we discuss in one of the case studies in the book, a Home Office minister who is implacably opposed to the liberalisation of drug policy is unlikely to be interested in the evidence (even when it is provided by his own special advisor) that such an approach would reduce harm. Equally, a politician who wants to prove his 'tough on crime' credentials to an electorate that fears that crime is rising may decide to seek out policy ideas and strategies and theories from other jurisdictions (particularly the USA) that will provide sound bites such as 'three strikes and you're out' that are likely to attract sympathetic press coverage.

What is criminal justice policy?

Criminal justice policy-making is difficult. There are competing demands to be balanced – a selection of available benefits – and it is rarely possible to achieve them all. There are risks, and the costs of failure can be high – a victim's life and an offender's liberty. As Jonathan Wolff points out (Wolff 2011), what distinguishes public policy from philosophical inquiry is that a decision *has to be made*. In conditions of uncertainty, with incomplete data, with untested theories, with the clamour of the media, the decision-makers have to make decisions. Where Wolff is wrong, though, is to say that there is a bias towards the status quo – at least in the policy area of crime. The emotive, vivid and personal nature of crime, the impact of seeing victims' photographs in newspapers, the guilt and feeling that had we been there we would have, for example, saved the child from the abusive carers, means that politicians are frequently placed under intense pressure to do something, *anything*.

When talking about policy-making, we need, therefore, to be mindful of the degree to which the policy agenda is shaped by 'events which explode in such a way in which unusual responses are called for by "public opinion" ' (Downes and Morgan, 2002: 310). Few would deny that some extraordinary national and international events have preceded the outpouring of increasingly punitive law and order measures over the last 20 years in the UK. However, while most would agree that governments on both sides of the Atlantic were under pressure to be seen to take decisive action in the wake of the attacks on New York and Washington on 11 September 2001, and the subsequent attacks in London on 7 July 2005, we need to pause a moment and consider the degree to which the frenetic pace of counter-terrorism legislation led to proportionate and fair policy-making. What is more, we should maintain a sceptical curiosity about the way in which politicians seemingly built upon public fear and risk aversion to legitimate the plethora of more general law and order policy-making that characterised this period, a period when a series of criminal justice Bills were debated and passed in parliament with a frequency and speed that seemed out of kilter with any form of ordered, reasoned, evidence-based policy-making, and whose content was all too often draconian in nature.

When studying criminal justice policy, we need to constantly remind ourselves that criminal justice policy raises serious moral questions about the state's power to punish. Coercion and the deprivation of liberty implicit in penal and criminal justice policy set it apart from other areas of public policy. Although it is not the authors' intention to give a blow-by-blow account of specific policy and legislation changes, students should reflect upon the wider issues of social justice when reading the debates about the way in which different individuals and groups seek to shape the policy agenda by exerting pressure on the government to adopt their model of causation of a problem and their recommendations for its solution. Decisions that involve locking up more people for longer or allow the private sector to profit from punishment should make us think about fundamental questions of the moral purpose of government actions and the limits of legitimacy.

The authors are indebted to Hill (2013), who makes the point that although there is no one universally accepted definition, it is generally agreed that 'policy [is] something more than simply a decision: it embodies the idea of action' (p. 14). It is about seeking solutions to problems and turning ideas into action. What is more, policy is rarely the outcome of a single decision, but rather encompasses a series or 'web of decisions'. When we are studying policy, we need to be aware that different stakeholders can exert different levels of influence at different stages of the decision-making process. As a consequence of this, we frequently find ourselves engaged in a dynamic (and at times fast-moving) political process in which existing policies that appear to be changing incrementally can suddenly change direction (often in response to a particular event or pressure exerted by a particularly powerful interest group). A recent example of the pressure that sectional commercial interests can exert over policy-making is the case of the government's decision to 'kick into the long grass' the requirement for the tobacco industry to use plain packages for cigarettes in response to pressure exerted by the tobacco lobby.

Who makes criminal justice policy?

The two principal government ministries with responsibility for criminal justice policy-making are the Home Office and the more recently established Ministry of Justice. Based at the heart of government in central London, these departments jointly preside over the law and the justice system. They share the ultimate responsibility and accountability for the agencies under their respective controls.

The origins of the Home Office date back to 1782, and from the Department's inception it was dealing with matters of national security, the safeguarding of civil liberties and public safety. At the time of writing, the Home Office employs 27,546 people (Home Office, 2013). The Ministry of Justice was formed in 2007, with the stated purpose of improving access to justice and increasing public confidence in the justice system. The Ministry of Justice currently employs 25,846 people (Ministry of Justice, 2013). As a 'barometer' of the scope and range of their respective portfolios, it would be useful here to examine the current multitude of operational briefs attached to each organisation.

The Home Office

The work of the Home Office concentrates on five principal areas of practice: borders and immigration; crime and policing; law and the justice system; national security; and equality, rights and citizenship.

To undertake this work, the Home Office currently draws on the expertise of 26 government agencies and public bodies. With a similar structure to the Home Office, these comprise an executive agency, executive non-departmental public bodies, advisory non-departmental public bodies, tribunal non-departmental public bodies, and departments listed as 'other'.

Home Office (HO) executive agencies

- HM Passport Office
- National Fraud Authority

HO executive non-departmental public bodies

- Office of the Immigration Services Commissioner
- Security Industry Authority
- Independent Police Complaints Commission
- Disclosure and Barring Service

HO advisory non-departmental public bodies

- Advisory Council on the Misuse of Drugs
- Police Advisory Board for England and Wales
- Technical Advisory Board
- Migration Advisory Committee
- National DNA Database Ethics Group
- Police Negotiating Board
- Animals in Science Committee

HO tribunal non-departmental public bodies

- Investigatory Powers Tribunal
- Police Arbitration Tribunal
- Police Discipline Appeals Tribunal
- Office of Surveillance Commissioners

HO Departments and bodies listed as 'other'

- HM Inspectorate of Constabulary
- Independent Chief Inspector of Borders and Immigration
- Security Service
- Independent Reviewer of Terrorism Legislation
- Intelligence Services Commissioner
- Interception of Communications Commissioner
- Surveillance Camera Commissioner
- Forensic Science Regulator
- Biometrics Commissioner

Source: Government UK (2013)

The Ministry of Justice

The work of the Ministry of Justice is broadly cited as 'law and the justice system', and at the time of writing eight principal Ministry of Justice policy areas were listed: creating a transparent justice system; making the criminal justice system more efficient; making legal aid more effective; preventing more young offenders from re-offending; making the family justice system more effective; protecting the UK against terrorism; helping and supporting the victims of crime; and making sentencing more effective.

To undertake this work, the Ministry of Justice currently draws on the expertise of 37 government agencies and public bodies. As with the Home Office, these comprise an executive agency, executive non-departmental bodies, advisory non-departmental public bodies, tribunal non-departmental public bodies, and departments listed as 'other.' However, remarkably, despite working in spheres that would appear closely interrelated, there is no explicit crossover between the agencies and bodies listed as utilised by the Home Office above and those utilised by the Ministry of Justice, which are shown in the following box.

Ministry of Justice (MoJ) executive agencies

- National Archives
- National Offender Management Service
- Office of the Public Guardian
- HM Courts and Tribunals Service
- HM Prison Service
- Legal Aid Agency

MoJ executive non-departmental public bodies

- Criminal Injuries Compensation Authority
- Judicial Appointments Commission
- Parole Board of England and Wales
- Youth Justice Board for England and Wales
- Criminal Cases Review Commission
- Legal Services Board
- Probation Trusts
- Information Commissioner's Office

MoJ advisory non-departmental public bodies

- Civil Justice Council
- Law Commission
- Sentencing Council for England and Wales
- Victims' Advisory Panel

- Advisory Committees on Justices of the Peace
- Advisory Council on National Records and Archives
- Civil Procedure Rule Committee
- Family Justice Council
- Family Procedure Rule Committee
- Independent Advisory Panel on Deaths in Custody
- Insolvency Rules Committee
- Prison Service Pay Review Body
- Tribunal Procedure Committee
- Advisory Panel on Public Sector Information

MoJ departments and bodies listed as 'other'

- HM Inspectorate of Prisons
- HM Inspectorate of Probation
- Victims' Commissioner
- Prisons and Probation Ombudsman
- Official Solicitor and Public Trustee
- Legal Ombudsman
- Judicial Appointments and Conduct Ombudsman
- Independent Monitoring Boards of Prisons, Immigration, Removal Centres and Short Term Holding Rooms
- Criminal Procedure Rule Committee

Source: Government UK (2013)

Theories of the public policy process

'Any discussion of the public policy process needs to be grounded in an extensive consideration of power. Any consideration of how the process works will tend to involve propositions about who dominates' (Hill, 2013: 8).

Despite the fact that we have chosen to omit from our discussions *seriously* improper forms of policy-making, for example, corrupt officials seeking to influence policy because of illegal payments (so-called 'cash for questions'), our aim is to identify different sources of influence over criminal justice policy-making, and to explore how successful different actors are in persuading politicians to do something that furthers their interest. This invariably leads us to consider issues related to the dispersal of power within the state and the ways in which spheres of influence are historically contingent, and the dominance of the policy agenda fluctuates over time with groups going in and out of fashion.

With this in mind, an important starting point for students of the criminal justice process is the study of power – its sources, its distribution and its day-to-day exercise. It involves identifying which groups have a stake in a specific policy issue, and how they vie with one another, or form collaborative alliances with others, to gain domination over the policy debate and thereby to ensure the adoption of solutions and resource allocation that serve their interests. It also involves accepting that the operation of power is simultaneously visible and invisible to the outsider. While students can gain valuable insights from studying the public face of policy-making (such as party political manifestos, party conference speeches, public consultation papers, government White and Green Papers, and transcripts of parliamentary debates and select committee inquiries), they need to remain alert to the covert and subtle face of the exercise of power that remains hidden from scrutiny. A recent example of this is ministerial special advisors on the Home Office policy of removing illegal immigrants from the UK having a series of lunches (away from the public gaze) with lobbyists from the 'controversial' MigrationWatch think tank (Boffey, 2013).

The following constitutes a short introduction to key aspects of the main theories, as described by Hill (2013) and Dorey (2005), that provide a framework for the analysis of power and the policy process.

The pluralist model

While it is the case that there are different variants of pluralism, the key components of the model are that, despite the fact that power to devise and implement policy remains essentially with the state, society comprises a wide range of different and competing interest groups who have a stake in policy-making and wish to exert their influence over the process. These groups see policy issues in different ways, adopt different models of causation of crime problems and adopt opposing views on how policy to address the problem should be framed. From this perspective, power is both diffuse and fragmented, and widely (and relatively equally) distributed throughout the different groups in society. All groups have some access to power and resources, and as a consequence no group is powerless. Everyone has access to the political stage, and all groups have the capacity to be heard at some point during the policy-making process. That said, groups that exert the greatest influence are those that have access to the most resources (such as the mass media) and shout the loudest.

In the different versions of this model, the role of the government takes two forms. It is portrayed either as a neutral conflict manager or arbitrator/negotiator that acts as a referee balancing different interest groups, or as an interested party whose agencies constitute one set of pressure groups that seek to promote their own views on a problem and its solution.

The elite model

Elite theory suggests that power is not distributed throughout society but rather is concentrated in the hands of a small elite group. The classical elite perspective maintains that all societies are divided into two groups – the ruling class and the ruled. The former group is always numerically the smaller. It dominates all political functions, monopolises power and enjoys the privileges that power brings. The latter group is the more numerous, but is devoid of power. It is regulated and controlled by the former.

In modern states, elites gain their power from a variety of sources: the occupation of formal office (e.g. in business, the government or a trade union), wealth and/or technical knowledge and expertise. From a Weberian perspective, power is acquired through the development of large-scale organisations and bureaucracies that are involved in the administration of government functions (such as the civil service). Bureaucracies have both positive and negative features. The positive aspects are that they provide an effective and efficient means of delivery of administrative tasks. The negative aspects are that they create the potential for power to be concentrated in the hands of unelected and unaccountable officials. From a Marxist perspective, political power is economically determined by the structural relationship to the means of production. In capitalist countries, economic power is concentrated in the hands of a small group who own the means of production (the bourgeoisie). The primary function of the state is not to act as a neutral agent; instead, it functions to create the conditions that will ensure the production of profit and capital accumulation, and class domination. For a Marxist like Ralph Miliband, there are three reasons why the state adopts this stance. These are: the similarities in background of the bourgeoisie and the members of the state elite – senior civil service, judiciary, government officials; the power that the bourgeoisie can exert through the maintenance of 'old boy' networks, personal contacts and organisations such as the business lobby group the Confederation of British Industry and the neoliberal Adam Smith think tank that promote their interests; and the constraints that the objective power of capital places on the state.

Although some proponents of this model argue that elites are the best guardians of society and are uniquely placed to use their power to create policy on behalf of the masses, others argue that in a class-based society the ruling class will always promote policies that reflect their own values, promote the interests of others like themselves, uphold the status quo and ensure the subordination of the working class.

The policy network model

This model draws attention to the way in which different pressure groups relate to one another. It explores 'systems of linking' that are established between groups within government and groups outside government. In analysing the different types of relationships and 'linkings' that develop, a distinction is made between policy communities and issue networks.

The main features of policy networks are: shared values and frequent interaction; the exchange of resources with group leaders to regulate this; and a relative balance of power among members. In contrast, issue networks are large and diverse, they have a fluctuating level of contact and lower levels of agreement, they have varying resources that are rarely shared on a collective basis, and the power is unequal.

Issue networks and policy communities differ from simple pluralist clusters of organisations in as much as the state has an interest in fostering them. Their value to the state lies in their capacity to facilitate the consultative process; to reduce conflict between groups; to make policy more predictable; and to relate well to government departments. The benefits for different special interest groups of forming policy communities lie in their potential to ensure control over the policy.

One variant of this model is the advocacy coalition approach, which sees the policy-making process – from inception to implementation – as being driven by the coordinated activities of a collation of actors from all parts of the policy-making system who share the same vision, objectives, policy goals, preferences and perceptions.

Critics of the overall model argue that the problem with policy community and policy network theory is that it is descriptive rather than analytical. While it tells us why and how collaborative relationships are formed, it fails to analyse how they influence the policy-making process, and does not fully explain their power.

The institutional model

This model is predicated on the concept that certain institutions are tasked with determining public policy objectives and processes. They function as strategic planning departments. This model focuses on the structure and organisational behaviour that develop within these institutions and how this impacts on the policy-making and implementation process. It acknowledges that although organisations are designed to attain certain stated goals and objectives, and seek to mobilise human and technical resources as means of achieving these goals, the formal structures that are put in place to achieve this can never fully control organisational behaviour. The actions of individuals within organisations are not merely determined by organisational structures, roles and procedures, and can at times act in ways that are at odds with institutionally stated goals. From this perspective, organisations can be seen as having a life of their own, adapting to intrinsic pressures and problems.

Individuals within a system have a tendency to resist being treated as a means to an end. As a consequence, it is important for us to recognise that professionals within an organisation (e.g. judges and youth workers), despite the application of structural constraints, retain a degree of agency and exercise their ability to resist institutional demands and expectations. They have the power to shape policy to fit with professional values and culture. Youth workers may choose to prioritise young offenders first and foremost as children in need of care, rather than as offenders in need of control. Similarly, judges may use their discretion to resist attempts by governments to determine sentencing outcomes.

A key aspect of this perspective is the relationship between types of capitalist economies and their institutional configurations. While the casual relationship remains contested, the identification of similar institutional characteristics between political economies is an important feature of the study of comparative social and penal policy.

The rational decision model

This model is the most widely held view of the way in which policy is made. It approaches policy-making as a process of problem-solving that is rational, impartial, fair and analytical. In the model, decisions are made in a series of phases that proceed in a logical sequence. It starts with the identification of a problem or issue, and ends with a set of activities to solve or deal with a policy issue. The phases are:

- recognising and defining the nature of the issue to be dealt with;
- identifying possible courses of action to deal with the issue;
- weighing up the advantages and disadvantages of each of these alternatives;
- choosing the option that offers the best solution;
- implementing the policy;
- possibly evaluating the outcome.

The rational choice model also embraces the view that policy-making mirrors the market place and offers the prospect of choice. From this perspective, assumptions about choice in the market place are applied to the political process. It is predicated on notions of rational behaviour and sees individuals as essentially motivated by the satisfaction of their wants and needs. Although it is not possible for all their wants and needs to be met, rational individuals calculate the consequences of alternatives, and invariably choose the ones that are of benefit to them. It also presupposes that all potential policy options are on the table, are afforded equal weight and have the same chance of being adopted if they constitute the best response to a problem.

The idea of politics as a marketplace extends to the notion that parties compete for power in the marketplace by responding to the demands of pressure groups. This perspective is a development of pluralist theory and adds the concept of economic reasoning to politicians' actions. Parties that seek to secure pressure group support are acting in a rational way to ensure that their best interests (the wish to secure votes) are served. In this model, where groups are seen as competing to accrue benefits for themselves (e.g. commercial interests), the state is portrayed as an autonomous actor. Some argue that one of the consequences of the state responding to plural demands is that the state grows, becoming overly powerful (with bureaucrats and officials gaining monopoly power). This is seen as damaging to the effective operation of capitalism. This concept of a powerful, autonomous state is at odds with the classical pluralist model that sees power distributed evenly throughout society.

Incrementalism

In this model, policy is rarely absolutely new, but instead emerges incrementally and over time through a series of small changes, adaptations or revisions to existing policy. The roots of any policy problem remain unaddressed because the original policy response to an issue is not challenged. The primary objective is to solve problems that have arisen from the implementation of an existing policy. Success is measured in terms of the degree of agreement that is reached between those involved in the policy-making process.

Some refer to incrementalism as policy-making that proceeds in successive limited comparisons. Policy-making is limited in scope and range to the consideration only of those policies that differ in a small degree from the one under consideration. From this perspective, instead of identifying policy objectives and then deciding which policies would be most effective in achieving these, policy-makers reach decisions through the process of comparing specific policies and deciding on the extent to which they are likely to achieve the desired ends. With this form of policy-making, the policy process progresses through a succession of 'small steps'. This has the advantage of providing a degree of policy stability as policies that would involve making 'root and branch' changes are excluded from the policy-making process. There is no optimum policy outcome, but rather a series of compromises in which a policy emerges that is something that is most agreeable/palatable to the various policy analysts and decision-makers. It constitutes the art of 'muddling through'. By making small incremental changes, policy-makers avoid making serious mistakes and can better predict outcomes. They can test the water and assess whether or not to make further changes.

The structure of the book

The book focuses on various aspects of the criminal justice-making process. It describes both the formal and informal processes of policy-making, explores debates about the power and influence of a range of key stakeholders, and locates changes in policy-making within wider social and economic contexts.

In Chapter 2, the building blocks of social policy-making, and specifically how criminal policy has developed historically are discussed. The chapter starts by outlining social change theory and the ways in which modern society classifies and deals with emerging social problems via formal and informal social controls. Within this analysis, the role of the modern nation state, in particular its protectorate role, its operation in maintaining power, managing consensus and protecting the populace, is examined. As part of this, the role of the state in acknowledging prevailing norms, mores and sensibilities, and the codification of these norms into rules is outlined. The chapter concludes with an analysis of the complexity of policy-making in the twenty-first century and an examination of the concept of living in a globalised 'risk' society, with an alert omnipresent media tuned to the harnessing of public disposition and anxieties.

In Chapter 3, criminal justice and penal policy are placed within a broader public policy landscape. The perspective adopted is that criminal justice policy should not be treated as distinct or separate from other social policy realms; rather criminal justice policy and wider social policy should be approached as interrelated aspects of public policy that seek to regulate behaviour. The chapter develops the constructionist perspective that behavioural norms are socially constructed and historically contingent, and explores the way in which behaviour becomes defined as a social problem requiring a public policy response. The changing political landscape of government responses to social welfare problems is explored from a political economy perspective that traces key developments from post-war penal welfarism to present-day neoliberalism. Bourdieu's concept of the left hand and right hand of state solutions is applied to examine the shifting boundaries between penal and social welfare policy, with a particular emphasis on New Labour's social inclusion policy and the 'criminalisation of social policy'. The chapter concludes by focusing on the Coalition's approach to social welfare and the emergence of the 'punitive welfare state'.

In Chapter 4, both the formal and informal processes of the criminal justice policy-making process are described. Tracing the trajectory of public policy-making through parliament, the chapter identifies the key official actors (government ministers and civil service mandarins) in the criminal justice policy-making process, and summarises how crime policy has been 'harnessed' by politicians over the past 50 years. Taking as its starting point the notion of 'policy from below', the important role that various pressure groups, special interest groups and think tanks play in lobbying both the media and politicians in order to promote their position on preferred policy is examined in detail. The chapter also discusses politicians, political power and ideology with particular attention to the political commitment to crime policy, and the recent drive to 'join up' public policy across government departments in the associated policy spheres.

In Chapters 5, 6 and 7, the focus is the identification of different stakeholders in the criminal justice system, and key debates about the degree of influence that they have over the policy-making process.

Chapter 5 explores the role that expert research plays in justice policy-making. In recent years, there has been considerable academic debate about the relationship between research expertise and public policy-making. The chapter traces the rise and fall of evidence-based policy-making as a primary influence on policy-making. It explores what is meant by the policy advisory 'expert', what counts as research evidence and the degree to which governments tend to favour those experts who provide evidence that fits with their ideological predilections and electoral prerogatives. The case of Professor David Nutt is highlighted as an example of what happens when a government special advisor seeks to promote scientific evidence that is at odds with government policy imperatives. The chapter concludes with an overview of key contemporary debates about public criminology.

Chapter 6 develops themes covered in the preceding chapter relating to the marginalisation of the academic expert. It focuses on the changing nature of the 'penal axis', with a particular emphasis on the decline of the 'liberal elite' as a key influence on policy-making, and the emergence of the public, victims and the mass media as new, influential stakeholders. A link is made to wider debates about populist policy-making, participatory policy-making and democratisation. With the decline of the expert as the source of information about crime and punishment, the role of red-top newspapers is discussed in the context of 'new punitiveness'. This is placed alongside the politicisation of the victim and the hijacking of the victims' agenda by right of centre politicians. The chapter concludes with a discussion of single-issue campaigns and the *News of the World*'s championing of Sarah's Law.

In Chapter 7, key ideas, themes and concepts about the similarities between penal policies in different advanced, industrial western states and international influences on domestic policy-making are discussed. Linked to the notions of globalisation and the spread of neoliberalism, the interaction between macro-level economic and social changes that characterise 'late modern' capitalist societies, and the micro-level decision-making of individual political actors in nation states are explored. A particular emphasis is on policy transfer and debates about the importance of the USA as an exporter of ideas on crime control and punishment to England and Wales. A distinction is made between the symbolic politics of the rhetorical and the real.

How to approach reading the book

The authors would like you to approach this book in the same manner that you approach lectures. Although we aim to provide you with an outline of the key themes and debates, we acknowledge that this is not the definitive text. That said, we hope that, by highlighting the main arguments and counterarguments to be found in the literature, we will help you to appreciate that studying criminal justice policy-making, in common with other aspects of criminology, involves engaging with different perspectives and truth claims. We trust that we will inspire you to carry out your own further research and reading. With this in mind, you will find that we have included an additional recommended reading section in each chapter.

Special features of the book

At the end of each chapter, you will find a summary of key points and a set of critical thinking questions. Both of these are intended to help you consolidate your learning by reflecting on the main issues addressed in the chapter.

Integral to each chapter is a case study. The case studies illustrate the different ways in which policy evolves. They provide 'real' examples that will help you to understand and critically evaluate ideas that feature in the body of the chapter. They also provide additional case-specific academic observations and commentary.

Glossary

At the end of the book, you will find a glossary of key terms used in the book. In this, there is an explanation of terms used. In addition, related ideas are grouped together to help you to understand the interconnectedness of concepts. For example, under 'privatisation', you will also be introduced to the closely related concept of contestability.

Brief summary of key points in the chapter

This chapter has stressed that this book focuses on the criminal justice policy-making process and the different interest groups that have a stake within this. In the chapter, we have outlined our working assumptions and our particular perspective. While we acknowledge that there are a range of theories of policy-making and provide you with a brief synopsis of these, we recognise that the book reflects the bias of the writers whose work we have used. Inevitably, this has curtailed a detailed discussion of all the models.

Critical thinking discussion topic

To get you to start to think about stakeholders and policy-making decisions, consider the recent decision by the Home Office to set up checkpoints manned by police and immigration in railway stations to question passengers and others in the vicinity about their right to be in the UK.

From what you have read in this chapter and elsewhere, consider the following questions:

- Who do you think are the key stakeholders in this policy?
- Which of these stakeholders do you think had the most influence over this policy decision (rate them individually from 1 to 5, with 5 as the most influential)?
- What part has the government played in the decision?
- What model of policy-making do you think best explains this policy development.

Recommended further reading

Downes, D. and Morgan, R. (2002) 'The skeletons in the cupboard: the politics of law and order at the turn of the millennium'. In M. Maguire, R. Morgan and R. Reiner (eds) *The Oxford Handbook of Criminology* (3rd edn). Oxford: Oxford University Press.

Hill, M. (2013) *The Public Policy Process* (6th edn). Harlow: Pearson.

References

Baxter, S. (2011, June 9) 'Why the *Sun* has turned Ken Clarke into a Teletubby'. *New Statesman*.

Boffey, D. (2013, August 4) 'Adviser warns Coalition over migrants'. *The Observer*.

Dorey, P. (2005) *Policy Making in Britain: An Introduction*. London: Sage.

Downes, D. and Morgan, R. (2002) 'The skeletons in the cupboard: the politics of law and order at the turn of the millennium'. In M. Maguire, R. Morgan and R. Reiner (eds) *The Oxford Handbook of Criminology* (3rd edn). Oxford: Oxford University Press.

Government UK (2013) Departments, Agencies and Public Bodies. [Online]. Retrieved from https://www.gov.uk/government/organisations (accessed 10 October 2013).

Hill, M. (2013) *The Public Policy Process* (6th edn). Harlow: Pearson.

Home Office (2013) *FOI Release Case number: 25942*, 1 January 2013. [Online]. Retrieved from https://www.gov.uk/government/publications/home-office-staff-employed-as-of-1-january-2013 (accessed 11 October 2013).

Jones, T. and Newburn, T. (2002) 'Policy convergence and crime control in the USA and UK'. *Criminal Justice*, 2(2): 173–203.

Ministry of Justice (2013) *Diversity Report 2011/12*. London: TSO.

Muncie, J. (2005) 'Globalisation of crime control: the case of youth and juvenile justice'. *Theoretical Criminology*, 9(1): 35–64.

Naylor, R. (2004) *Wages of Crime: Black Markets, Illegal Finances, and the Underworld Economy*. London: Cornell University Press.

Page, E. (1999) 'The insider/outsider distinction: an empirical investigation'. *British Journal of Politics and International Relations*, 1(2): 205–14.

Pratt J. (2007) *Penal Populism*. London: Routledge.

Vidal, J. (2013, September 19) 'Russian military storms Greenpeace Arctic oil protest ship'. *The Guardian*.

Wolff, J. (2011) *Ethics and Public Policy: A Philosophical Inquiry*. Abingdon: Taylor & Francis.

2 Social change and criminal justice policy-making

Chapter summary

This chapter provides a foundation for considering the building blocks of social policy-making, and specifically how criminal policy has developed historically. The starting point for consideration is social change theory and the ways in which modern society classifies and deals with emerging social problems via formal and informal social controls. Within this analysis, the role of the modern nation state is key, as is its operation in maintaining power, managing consensus and protecting the populace. Criminal policy is fundamental to this protectorate role, and the state requires an ongoing awareness of prevailing norms, the codification of norms into rules and the public perception of its ideology. The chapter also examines the complexity of policy-making in the twenty-first century and the concept of living in a globalised 'risk' society, with an alert omnipresent media tuned to the harnessing of public disposition and anxieties.

This chapter looks at:

- the way in which societies develop policy linked to social change, considering functionalist and Marxian perspectives;
- the social discovery and content of social problems, and the use and features of social control in modern society;
- globalisation as emancipation and constraint, neoliberalism and transnational cooperation in crime policy;
- definitions of the state, consensus, state paternalism and state power;
- the content of criminal law and criminal justice, definitions of crime and deviance;
- considering crime as a social construct and the role of norms, rules and policies in maintaining this construct;
- the discovery and management of risk in the twenty-first century;
- public perception and policy influence, moral panic and deviancy amplification.

Case study: The deportation of Abu Qatada – social change, moral panic and the globalisation of crime

In the case study, you will be provided with the background to a number of policy areas that have converged to complicate contemporary terrorism policy in the UK, in this case the attempted deportation of Abu Qatada, a Jordanian national and terrorism suspect granted asylum in the UK. The human rights backdrop to the case is provided, along with a summary of the accompanying drawn-out political and legal battle, which took place under the gaze of a critical media and increasingly exasperated public. The case study illustrates the speed of social change in contemporary criminal policy-making, the move towards globalised policy in areas of risk, and the interrelated theories of moral panic and deviancy amplification.

Considering social change theory

Social change theory seeks to examine how society is constructed, and how it evolves. Each human society is reliant on a number of social institutions, ranging from basic institutions (such as family or kinship) through to highly complex institutions (such as religious, political or legal systems). Societies are seen to develop and change over time, becoming more complex and requiring more sophisticated means of administration and social control, a process known as 'differentiation'. Much modern sociology has concerned itself with this concept of social change and the tools that allow change to be instigated and crafted by way of social norm, social policy and legislation. As Roach-Anleu argues: 'The formative period of sociology as a distinct discipline was characterized by large-scale economic, political, and social transformation. There is often an assumption, either implicit or explicit, that social change is tantamount to social progress' (2000: 2).

Social change

Within sociology, the concept of social change is traditionally considered from functionalist and Marxian perspectives. Functionalists see social change as akin to biology in that the various institutions of society function, and initiate/incorporate change for the benefit of the whole, like a human body (an organismic analogy). With this model, change is seen to be evolutionary, and occurring via adaptation or integration. For example, the family is a site for early socialisation and child development that feeds into the function of the education system, which in turn functions to prepare young people to be productive and functional members of society in the workplace.

Like an organism, society consists of a large number of complex interrelated components to make a functioning whole. This concept of society as an integrated whole is most evident in the work of Talcott Parsons, who argued that, like biological organisms, society is constantly striving to achieve homeostasis, the maintenance of a stable state (equilibrium). Furthermore, while the institutions and elements of a society can be separated for the purpose of study or examination, they can only be fully understood as a whole. In this environment, social change occurs when there is a functional impetus for that change. For example, in the 1970s and 1980s, the invention of the personal computer and its proliferation in the workplace led to a need for computer literacy to be added to the school curriculum as education policy. A generation on, concerns over cybercrime have required consecutive governments to consider policy and legal changes to combat computer misuse (Yar, 2006; Jewkes and Yar, 2010). Here, social change is driven by the perceived need to educate and protect the public in the light of significant technological change.

Marxism offers the polar view, that the default state of society is conflict rather than equilibrium, and that the various institutions within are fragmented rather than founded on consensus. With this model, society exists as a form of class conflict, with the bourgeoisie (property-owning class) and the proletariat (working class) diametrically opposed and pursuing self-interest. Fundamental to this concept is power, specifically the power to control the means of production and defend it. Here, class conflict is seen as the driving force behind social change, as Simons and Stroup suggest: 'Conflict perspectives to the study of society, on the other hand, do not see disruption or conflict as pathological, but rather as the moving force behind social changes needed to address injustices and inequalities within society' (Simons and Stroup, 1997: 113). Thus, social change follows class conflict, and the resulting social policy and legislation cannot be seen as neutral or non-partisan.

Social problems

These functionalist and Marxist perspectives on social change provide background and insight into the controversy which often surrounds behaviour that society perceives as a social problem – and moreover, a social problem worthy of social action in the form of censure, policy or legislation. Consequently, government policy is a reasonably reliable barometer and conduit of the concerns and conflicts that exist in modern society. The recent financial crisis and global downturn has provided the chance to reflect on both function and conflict when considering whether the root of the problem lies with overpaid, careless, cavalier bankers or the idle, welfare-reliant poor. As Edelman suggests when considering an earlier recession:

> When we name and classify a problem, we unconsciously establish the status and roles of those involved with it, including their self-conceptions. If the problem is an economic system that yields inadequate monetary and psychological benefits, then the working poor and the unemployed are victims; but if the problem is personal pathology, they are lazy and incompetent. How the [social] problem is named involves alternative scenarios, each with its own facts, value judgements, and emotions.
>
> (Quoted in Considine, 2005: 63)

What is clear at the outset is that the concept of the social problem is both subjective and controversial. There is a numerical consideration in that, for that perceived problem to be addressed, a significant part of the population must believe that there is a social problem. Concerns over banking practices, benefit fraud or anti-social behaviour per se require a collective response to commence the transposition from problem to policy. Put simply, a *bona fide* social problem requires a large section of the public to perceive the behaviour or practice as problematic. Robertson provides an excellent succinct definition: 'A social problem is whatever a significant part of the population perceives as an undesirable gap between social ideals and social realities and believes can be eliminated by collective action' (1980: 4).

A social condition in isolation does not constitute a social problem, even if that social condition has existed for many years and is seen by many as undesirable. Historically, many issues perceived as social problems drawing collective social action and resulting in socio-legal change have been slow burn, such as racial discrimination and female emancipation, with an evolutionary timescale that can be measured in centuries. However, with the fast-paced nature of modern society, under the constant focus of globalised on-demand media, which no longer merely highlights social problems but commentates and mobilises campaigns to address them, the incubation period between collective perception and collective action can in some cases now be measured in days. An example of this would be the hasty manufacture of the Dangerous Dogs Act 1991, which came hot on the heels of a series of sensationalist stories in the media regarding attacks by newly imported 'fighting' breeds of dog, such as the Pit Bull Terrier and the Japanese Tosa in the late 1980s. The Dangerous Dogs Act can be seen as an example of 'knee-jerk' legislation.

Social control

With social change and the discovery of social problems, there is a perceived need within societies for 'social control'. Social control theory examines what it is that makes individuals conform within society or rebel against it. The default position is that human nature itself is anti-social, and that it is the institutions within society that provide opportunity, impetus and coercion for compliance. Our social lives in contemporary society are subject to a number of ever-increasing controls, both formal and informal; as Black reminds us, such controls are both normal and expected: 'social control is the normative aspect of social life, or the definition of deviant behaviour and the response to it, such as prohibitions, accusations, punishment, and compensation' (1976: 2).

The fundamental question is the consideration of why the majority seek to conform rather than deviate, particularly in a society of individuals that apparently seek freedom rather than control. Sociologists have explained this conformity via the examination of social institutions, such as the family, education and the workplace. The most enduring fully formed social control theory is the 'social bond' theory proposed by Hirschi in 1969 (see, among others Akers and Sellers, 2008). Hirschi's starting point is that deviant or criminal behaviour is not linked to the acquisition of motivational factors such as social strain (poverty or aspiration 'gap') or differential association (deviant learned behaviour). Rather, every human being is born with the drive to commit deviant and criminal acts, but most hold this drive in check via reference to social bonds formed to pro-social values.

According to Hirschi, these bonds can be viewed in four forms: *attachment, commitment, involvement* and *belief.*

Attachment refers to how attached an individual is to important peers and social institutions, the most obvious examples being a child's attachment to parents and school. It follows that a child with strong attachment is likely to experience and endorse a higher level of social control, while those weakly attached are seen to be less concerned about social approval.

Commitment, according to Hirschi, refers to the value that individuals see in relationships, that might be jeopardised or weakened via deviant or criminal behaviour. This is directly linked to socialisation in that a child brought up to have respect for the law is much less likely to break the law. Consequently, a person is much less likely to jeopardise their chances of success in education or the workplace, or indeed in personal relationships, if they are a stakeholder, and have something to lose. Thus, conformity has benefits, whereas non-conformity has penalties.

Hirschi's third bond is *involvement*, which considers how an individual spends their time. Time spent on pro-social activities indicates that the person is involved in positive development, whereas time spent on anti-social or perhaps deviant activity is viewed in a negative context – the maxim 'idle hands are the devil's workshop' is applied.

The final bond described is *belief*, which refers to belief in society's laws, or respect for the values associated with legal conformity.

Source: Hirschi (1969)

The strength in Hirschi's theory is that the social bonds described indicate that while social control can refer on the one hand to direct control (whether the barriers are physical or legal), most social control that exists within society is indirect and autonomous, a consideration seldom lost on politicians and policy-makers. Innes interestingly describes this indirect autonomy as 'ambient' control:

The control capacity that was formerly implicit in social institutions and situations, is being formalized. This has involved the introduction of new modes of social control, alongside reconfigured and retooled older modes. The impact of which has been to contribute to a situation where social control appears more integrated, continuous and seamless. There are cross-cutting revisions too: 'hard' and 'soft' controls; reactive and proactive controls; targeted and untargeted controls; systematic and unsystematic controls; and coercive and non-coercive controls.

(Innes, 2003: 150)

Globalisation and criminal policy universalism

Globalisation can be, and has been, defined and described in a number of ways depending on the context. In general terms, despite merchant capitalism having historically possessed a worldwide reach (in terms of trade), the term 'globalisation' refers to relatively recent worldwide economic developments that have seen the creation of controversial organisations such as the World Bank and International Monetary Fund and led to the discovery of the multinational company and the global brand. This has led to the breaking down of barriers in terms of communication and movement, and the use of internationally sourced cheap labour to provide goods and services ranging from designer clothing and electrical goods to the voice on the end of the phone in a bank call centre. As Giddens has argued: 'Globalization may not be a particularly attractive or elegant word. But absolutely no one who wants to understand our prospects at century's end can ignore it' (2000: 25).

The contemporary view is that there is far more to globalisation than an economic ethos, as Waters suggests: '[globalisation can be seen as] A social process in which the constraints of geography on economic, political, social and cultural arrangements recede, in which people become increasingly aware that they are receding and in which people act accordingly' (1995: 5). A political accompaniment to this rapid economic social change and growing awareness has been 'neoliberalism', often seen as the driver for national deregulation in terms of privatisation, and as a potential assault on national identity, as Passas argues:

> neoliberalism refers to an economic and political school of thought on the relations between the state on the one hand, and citizens and the world of trade and commerce on the other. Because it espouses minimal or no state interference in the market and promotes the lifting of barriers to trade and business transactions across regional and national borders, it certainly becomes a motor of globalisation.
>
> (Passas, 2000: 21)

A further byproduct of the removal of barriers, both real and virtual, has been the development of globalised crime. This includes such behaviours as transnational organised crime and cybercrime, with both types of crime at the forefront of contemporary criminal policy. Transnational organised crime is, broadly speaking, crime that crosses national boundaries, including the trafficking and sale of both goods and human beings and the supply of the global market in drugs, weaponry and items prohibited within individual nation states. The growing spectre of cybercrime has raised the stakes yet higher, with the ability to utilise global networks remotely to commit fraud, steal, circumvent indecency laws, commit hate crime or instigate and engage in acts of terrorism. In a speech to the London Conference on Cyberspace in November 2011, the British Prime Minister David Cameron concluded:

> [A] cross-border problem needs cross-border solutions, which is why the world needs to act together ... international cyber security is a real and

pressing concern. Let us be frank. Every day we see attempts on an industrial scale to steal government secrets, information of interest to nation states, not just commercial organisations.

(Cameron, 2011)

Such cross-border solutions include increased cooperation in international policing and security policy, and a movement towards universalism in criminal policy and international criminal law. This suggests a rapidly changing role for the nation state in terms of policy-making in a number of key areas, which include national defence/security and crime, and a growing stimulus for politicians and civil servants to possess 'global consciousness' when planning policy.

A further constituent component of neoliberalism and democratisation is the rise of global consumer culture and a perceived 'free choice' in both product and information selection, as Baker and Roberts argue: 'Modern communications technology ensures that what were once alien beliefs and customs can be imported within the state's borders to intermingle with those of domestic origin, thereby threatening to dilute the indigenous cultural fabric upon which the sense of nation-hood thrives' (2005: 126). Contemporary society is a society that is increasingly focused on global solutions to global risk (both real and perceived) along the lines suggested by Beck (1986, 1999), in terms of potential 'borderless' pressures wrought by international financial instability, international terrorism and environmental disaster, with the policies to control such risks now at the forefront of the political agenda.

The state and intervention

While acknowledging the growing complexity of what it means to be a nation state at the start of the twenty-first century, it is clear that, as it is the primary vessel for public policy, we should try to define what the concept of 'the state' means or refers to. Fundamentally, the state is associated with the control of order within a society. This control of order requires both consensual and coercive strategies, and often the state crossing over from the 'public' to the 'private' in terms of new jurisdictional boundaries. This includes the instigation and implementation of policy, and the attachment of sanctions and punishment to such policy where appropriate. As such, the very notion of the nation state as a self-legitimising entity is controversial, and therefore an interesting proposition for analysis.

Defining the state

Mitchell describes the slippery concept of the state in the following terms: 'The state is an object of analysis that appears to exist simultaneously as material force and as ideological construct. It seems both real and illusory' (2006: 169). This description allows one to reflect on the notion of an invisible social contract holding the entire thing together. In traditional form, the state is the name given to sovereign authority over a designated area; this authority suggests no higher claim, and is backed by force, as Weber famously stated: '[A] monopoly of the legitimate use of physical force in enforcing its order within a given territorial area' (1946: 77). Such legitimacy can be transient, and there is a need to consider *de jure* sovereignty (the legal right to supreme rule) and *de facto* sovereignty (the actual distribution of political power) when considering validity.

In the traditional social contract model formulated by Hobbes (1588–1679), Locke (1632–1704) and Rousseau (1712–1778), human society is seen to be tied to the state by the device of an invisible social contract. For Hobbes, human existence as a state of nature was characterised as 'solitary, poor, nasty, brutish, and short', with people existing in a volatile insecure environment, bereft of social stability. As the nation state emerged, it was seen to be beneficial to forgo some individual rights for the greater good of the whole; thus, we see the appearance of Hobbes' all powerful sovereign state, *Leviathan* (1651; Hobbes, 2012).

Locke adapted Hobbes' model of the social contract to argue that individuals were not necessarily purely bound and driven by self-interest, but rather were in the main moral actors bound by the laws of nature. According to Locke, the populace required the state to be a 'neutral judge' to protect the life, liberty and property of its subjects (Locke, 1996 [1690]). Both Hobbes and Locke propose a version of social contract that advocates the free market with minimal state intervention in social life, a theory that has endured and formed the basis and impetus for the 'New Right' during the 1980s.

Rousseau's version of the social contract does not share this enthusiasm for the minimal state, outlining a system based on unlimited popular sovereignty. For Rousseau, the key is collectivism, where man must be forced to be free: 'Each of us puts his person and all his power in common under the supreme direction of the general will; and in a body we receive each member as an indivisible part of the whole' (1990: 139). In other words, the collective decides what is good for the whole and requires compliance from the individual; thus, public policy and law emanates from the general will of the people acting as a body. These theories form the bedrock of the modern liberal state, and most contemporary western liberal state models possess similar institutions, including a legislature, executive, judiciary, centralised and local political administration, backed by police and military force.

Consensus and state paternalism

The existence of a social contract confers a degree of consensus that allows for state paternalism. Paternalism, in this sense, can be seen as the limiting of an individual or group's liberty for their own good, or indeed the greater good. In practice, state paternalism in the British context since the Second World War has been founded on the inclusive notion of the welfare state, primarily the raft of social legislation formulated between 1944 and 1948 that still forms the basis of public welfare to this day. This foundation was founded on six principles; *full employment* (the guarantee of a job for job seekers), a *national minimum* (a monetary safety net), *equal and free access to health and education, a crucial role for the centre* (a renewed focus on central government), *state provision* and *continuity.*

One effect of this centralisation and move towards paternalism was a renewed faith in the notion of the social contract. However, as Glennerster makes clear, by the 1960s the state was loosening its grip in a number of areas:

> [By the 1960s] a new social policy agenda was emerging, outside of the normal range of party politics. It questioned the state's right to interfere in matters of personal concern: sexual relations between consenting couples of whatever sexual persuasion, the state's regulation of marriage and divorce, of women's right to abort a birth, the state's right to take life and its right to censor what people read. All these were challenges to paternalism and author-itarian state power.
>
> (Glennerster, 2007: 99)

However, the area of crime and criminal policy has generally retained the state's focus as an area where the social contract should be upheld and an arena where paternalism can be readily observed.

State power and state policy

The institutions of the criminal justice system as appendages of the state are rarely seen as neutral under the gaze of academic criminology, with a debate over whether the state is responding to social problems or precipitating them. The state's fundamental role as guarantor of peace and security means that it is constantly under scrutiny as being far too heavy handed or far too lenient, depending on the circumstances and personalities involved.

The fledgling science of criminology at the beginning of the twentieth century forged necessarily close links with the criminal justice system. Mainly positivist in nature, academic criminology was a policy-related discipline, looking to feed into criminal jurisprudence and penology and uphold the social order and state power. As the century progressed, this paternalistic relationship between academic social science and state-approved public policy gained momentum via the explo-ration of the work of Durkheim, which posited the state as the moral barometer of public will in criminal justice, as he argued: 'Crime is, then, necessary; it is bound up with the fundamental conditions of all social life, and by that very fact it is useful, because these conditions of which it is a part are themselves indispensable to the normal evolution of morality and law' (1982: 67). This theme of state neutrality was also apparent in the influential work of the Chicago School during the 1920s, and reinforced still further by the dominant functionalist sociology, led by Parsons, throughout the 1940s and 1950s (Parsons, 1955, 1960). Criminal policy and criminal justice practice by nature is an emotive subject, involving extremity in human interaction and interpersonal violence; it is at the very sharp end of state policy. Considering these variables, it is often comforting to view the state as paternalistic and protective, liberal and benevolent.

Such views and displays of consensus and solidarity are most apparent in times of civil conflict, or in extreme cases where politicians, leaders and the public at large unite to condemn or call for action. An appropriate recent case to illustrate this point are the riots that took place in England on 6–10 August 2011, which followed the police shooting of Mark Duggan in Tottenham, London, on 4 August. As the rioting intensified, it spread from Tottenham across several London boroughs, and into a number of major cities including Manchester, Birmingham and Bristol.

Throughout this four-day period, appeals were being made by local residents and business owners for increased state protection and swift intervention. Police resources were questioned, but criticism was tempered by a number of reports concerning the bravery of individual officers and members of the public. In the aftermath, five deaths were reported, over 3,100 arrests were made, and it was estimated that around £200 million of damage to property had been caused. Heated public dialogue with the state actors (the Coalition government and police) during the period of rioting had included calls for extreme policy change – paramilitary riot control methods to be utilised, and the right for the public to bear arms in self-defence of property. Both calls were rejected, with the Home Secretary Theresa May stating on 9 August: 'The way we police in Britain is not through use of water cannon. The way we police in Britain is through consent of communities' (Whitehead, 2012).

However, public anger was assuaged somewhat in the punitive sentencing round that followed, with reports that courts were being advised to circumvent sentencing guidelines and crown prosecutors instructed to oppose bail *en masse*. These unusual measures were publicly endorsed by the Prime Minister, David Cameron, and in a number of cases direct condemnation was forthcoming from the judiciary, including the Lord Chief Justice, Lord Judge, who concluded during an appeal case that there was:

> an overwhelming obligation on sentencing courts to do what they can to ensure the protection of the public . . . those who deliberately participate in disturbances of this magnitude, causing injury and damage and fear to even the most stout-hearted of citizens, and who individually commit further crimes during the course of the riots are committing aggravated crimes.
>
> (Blackshaw, R. v (Rev 1) [2011] EWCA Crim 2312)

The riots of August 2011 illustrate several aspects of the power behind state policy, in particular the powder keg that is criminal policy. The London School of Economics' Department of Social Policy report *Reading the Riots: Investigating England's Summer of Disorder* (Lewis *et al.*, 2012) suggests that the main causative factors behind the disorder were social deprivation, a feeling of social injustice and opportunism, allied to perceived negative policing methods. The shooting of Mark Duggan by the police certainly provided the catalyst, an emphasis of state monopoly of force and the power behind social control. For the majority of the British public, the sentencing that followed was a response to an assault on equilibrium, and a reaction by the 'whole' towards the individuals who had chosen to be involved.

This, however, is clearly not the only view, and criminal policy by its very nature invites challenges to its actions, power and legitimacy. In academic criminology and criminal justice activism, the momentum for challenge propagated during the 1960s, notably in the work of Becker, which focused on labelling and control culture, and that of Quinney, which problematised the role of the state, seeing it in the servitude of the power elite (Quinney, 1974, 1975). The studies that followed under the labels of radical and latterly critical criminology have provided a counterpoint for the analysis of crime policy and criminal justice activism that views the modern nation state as coercive, self-serving and inherently violent. This potential for state violence in the exercise of criminal justice is aptly illustrated by Cover (here reflecting on the US system):

> If convicted the defendant customarily walks – escorted – to prolonged confinement, usually without significant disturbance to the civil appearance of the event. It is, of course, grotesque to assume that the civil façade is 'voluntary' . . . There are societies in which contrition and shame control defendants' behaviour to a greater extent than does violence . . . But I think it is unquestionably the case in the United States that most prisoners walk into prison because they know they will be dragged or beaten into prison if they do not walk.
>
> (Cover, 1986: 1607)

The picture painted by Cover rejects the notion of ideological consensus, institutional coherence or indeed a functional system, which raises questions of the validity of what at first sight appear to be clear, common-sense definitions of crime and criminal justice. At the source of this are the building blocks that provide us with our definitions of crime and deviance, and the foundations of the institutions that make up the criminal justice system.

Criminal law and criminal justice

Having discussed social change and the development of social problems, and provided a definition of the state, we will now examine the basis of defining the content of criminal law and criminal justice.

Defining crime and deviance

Crime is a contested concept: what is deemed to be criminal differs from society to society, is subject to social change and is dependent on who is making the definition. If we consider the concept of crime in western liberal democracies, several variables need to be considered. The first is the legal consensus view; this consists of three main elements: (a) social harm, (b) consensus of harm, and (c) official response/censure. These elements appear as a thread in criminal law codes, with a focus on the specific harm caused to a specific victim, followed by a group consensus that harm has been caused, which requires the transgressor to be answerable to a criminal rule, code or punishment. Here, essentially, crime is behaviour forbidden by criminal law – a social construct – and with this definition we can say that, to understand crime in England and Wales in 2013, one should simply head to a law library and consult the statute books. However, while there we may find ourselves disagreeing with what is currently given criminal status at law or not, depending on our personal view of human conduct.

Human conduct is the key element for conflict theorists, with a view that criminal harm should be linked to human rights to provide universal protection free from individual power or the protection of an elitist state (Schwendinger and Schwendinger, 1970; Quinney, 1977). Next, we might argue who or what is to adjudicate the harm threshold or indicate the level of moral outrage that forms the consensus required to identify criminal behaviour. This indicates that what is considered to be harm and morally repugnant is dependent on both social and cultural change. This is certainly the case when you bring *deviance* into the frame, as the term covers fringe behaviour in terms of appearance, attitude, belief identity and manner, those whom Becker labelled 'outsiders' (Becker, 1963). Media influence in contemporary society plays a pivotal role in leading perceptions of deviance, sometimes descending into witch hunts while reporting on emotional cases.

Two recent examples are the treatment of Robert Murat during the Madeleine McCann abduction investigation in 2007, and the vilification of Christopher Jefferies in the aftermath of the murder of Joanne Yeates in 2010. As Surette argues:

> As the distributors of social knowledge, the media also legitimize people, social issues, and social policies for the general public. And though the media do not control the process of cultural change, the fact is that in large industrialized nations with hundreds of millions of people, cultural change without media involvement does not occur. The media simultaneously change, react to and reflect culture and society.
>
> (Surette, 1998: 11)

This allows us to view the concept of crime as something of a paradox, in that it appears to be a rigid set of rules subject to constant change. In reality, as we discovered earlier in the chapter, change, while constant, tends to be evolutionary when applied to social problems, and consequently when translated into social policy.

Norms, rules and policies

If we consider crime as a social construct, we should examine the beliefs that underpin that construct; we can start by examining normative standards of behaviour, or 'norms' for short. As we have seen when considering Hirschi's social bond theory, norms have an important part to play in social control as they are linked directly to social approval, social attainment and social status. If an individual decides to act in an abnormal way by breaking rules, informal or formal sanctions may apply. An example would be a student talking loudly into her phone in a university library, who may receive glares, verbal prompts or exclusion from her peers (an informal sanction), or be subject to a fine, suspension or ban from the library for her actions (a formal sanction). Here, norms provide common guidelines for 'correct' or 'proper' social behaviour – 'common' being the key word as the norm often merely refers to the most commonly occurring pattern of behaviour. Similarly, attitudes and tolerances to behaviour are subject to a number of factors, as Henry states: 'What is defined as "deviance" can also vary according to one historical time period to another, one context versus another, and, within the same society, from one social circle or community to another' (2009: 4).

For the majority of people, behaviour is linked to familiarity with the situation or the social group; norms are acquired to cope with expectation. Often, to avoid ambiguity, rules are provided, and by nature, norms imply legitimacy with conduct subject to rules. According to Winch (1958), social behaviour is directly linked to rule-following, with human actors reliant on the knowledge of rules to govern their words and actions, with past experience governing current behaviour. Past knowledge and experience of accepted norms and rules are also often a catalyst for formalisation when considering policy changes or amendments to legislation.

The formal rules that exist within the criminal law and criminal justice on matters such as sentencing guidelines require constant state scrutiny and agency in their development and enforcement. This is the watchman state in operation, with a continuous consideration of accepted norms and rules of conduct, and the scrutiny of behaviour likely to cause offence or harm. While the state considers the populace are to be aware and realistic, as Box reflects:

> We don't want to be murdered, raped, robbed, assaulted, or criminally victimised in any other way. Reassured that our political leaders are both aware of the problem's growing dimensions and receptive to our rising anxieties, we wait in optimistic, but realistic anticipation for crime to be at least effectively reduced.
>
> (Box, 1983: 1)

Managing risk

Risk is something that appears to be synonymous with living in a developed globalised world in 2013. We live daily with apparent risks to our health and personal safety: risks in the workplace, risks concerning the environment, our finances, and the risk of becoming a victim of crime. Risk has been used since the 1970s as a driver for 'forward thinking' policy-making in crime and security. This perception has developed alongside globalisation, and has been fuelled by significant and rapid social change.

The work of Beck (1986, 1992, 1999) has been highly influential in developing the notion that we are now living in a full-blown 'risk society' characterised by a movement from state social policy that aims for relative stability, towards suprastate social policy that aims to anticipate and control risks:

The argument is that, while in classic industrial society the 'logic' of wealth production dominates the 'logic' of risk production, in the risk society this relationship is reversed ... The gain in power from techno-economic 'progress' is being increasingly overshadowed by the production of risks.

(Beck, 1992: 12)

According to Beck, risk is linked to modernisation, and the very process of modernisation provides an irresistible and irreversible threat to ecology and human and animal life. Here, life lacks surety, and there is a growing concern for future prospects with an awareness that scientific and technological advancement confers disadvantage as well as advantage. Another aspect of risk society is increased individual awareness, both in concern for global social order and personal threats:

We live in an age in which the social order of the nation state, class, ethnicity and traditional family is in decline . . . The choosing, deciding shaping human being who aspires to be the author of his or her own life, the creator of an individual identity, is the central character of our time.

(Beck and Beck-Gernsheim, 2003: 22)

This centrality is also observable in criminal policy, with a great deal of research undertaken into risk, risk factors and risk management – this focuses on both the 'local' and the 'global'. In terms of the transnational alerts, recent emphasis has been placed on international terrorism, organised crime (which includes people trafficking and cybercrime), environmental pollution, the transmission of diseases such as 'mad cow disease' and 'avian flu' and the contamination of processed food by horsemeat. All of these ongoing causes contribute to a heightened aware-ness of both risk and potential victimisation, a state of affairs not lost on the globalised mass media:

Terrorist attacks on 'innocent' civilians chime with the postmodern idea that we are all potential victims. Postmodern analyses reject traditional crimino-logical concerns with the causes and consequences of crime, pointing instead to the fragmentation of societies, the fear that paralyses many communities, the random violence that seems to erupt at all levels of society, and the apparent inability of governments to do anything about these problems. This concern with a lurking unpredictable danger is fortified by an omnipresent media.

(Jewkes, 2004: 28)

In the British context, a good illustrative case in point here is contemporary terrorism policy (see Mythen and Walklate, 2012). Between the late 1960s and late 1990s, the primary terrorist threat to Britain was Provisional Irish Republicanism, linked to the ethno-nationalist conflict known as 'The Troubles' (*Na Trioblóidí*). Following the US-brokered Good Friday Agreement in 1998, the conflict that had led to over 3,500 deaths was brought to an end, and the threat of terrorism receded. However, three years later, in the aftermath of the coordinated airliner attacks on the Twin Towers in New York by the Islamic fundamentalist group al-Qaeda on 11 September 2001, the British government was quick to assess the potential risk to the British population from this new form of terror and instigate policy. Building on the provisions of the Terrorism Act 2000, which included al-Qaeda and a large number of other Islamist organisations as 'proscribed' terrorist groups, the far-reaching and uncompromising Anti-Terrorism, Crime and Security Act 2001 was introduced. Coming just two months after the 11 September attacks, the scope of the act was remarkable, leading Tomkins to describe the legislation as 'the most draconian legislation parliament has passed in peacetime in over a century' (Tomkins, 2002: 205).

Response to risk and potential risk has also passed into mainstream crime policy and planning, with movement towards crime prevention schemes, crime avoidance programmes, offender risk management and offender profiling now all familiar within the criminal justice discourse. A further feature of this discourse is the growing use of risk assessment in offender management, a policy with links to notions of speculative 'actuarial' justice with assumed (potential) risk and actual risk open to speculation and hypothesis (Ericson and Haggerty, 1997; Rigakos, 1999).

Public perception and policy

An enduring feature of contemporary society is the power of the public in influencing social policy. Two important theories used widely within the criminal justice context that highlight this phenomenon are moral panic theory and deviancy amplification theory.

Of policies and moral panics

Stan Cohen's classic theory of 'Folk Devils and Moral Panics' has permeated all areas of social science, and is now as likely to be used by a student of politics or social policy as by the sociologists and criminologists for whom it was originally intended. In terms of criminal justice policy, Cohen's work, which originally formed the basis of his famous 'Mods and Rockers' PhD thesis in 1969, runs parallel with the growth of party political interest in the 'crime problem' and the perceived need for a rapid response to public outcry (a social reaction to a social problem). The theory itself has been widely used to highlight how contemporary public policy, particularly criminal justice policy, is often instigated as a result or consequence of a dramatic event, or series of events, that captures the public imagination.

The 'folk devil' in Cohen's theory is the generic criminal or deviant – the out of control youth, the dangerous immigrant, the mugger, the drug dealer, the sex offender, the terrorist, to paraphrase Becker, society's 'outsiders' (Becker, 1963). Such folk devils represent a threat to the moral fabric of civil society and provide an embodiment of social decline. Once a folk devil has been brought to the attention of the public, most often by a media tuned to the prevailing ideological climate, the negatives are accentuated and a 'trial by media' commences (these concepts are further explored in Chapter 6). In these circumstances, resulting public hysteria (moral panic) is harnessed and massaged by the media, amidst calls from the great and the good to man the cultural and moral barricades. The initial reaction on the part of the media, police and politicians can often be identified as exaggerated, and the moral panic is quickly forgotten. However, when moral panic occurs during times of rapid social change, particularly when society has not had time to adapt to such change (Furedi, 1994), the hostile reaction becomes galvanised and can influence both policy and law.

A tragic example of this was the murder of a two-year-old toddler, James Bulger, by two 10-year-old boys following his abduction from a shopping centre in Bootle, Liverpool, on 12 February 1993. The horror was exacerbated as CCTV images from the shopping centre appeared to show the two 10-year-olds searching for a suitable target, and subsequently leading James Bulger by the hand from the centre to his death. In the immediate aftermath of the case, both the public and the press furiously debated the very concept of 'childhood' in contemporary Britain, and cultural notions of moral innocence and moral evil were played out (Scraton, 1997). At the boys' initial Magistrate's Court hearing, police had to hold back over 500 furious protesters, and the *Sun* newspaper collected a petition of 280,000 signatures requesting harsh sentencing in the case. The subsequent public policy response was predictably dramatic and chimed with public requests for a harsher and 'more traditional' approach to youth justice that 'condemned more and cared less', more CCTV cameras in public spaces and stricter controls on screen violence and 'video nasties'.

Since the Bulger case, child safety has been a perennial media topic and regular source of moral panic in the UK, following a number of shocking cases and the social discovery, or rediscovery, of paedophilia due in a large part to large-scale internet use, and associated fears (Davidson and Gottschalk, 2011; Yar, 2013). As Cohen (2002) points out, moral panic can be related to a 'disaster' analogy with three principal stages apparent. First is *taking stock* – a crucial phase in which the public's imagination or attention is harnessed. There is likely to be an exaggeration of the deviant behaviour or the numbers involved, accompanied by dramatic headlines and sensationalist reporting. Phase two is *prediction* – here the offensive behaviour is identified as the 'tip of the iceberg', with the moral future seen as bleak. The final phase is *symbolisation* – with a link to deviance drawn via a particular identifying factor (such as clothing) or the membership of a particular social group.

In terms of the current Coalition government, alongside the seemingly perpetually perceived threat of youth deviance (the most recent incarnation being 'hoodies' and 'knife gangs'), the disaster analogy is most appropriately applied to certain aspects of the response to the policy of increased immigration to the UK since the mid-1990s. This fear has been exacerbated by the emergent risk and danger associated with radical Islamist terrorism post 9/11, 7/7 and the apparently open-ended 'war on terror.' Currently, the fear of a 'new wave' of immigration from Eastern Europe, specifically Romania and Hungary in 2014, linked to domestic concerns over pressure on jobs and services, has appeared as a popular political and media theme. The political response to this theme in particular has been theatrical at times, and alongside the rhetoric has included the government funding of a video warning would-be Polish immigrants of the dangers associated with moving to Britain, and a fleet of Home Office 'Immigration Vans' (which the public quickly dubbed 'Racist Vans') warning illegal immigrants to 'go home or face arrest' (*Economist*, 2013). This kind of moral panic response has been seen before, and can be linked to another important criminological theory with policy implications, that of 'deviancy amplification'.

Deviancy amplification and self-fulfilling prophecy

Deviancy amplification theory (a term first coined by Wilkins, 1964) refers to a political or media reaction to perceived deviance or criminality (often moral panic), which has the effect of exacerbating or increasing the problem rather than resolving it – the problem thus becomes self-perpetuating. Deviancy amplification is seen to occur most often during periods of social strain and economic hardship, when public levels of tolerance and intolerance towards lifestyles and cultures perceived as deviant or different are heightened.

In these circumstances, public intolerance can lead to a widespread negative reaction, which may in turn lead to policy change, often with populist overtones. A powerful example of deviancy amplification in action is the work of Stuart Hall *et al.* (1978), *Policing the Crisis: Mugging, the State and Law and Order*. The 'crisis' in *Policing the Crisis* refers to public fears over the apparent growth of street robbery in London in the mid 1970s, and in particular the adaptation of the American slang term 'mugging' by the British media and subsequent deviancy amplification. The real power of the media in such circumstances is that of defini- tion, as Hall *et al.* state:

> If the world is not to be represented as a jumble of random and chaotic events, then they must be identified (i.e. named, defined, related to other events known as the audience), and assigned to a social context (i.e. placed within a frame of meanings familiar to the audience). This process – identification and contextualisation – is one of the most important through which events are 'made to mean' by the media.
>
> (Hall *et al.*, 1978: 54)

The research points out that Britain in the late 1970s was a society in steep socio-economic decline, and as such was ripe for the creation of new scapegoats and folk devils, including the 'black mugger'. Hall *et al.* point out that popular opinion of the time supported the view that white youths were able to cope with the economic crisis, whereas black youths were not, leading to the adoption of a 'false enemy' by the media, politicians and the public. This stereotyping and negative reaction resulted in over-policing and an indiscriminate use of stop and search and raiding in certain areas of London, predominantly areas with large African-Caribbean populations.

In turn, this form of heavy-handed policing policy was linked to the Brixton Riots of 1981 (Scarman, 1982), and was identified as a catalyst for a series of serious race-related disturbances that followed Brixton in a number of other large British cities – notably Handsworth in Birmingham, St Pauls in Bristol and Toxteth in Liverpool (see Hall, 1999). Accordingly, the primary value in the recognition of the potential effect of moral panic and deviancy amplification for criminal justice policy-makers would appear to lie in the requirement to consider the implication of instigating policy change as a knee-jerk reaction to public pressure, or the political reinforcement of a negative media stereotype.

Case study: The deportation of Abu Qatada – social change, moral panic and the globalisation of crime

This case study illustrates the development of human rights policy and protective legislation in the UK since the Second World War, by considering it alongside the eight-year legal battle to deport the terrorist suspect Abu Qatada back to his native Jordan to stand trial. It also highlights how the public and media perception of social policy changes over time, sometimes a very short time, and the relevance of moral panic theory to contemporary policy debates.

UK social policy and the universal human rights project

Reflection on the case of Abu Qatada raises a number of interesting issues when considering public policy. A foundation of British social policy since the end of the Second World War has been the human rights project, with a number of significant social changes underpinned by human rights guarantees.

During the Second World War, the allies agreed on four human rights principles that would form the basis of a post-war declaration: *freedom of speech, freedom of religion, freedom from fear* and *freedom from want*. In December 1948, these principles formed the basis for the Universal Declaration of Human Rights (UDHR), which was signed by 48 countries, giving strength to the United Nations aim of the adoption of fundamental human rights worldwide. While the UDHR did not have the power of a treaty, it acted as a catalyst for the human rights debate.

The UDHR provided the inspiration for the European Convention on Human Rights (ECHR) 1953, which was seen as a regional foundation for the post-war human rights agenda and a reflection on the serious human rights violations that had occurred during the war. During the 1970s and 1980s, several pressure groups lobbied parliament to adopt a British bill of rights that would act to guarantee treaty rights under the ECHR, and in the run up to the 1997 election the Labour opposition pledged to provide an act

---

to fully incorporate the Convention into domestic law. The creation of the Human Rights Act 1998 ensured that, wherever possible, British legislation (and therefore indirectly, social policy) should comply with the rights laid down in the ECHR.

Since its adoption, the Human Rights Act 1998 has proved controversial, and has attracted criticism from both sides of the political divide. A particularly rich area of debate has centred on the treatment of terrorism suspects and public safety. The concept of terrorism in the UK has changed dramatically over the past 15 years, with the 'traditional' threat of Irish Republican terrorism diminishing following the Good Friday Agreement in 1998, to be replaced with the 'globalised' threat of Islamic terrorism, particularly in the aftermath of the attacks on New York on 11 September 2001.

The social discovery of this new, apparently ubiquitous form of risk has led to growing concerns over potential terrorist operations and recruitment in Britain, and a crackdown on the preaching of religious hatred. This situation does not sit easily in a country with a social history of freedom of speech and religion, and a protective stance towards refugees and asylum-seekers. Attempts to fight global terrorism while upholding the principles of the Human Rights Act have seen politicians under increasing media scrutiny, with the former Labour Government Home Secretary John Reid arguing: 'I am the first to admit that the means we have of fighting it are so inadequate that we are fighting with one arm tied behind our backs' (Travis and Dodd, 2007).

The case of Abu Qatada

Omar Mahmoud Mohammed Othman, better known simply as Abu Qatada, was born in Bethlehem in 1960, a Jordanian citizen with Palestinian ancestry. In September 1993, Qatada arrived in Britain as a 'Muslim cleric' bearing a forged passport and claiming political asylum as a refugee. His basis for asylum was that he had been subject to torture by the Jordanian government after being accused of planning terrorist attacks. Subsequently, Qatada was granted asylum and refugee status in Britain, and in 1998 he applied for indefinite leave to remain.

Prior to his application for indefinite leave, Qatada had publicly made a number of threats from his London base, *inter alia* agreeing with the killing of converts from Islam in Algeria, and in 1999 stated in a speech that he supported the killing of 'Jews and Americans', episodes that brought him to the attention of the British media and public as a 'radical cleric' and 'hate preacher'. In the wake of this publicity, Qatada was convicted *in absentia* of terrorist charges in Jordan, with a life sentence imposed.

During 2001, the Metropolitan police questioned Qatada about his relationship with a number of terrorist organisations, and after searching his home found a large amount of money (£170,000) and evidence linking him to Chechen terrorists. Late in 2001, while being investigated by the police, Qatada absconded, and after being found and arrested in October 2002, he was detained in Belmarsh High Security Prison. After being held in Belmarsh for two and a half years, Qatada was granted bail and returned to London to once again face media scrutiny. In August 2005, the British government re-arrested Qatada, and he was sent to Full Sutton Prison to await deportation to Jordan. However, these government attempts to deport him were unsuccessful, and in April 2008 the Court of Appeal expressed concerns over his human rights status should he be returned to Jordan; again he was granted conditional bail.

Late in 2008, Qatada was again arrested and his bail revoked by the Special Immigration Appeals Commission (SIAC) following concerns over absconding risk. During February 2009, the House of Lords passed a ruling in support of the government's policy to permit the removal of terrorism suspects from British jurisdiction to face trial abroad, on the proviso that assurances over treatment and due process were agreed before-hand. On this basis, it appeared that Qatada could finally be deported to Jordan to face the historical terrorism charges. This position was strength-ened in January 2012 after the European Court of Human Rights (ECtHR) ruled that Qatada could be deported to Jordan providing that assurances were received, but significantly not while any risk remained that torture would be used against him.

In the aftermath of these landmark rulings, Qatada was released from prison by the SIAC despite security fears and media uproar. In May 2012, Qatada failed in an attempt to appeal his deportation at the ECtHR, leading the Home Secretary Theresa May to state triumphantly to the media that 'Qatada will soon be out of Britain for good!' (Home Office, 2013). After two further unsuc-cessful attempts to appeal his bail conditions at SIAC and the High Court, Qatada won a SIAC appeal in November 2012 on the grounds that he would be unable to receive a fair trial in Jordan, an outcome Theresa May described as 'deeply unsatisfactory' while questioning the legal basis used by the tribunal. Subsequently, Qatada was once again released, with the press revealing that his legal aid bill to date stood at over half a million pounds.

Public anger increased once more in February 2013 when it was revealed that Qatada had been granted an injunction preventing harassment or protest outside his home. Public feelings again ran high during March 2013 when Theresa May lost an appeal to force the deportation, the court once again expressing its concern over human rights and the potential for the torture in Jordan, this time the torture of witnesses in any subsequent case. After being refused permission to appeal by the Court of Appeal in this instance, the government stated that it would apply directly to the Supreme Court for permission to deport, and the following month revealed that a 'mutual assistance treaty' had been signed with Jordan containing human rights and procedural guarantees. The treaty became law in June 2013, and thus provided an immediate outlet for the deportation of Qatada. On 7 July 2013, following eight years of legal wrangling, Abu Qatada was deported from Britain to face terrorism charges in Jordan. In a speech to the House of

Commons on 8 July, the Home Secretary Theresa May stated that she was 'immensely proud' of her role in his deportation in the face of 'real problems with our human rights laws' (Home Office, 2013).

Reflections on the Qatada case

In the aftermath of the deportation of Abu Qatada, a drama that the British public had watched unfold for two decades, he was variously described as 'Osama Bin Laden's right hand man', 'Britain's nastiest Islamist' and 'refugee turned detainee'. This last description allows us to consider his case outside the media bubble that has sometimes approached hysteria over the past decade.

Qatada was destined to be a difficult figure given the timing of his arrival and subsequent stay in Britain. He arrived at a time when the politics of law and order had become a key debate in the electability of politicians, and was granted asylum in the UK as Tony Blair's New Labour were riding to a landslide victory by being tough on crime and its causes. New Labour's election in 1997 also coincided with a growing political awareness of the need to participate in global business and of policy and legislative activism in immigration matters. Mulvey (2011) argues that this activism extended to the characterisation of migrants according to 'type' adopting a dual approach whereby migrant workers were viewed as desirable, and asylum-seekers and refugees were seen as undesirable. Thus, the social policy discourse surrounding immigration under New Labour has had the consequence that the media and public see the immigration system as being in crisis, which has in turn led to migration, and in particular undesirable migration, being identified as placing increasing strain on public services (Mulvey, 2011). Clearly, this has not been lost on politicians or the media, and immigration policy is now a continuing theme.

The Qatada case can also be viewed in terms of a classic moral panic, with Cohen's disaster analogy providing an appropriate vehicle for the examination of both immigration policy and the perceived threat of Islamic terrorism. Having seemingly been freed from the threat of Irish republicanism, the British public have over the last decade been asked to *take stock* and focus on a new, and potentially more serious, threat; to *predict* the future for Britain as a 'partner' in the 'war on terror'; and to *symbolise* the identifying factors that classify and characterise these new folk devils. As Cohen argues, the social response to new folk devils will often include declarations about moral boundaries and how much diversity can be tolerated:

> [Thus] the community begins to censure forms of behaviour which have been present in the group for some time but have never attracted any particular attention before, and . . . certain people in the group who have already acquired a disposition to act deviantly move into the breach and begin to test the boundary in question.
>
> (Cohen, 2002: 162)

The debate on how much diversity can be tolerated in terms of future social policy and legislation on immigration and national security is one that is likely to run and run, and may yet lead to the repeal of the Human Rights Act, a hard-fought 'guarantee' over 50 years in the making.

Key points summary

This chapter explores a number of key areas that provide the foundation for the creation, development and management of criminal policy-making in contemporary globalised society. It argues the following:

- The complexity and technological pace of modern society means that social change is occurring at an unprecedented rate, and that the frequent social discovery of new or augmented social problems is subject to a reactive global media and critical public audience. This has led to a proliferation of informal and formal social control strategies that are increasingly geared to globalisation and burgeoning attempts at criminal policy universalism.
- As witness and contributor to this rapid social change and globalisation, the identity of the individual nation state has become complicated. The nation state remains the primary vessel for prevailing ideology, domestic public policy and censure, in order to maintain consensus and social order. However, the wide range of social policy initiatives requires the state regularly to reconsider the efficacy of its provision, resulting in policy seemingly in perpetual flux. This instability means that the definition of crime and deviance is often left to politicised criminalisation and decriminalisation strategies without an adequate consideration of normative standards or social stability. This can in turn increase fear of crime and intensify perception of risk.
- The management of risk has in many ways replaced attempts to suppress or eradicate crime, meaning that much contemporary social policy is tuned to risk rather than progress. The global nature of risk has also garnered rapid change in social order and fluid perceptions of nation state, national security, culture and ethnicity.
- The organisation and proliferation of contemporary media has ensured that the public audience is highly tuned to materials that expose deviance, criminality, risk and unfamiliar social change. This tuning ensures that both moral panic and deviancy amplification regularly occur, and that both politicians and policy-makers see the media spectacle as a guide to public mood and a sounding board for the production of popular policy.

Critical thinking discussion topics

1   What are the distinctive features of social change theory, and what role does social policy play in addressing social problems and instigating social change?

2   Do you agree or disagree with the argument made by Black (1976) that social
     control is the normative aspect of social life? Give reasons for your answer.
3   To what extent has the spread of neoliberalism accelerated globalisation and
     increased our risk of becoming victims of crime?
4   What is the 'purpose' and 'role' of the nation state at the start of the twenty-
     first century with regard to crime policy and security?
5   Cohen (2002) argues that 'One of the most recurrent types of moral panic in
     Britain since the war had been associated with the emergence of various
     forms of youth culture (originally almost exclusively working class, but
     often recently middle class or student based) whose behaviour is deviant or
     delinquent.' Why might this be the case?

Seminar task

You are shipwrecked on a remote desert island with 300 others, and on realising
that it could be some time before you are rescued, you form a social policy
committee. You are tasked with writing a set of six universal social rules to form
a basic constitution for the community – which six social rules will you enshrine
as laws to protect/regulate yourself and your community?

Recommended further reading

Beck, U. and Beck-Gernsheim, E. (2003) *Individualisation: Institutionalised Individualism
    and its Social and Political Consequences.* London: Sage.
Cohen, S. (2002) *Folk Devils and Moral Panics* (3rd edn). London: Routledge.
Hall, S., Criticher, C., Jefferson, T., Clarke, J.N. and Roberts, B. (1978) *Policing the Crisis:
    Mugging, the State and Law and Order.* London: Palgrave Macmillan.
Mythen, G. and Walklate, S. (2012) 'Global terrorism, risk and the state'. In S. Hall and
    S. Winlow (eds) *New Directions in Criminological Theory.* London: Routledge.
Schwendinger, H. and Schwendinger, J. (1970) 'Defenders of order or guardians of human
    rights?' *Issues in Criminology*, 5(2): 123–57.

References

Akers, R. and Sellers, C. (2008) *Criminological Theories: Introduction, Evaluation and
    Application.* London: Oxford University Press.
Baker, E. and Roberts, J. (2005) 'Globalisation and the new punitiveness'. In J. Pratt,
    D. Brown, M. Brown, S. Hallsworth and W. Morrison (eds) *The New Punitiveness:
    Trends, Theories, Perspectives.* Cullompton: Willan.
Beck, U. (1986) *Risikogesellschaft.* Frankfurt: Suhrkamp.
Beck, U. (1992) *Risk Society: Towards a New Modernity.* London: Sage.
Beck, U. (1999) *World Risk Society.* Cambridge: Polity Press.
Beck, U. and Beck-Gernsheim, E. (2003) *Individualisation: Institutionalised Individualism
    and its Social and Political Consequences.* London: Sage.
Becker, H. (1963) *Outsiders: Studies in Sociology of Deviance.* New York: Free Press.
Black, D. (1976) *The Behaviour of Law.* New York: Academic Press.
Box, S. (1983) *Power, Crime, and Mystification.* London: Tavistock.

Cameron, D. (2011) 'Prime Minister's speech on cyberspace'. [Online]. Retrieved from https://www.gov.uk/government/news/prime-ministers-speech-on-cyberspace (accessed November 2013).

Cohen, S. (2002) *Folk Devils and Moral Panics* (3rd edn). London: Routledge.

Considine, M. (2005) *Making Public Policy: Institutions, Actors, Strategies*. Cambridge: Polity Press.

Cover, R. (1986) 'Violence and the word'. *Yale Law Journal*, 95: 1601.

Davidson, J. and Gottschalk, P. (eds) (2011) *Internet Child Abuse: Current Research and Policy*. London: Routledge-Cavendish.

Durkheim, E. (1982) *The Rules of Sociological Method*. New York: Free Press.

Economist (2013, August 3) 'Comments on the Coalition: enter the van men'. *Economist*.

Edelman, M. (1977) *Political Language: Words that Succeed and Policies that Fail*. New York: Academic Press

Ericson, R. and Haggerty, K. (1997) *Policing the Risk Society*. Toronto: Toronto University Press.

Furedi, F. (1994) 'A plague of moral panics'. *Living Marxism* (73). [Online]. Retrieved from http://web.archive.org/web/19991005032410/www.informinc.co.uk/LM/LM73/LM73_Frank.html (accessed November 2013).

Giddens, A. (2000) *Runaway World*. New York: Routledge.

Glennerster, H. (2007) *British Social Policy: 1945 to the Present*. London: Blackwell.

Hall, S. (1999) 'From Scarman to Stephen Lawrence'. *History Workshop Journal*, 48(3): 187–97.

Hall, S., Criticher, C., Jefferson, T., Clarke, J.N. and Roberts, B. (1978) *Policing the Crisis: Mugging, the State and Law and Order*. London: Palgrave Macmillan.

Henry, S. (2009) *Social Deviance*. Cambridge: Polity Press.

Hirschi, T. (1969) *Causes of Delinquency*. Berkeley, CA: University of California Press.

Hobbes, T. (2012 [1651]) *Leviathan*, Malcolm, N. (ed). Oxford: Oxford University Press.

Home Office (2013) *Home Secretary addresses Parliament on Abu Qatada*, 8 July 2013. London: HMSO.

Innes, M. (2003) *Investigating Murder: Detective Work and the Police Response to Criminal Homicide*. Oxford: Clarendon Press.

Jewkes, Y. (2004) *Media and Crime*. London: Sage.

Jewkes, Y. and Yar, M. (eds) (2010) *Handbook of Internet Crime*. Cullompton: Willan.

Lewis, P., Newburn, T., Taylor, M., McGillivray, C., Greenhill, A., Frayman, H. and Proctor, R. (2012) *Reading the Riots: Investigating England's Summer of Disorder*. London: LSE.

Locke, J. (1996 [1690]) *Two Treatises of Government*, Laslett, P. (ed.). Cambridge: Cambridge University Press.

Mitchell, T. (2006) 'Society, economy, and the state effect'. In A. Sharma and A. Gupta (eds) *The Anthropology of the State: A Reader*. Oxford: Blackwell.

Mulvey, G. (2011) 'Immigration under New Labour: policy and effects'. *Journal of Ethnic and Migration Studies*, 37(9): 1477–93.

Mythen, G. and Walklate, S. (2012) 'Global terrorism, risk and the state'. In S. Hall and S. Winlow (eds) *New Directions in Criminological Theory*. London: Routledge.

Parsons, T. (1955) *Family, Socialization and Interaction Process*. New York: Routledge.

Parsons, T. (1960) *Structure and Process in Modern Societies*. Michigan: Free Press.

Passas, N. (2000) 'Global anomie, dysnomie, and economic crime: hidden consequences of neoliberalism and globalisation in Russia and around the world'. *Social Justice*, 27(2): 16–43.

Quinney, R. (1974) *The Social Reality of Crime*. New York: Little, Brown.

Quinney, R. (1975) *Criminology*. New York: Little, Brown.

Quinney, R. (1977) *Class, State, and Crime*. New York: David McKay.

Rigakos, G. (1999) 'Risk society and actuarial criminology: prospects for a critical discourse'. *Canadian Journal of Criminology*, 41(2): 137–51.

Roach-Anleu, S. (2000) *Law and Social Change*. London: Sage.

Robertson, I. (1980) *Social Problems*. New York: Random House.

Rousseau, J. (1990 [1762]) *The Collected Writings of Rousseau*, Kelley, C. and Masters, R. (eds). Hanover, NH: University Press of New England.

Scarman, L. (1982) *The Brixton Disorders 10–12 April 1981: Report of an Inquiry*. London: Penguin.

Schwendinger, H. and Schwendinger, J., (1970) 'Defenders of order or guardians of human rights?' *Issues in Criminology*, 5(2): 123–57.

Scraton, P. (1997) *Childhood in Crisis*. London: Routledge.

Simons, G. and Stroup, W. (1997) 'Law and social change: the implications of chaos theory in understanding the role of the American legal system'. In D. Milovanovic (ed.) *Chaos, Criminology, and Social Justice*. Westport, CT: Praeger.

Surette, R. (1998) *Media, Crime and Criminal Justice*. Belmont, CA: Wadsworth.

Tomkins, A. (2002) 'Legislating against terror: the Anti-Terrorism, Crime and Security Act 2001'. *Public Law*: 205–20.

Travis, A. and Dodd, V. (2007) Reid Warning to Judges over Control Orders. [Online] Retrieved from http://www.theguardian.com/politics/2007/may/25/uk.topstories3 (accessed November 2013).

Waters, M. (1995) *Globalization: Key Ideas*. London: Routledge.

Weber, M. (1946) *Max Weber: Essays in Sociology*. New York: Oxford University Press.

Wilkins, L. (1964) *Social Deviance*. London: Tavistock.

Winch, P. (1958) *The Idea of a Social Science*. London: Routledge & Kegan Paul.

Whitehead, T. (2011, August 9) 'Theresa May rejects calls for water cannon'. *Daily Telegraph*.

Yar, M. (2006) *Cybercrime and Society*. London: Sage.

Yar, M. (2013) *Cybercrime and Society* (2nd edn). London: Sage.

3   Criminal justice and social policy

Chapter summary

This chapter provides an overview of major ways of thinking about criminal justice policy that seek to locate it within a broader policy landscape. It takes as its starting point the perspective that criminal justice policy should not be treated as distinct or separate from other social policy realms. Instead, criminal justice policy and wider social policy should be approached as interrelated aspects of public policy that can be applied interchangeably to regulate behaviour. It discusses the claims that the recent tendency to separate the two removes the understanding of crime from its social context, and legitimises policies that promote the incursion of traditional criminal justice agencies into ever-widening circles of social activity.

When reading the chapter, you should consider the implications for victims, offenders and the public of favouring criminal justice over alternative forms of public policy intervention.

The chapter looks at:

- the problematisation of behaviour and the contingent nature of state responses;
- the relationship between penal and welfare policy and the decline in the belief that welfare has any purchase on crime and punishment;
- the boundaries between social and criminal justice policy, and how these have shifted historically in the face of a changing political landscape marked by the demise of the social democratic welfare state and the rise of the neoliberal welfare state;
- debates about models of social inclusion and New Labour's record of tackling 'crime and causes of crime';
- the concepts of the 'penalisation of poverty' and the 'criminalisation of social policy';
- recent policy developments and the concept of the 'punitive welfare state'.

Case study: Criminalisation of poverty and ASBOs

In the case study, you will be introduced to key debates about the blurring of social and criminal justice as exemplified by the creation of Anti-Social Behaviour

Orders. The case study illustrates the concept of the criminalisation of social policy, and Cohen's (1985) dispersal of justice thesis.

Understanding social policy

What is meant by public policy?

Social policy is an aspect of public policy. It refers to 'the actions and positions of the state as the overriding collective entity in society' in relation to matters of social or collective concern, as opposed to the 'private concerns of individuals or small groups'. Its primary focus is the allocation of public resources and involves a 'set of inter related decisions taken by political actors or groups concerning the selection of goals and the means of their achievement within a specified situation where these actions should, in principle, be within the power of those actors to achieve' (Jenkins, 1998: 2). As Hill makes clear, the public policy process is a 'complex and multi-layered one'. It is a political process in the 'widest sense' that incorporates a range of different actors, including politicians, civil servants, publicly employed officials and pressure groups. What is more, it is the product of a series of decisions (it is not usually one decision) taken by political actors (Hill, 2013). These decisions are contingent upon a 'specified situation', are shaped by the boundaries of interpretation of the situation, and are restricted to matters over which the 'state has authority' and which are 'practically feasible' (Hill and Bramley,1986).

While there is considerable debate about the parameters of social policy (these include whether or not criminal justice policy constitutes a branch of social policy), there is a convincing argument to be made that penal and criminal justice policy should not be studied in isolation from the wider branch of social policy, since at an ideological level they share the same justifying objective of contributing towards social justice (Hudson, 1993), and at a pragmatic level policy decisions made in other social policy realms frequently have implications for crime rates and criminal justice policy. An example of this are recent changes to housing benefit payments that critics claim have increased the likelihood of individuals and families becoming homeless (Ramesh, 2013). This social welfare policy change not only raises philosophical and moral issues about fairness, equality and citizens' rights, but also has implications for offending rates and criminal justice policy as homelessness is a social factor widely acknowledged by academics and social policy advisors as being closely associated with a heightened risk of offending (Social Exclusion Unit, 2002). The concept of the interconnectedness of wider social policy and crime is eloquently illustrated in the following quote from Dorling in his paper on murder:

> Behind the man with the knife is the man who sold him the knife, the man who did not give him a job, the man who decided that his school did not need funding, the man who closed down the branch plant where he could have worked, the man who decided to reduce benefit levels so that a black economy grew. . . . Those who perpetrated the social violence that was done to the lives

of young men starting some 20 years ago are the prime suspects for most of the murders in Britain.

(Dorling, 2008: 42)

What is meant by social policy?

Defining social policy in a theoretically coherent way is problematic as there is no one definition of social policy that is universally accepted. Despite this, however, it is generally agreed that its primary focus is the identification of a social problem or need and its amelioration through state action. Although, as an area of study, social policy is traditionally associated with the activities of the state that seek to enhance the welfare of its citizens, opinions are divided over the specific aspects of public policy that this incorporates. Some maintain that the scope of social policy should be restricted to the activities of state institutions charged with the administration of public services under Beveridge's original configuration of the welfare state (the 'Big Five' of income maintenance and social security, health, education, housing, personal social services and employment). Others argue that areas of public policy such as employment, which fall within the Big Five, should not be located within the social policy realm, but should rather occupy the realm of economics, while yet others make the case that criminal justice policy, which falls outside the Big Five, should be understood as a branch of public policy that straddles the realms of both social policy and criminal law (Alcock *et al.*, 2008).

To help explain the contested nature of the definition of social policy, Hill and Bramley (1986) identify three key competing perspectives: the *social administration perspective*, the *welfare economics perspective* and the *political economy perspective*. Between these perspectives there are few common elements, and considerable differences in terms of boundaries. Indeed, while some favour narrower definitions, others are broader and more unwieldy.

Social administration: social policy equates with a concern with welfare, and is closely related to the development of the welfare state. It adopts an institutional approach to social policy analysis. Its subject matter is the decisions, practices and institutions of the Big Five of the welfare state. The most influential writer within the post-war social administration tradition is Titmuss. His definition extends to 'all collectively provided services ... which implicitly includes things like defence' (p.7). It fits with the functionalist tradition in sociology, assumes social consensus on wants and needs, and places a high value on acts of altruism. Key elements of the tradition are: (a) positive attempts to promote the welfare of individuals; (b) the diversion of resources to and the promotion of care of dependent groups; (c) a more general redistribution of resources; (d) the promotion of altruism; and (e) the promotion of community and collectivism.

Welfare economics: equates social policy with the provision of welfare goods and services provided to individuals, and emphasises redistribution.

The provision of services is made necessary by the deficits of the market economy. The case for a state allocation of resources arises when the primary market for allocation – the competitive free market – fails to achieve efficient allocation. At the core of social policy is its 'distribution branch'. This can embrace (re)distribution in cash and in the form of services. This approach incorporates concepts of altruism and social justice.

Political economy: equates social policy with economic processes and capitalist interests. It fits within the critical or neo-Marxist tradition. Social policy is essential for the maintenance of capitalism: assisting the reproduction of labour power (e.g. through providing services that are important to the continued availability of a productive labour force); contributing to the budgets of working households in terms of cash benefits; and subsidising key commodities (e.g. housing). It encompasses a broad view of social policy and includes services such as water and sewage. Social policies such as health, housing, child benefit and family income support are viewed as pivotal to the physical maintenance of labour power, whereas education is concerned with its ideological reproduction. This tradition also focuses on the 'unreproductive' elements of the economic system that are necessary for its maintenance. Social policies embrace both negative and positive functions – the positive one of 'legitimation' (securing consent) and the negative one of control (overcoming dissent). A radical perspective on social work and community work views social policy as embracing both roles.

Source: Hill and Bramley (1986)

Despite the definitional and jurisdictional problems that emanate from the wider debates about the parameters of social policy, Hudson, writing in the 1990s, makes the still valid argument that penal and criminal justice policy constitute social policy as there are aspects of the criminal justice system that are intrinsically concerned with the welfare of the offender and victims. Also, more importantly, there is considerable policy symbiosis: social welfare and criminal justice policy are underpinned by the same ideological movements; are designed and delivered in the same socio-economic contexts; and deal with the same groups and individuals (e.g. the disadvantaged, the poor, the mentally ill, the addicted) (Hudson, 1993). This inevitably leads to an overlap between the policy realms.

The view that separate realms of public policy share common ideologically defined features has led Rose (2000) to talk about *family resemblances*. He argues that the key concepts and ideas that shape different public policies, practices and initiatives serve to create *strategic coherence*. To illustrate this point, he cites the prominence given to the notion of individual responsibility-taking ('responsibilisation') across the social policy realms of health, education and social housing, as well as criminal justice. A contemporary example of 'family resemblances' in public policy-making can be identified in the Coalition government's privatisation agenda, which has seen a wide range of public services being put out to private tendering (Cabinet Office, 2011).

The problematisation of behaviour and the contingent nature of state responses

Private troubles and public issues

The sociologist C. Wright Mills, writing in *The Sociological Imagination*, distinguishes between personal troubles and public issues. For him, *troubles* have to do with 'an individual's character and with those limited areas of social life of which he is directly and personally aware'. Hence, a trouble is an individual, private matter related to a perceived or real threat to values cherished by the individual. Public issues, by contrast, relate to 'matters that transcend those local environments of the individual and the limited range of his life' (Mills, 1959: 8). Private troubles become public issues when wider societal/public values are threatened. This invariably occurs when a problem is conceived as being a widespread trouble that can no longer be maintained in the private everyday environment. The construction of a problem as a public or social issue, as opposed to a private concern, provides the legitimacy for collective action by the state.

An aspect of the study of public policy that is of interest to students of both crime and social problems is the process by which behaviour becomes defined as a crime problem, moves from the private to the public realm, and falls under the auspices of the criminal justice system instead of the education, health or social welfare system. As Howard Becker (1963) reminds us, an act is not inherently deviant, rather the attribution of deviancy to behaviour represents the power of moral entrepreneurs to impose the label (see also Chapter 2). Furthermore, once behaviour is defined as deviating from socially acceptable norms or mores, it is a political decision as to whether (or not) it warrants a policy response, and if so, the type of public policy response that is appropriate. A recent example of behaviour that moved from the private realm of the family to the public realm of criminal justice is marital rape.

As Elias points out, social sensibilities and mores about acceptable and unacceptable behaviour are subject to change over time (Garland, 2012). Consequently, public perceptions of what constitutes a social problem are not fixed, but rather are both historically variable and situationally contingent. Similarly, beliefs and ideas about how to address a problem vary across historical periods. Examples of changes in public sensibilities that have had legal consequences include the decriminalisation of homosexuality and abortion, and the criminalisation of child labour and the abuse of women. The contingent, non-fixed nature of the public policy means that the boundaries between social welfare policy and criminal justice policy operate in flux, and frequently appear blurred and permeable.

Depending on how a 'problem' is defined, interpreted, conceptualised and theorised, social welfare expenditure can substitute for criminal justice expenditure, and vice versa (Rose, 2000). Pivotal to this distinction is the degree to which a problem is constructed as a threat to social order. Recent examples of this include the attribution of the label of 'gang activity' to a range of youthful activities and transgressions (Pitts, 2008), and the association of night-time economy binge-drinking with public disturbance and disorder (Hobbs *et al.*, 2003). As Simon (2007) reminds us, in modern, risk-averse societies, the discourse of disorder and threat creates a 'culture of fear' that legitimates the criminalisation of an increasing range of social problems, and thereby the expansion of the right hand of the state [see the later section on Anti-Social Behaviour Orders (ABSOs)].

As a consequence of this blurring of the boundaries, a public concern originally defined as being the exclusive preserve of the social welfare system (e.g. heroin use) can be redefined as the exclusive preserve of the criminal justice system through the adoption of the prohibition perspective, or may be redefined in such a way that it straddles both through the adoption of the harm reduction perspective. The decision of whether (or not) to criminalise a problematic behaviour, to apply a social welfare or a criminal justice solution and/or to medicalise rather than criminalise a 'problem' (transferring responsibility to health rather than criminal justice practitioners) is ultimately a political one that reflects a combination of ideological preferences (what should be done) and pragmatic considerations (what can be done).

That said, although it is manifestly the case that it is politicians who are mandated by the electorate to exercise judgement about the nature of the problem, the solution required and the resources to be allocated to it, the vagaries of modern politics means that politicians do not operate in a vacuum but need to take account of competing interests, both within and outside government, that seek to shape policy outcomes through the promotion of their own definition of the problem and its solution (see also Chapter 4). An example of conflicting definitions of a social problem and its resolution (e.g. drug misuse) is explored in the case study on David Nutt (see Chapter 5).

The left hand and the right hand of the state

Bourdieu (1998, as cited in Wacquant, 2001) states that when reaching a policy decision, the state has at its disposal both a *left hand* and a *right hand* of state solutions for addressing an identified social problem. The left hand of the state's solutions is predicated on the concept of social needs to be met, and is 'symbolised' by social welfare provisions of 'education, public health care, social assistance and social housing', whereas the right-hand solutions are predicated on the concept of risks to be managed, and are symbolised by law and order provisions of the 'police, the courts and the prison system' (Wacquant, 2001: 402). When deciding on which set of responses to adopt, politicians tend to favour those that fit best with their political party's own ideological predilections.

While some writers (Downes and Hansen, 2006a), adopting the social administration perspective, maintain that the left hand of the state and the right hand of the state provide distinctive, alternative and competing institutions and practices, encompassing fundamentally different values, imperatives and preoccupations, others (Wacquant, 2001) see them as essentially complementary, sharing the same overarching social regulation function. Writers favouring the former position argue that the distinctive, separate features of social welfare provision are too frequently dismissed; by contrast, writers favouring the latter position argue that the criminal justice system and the wider social welfare system cannot be separated as they function symbiotically to regulate and control the poor (Downes and Hansen, 2006a). Rose (2000), who adopts the regulatory perspective, argues that the social welfare and criminal justice systems have the same populations in their gaze, and share the same overarching aims and objectives to manage and control conduct through the implementation of strategies, programmes and techniques that serve to 'normalise' behaviour. Similarly, Wacquant (2001) argues that the spread of neoliberalism across Western Europe (and the ideological changes that it has brought about) has resulted in the right hand of state solutions superseding (in the USA) or supplementing (in the UK) the left hand of state solutions.

The welfare state and crime nexus: the relationship between social welfare and punishment

The decline in the belief that social provision reduces crime and punishment

Notwithstanding the debate about the key features, principles, ideology and normalisation function of social welfare provision, it is widely accepted by criminologists that the first two-thirds of the twentieth century were demarcated by a period of consensus among politicians, academics and penal reformers that '[W]elfare, "the welfare state" and allied forms of social provision for human needs' (Downes and Hansen, 2006a: 133) would reduce poverty and associated crime. Underpinned by a broadly social democratic political economy model (see also Chapter 7), the dominant belief was that crime was linked to social and economic deprivation, and that the solution was to pursue public policies that would create greater social and economic equality, and by so doing would redress the negative consequences of unregulated capitalism. Affluence, it was agreed, would bring about the end of crime: those not able to benefit from the new prosperity were defined as unfortunate, dysfunctional groups or individuals, who could be redeemed by the treatment strategies of the newly emerging army of welfare state professionals. Public policy was predicated on the pursuit of economic regulation based on Keynesian principles, and liberal social policy. Embracing an ethos of universalism and collectivism, governments accepted that the state had a dual responsibility to eradicate the structural causes of crime, and to provide for the welfare needs and the care of the offender. Garland calls this period *penal welfarism* (Garland, 2001; Ryan, 2005; Reiner, 2007).

However, despite the post-war bi-partisan consensus on crime, its causes and its solution, by the last third of the twentieth century the fundamental belief that welfare had any purchase on crime and punishment was in decline. Downes and Hansen (2006a) identify the key reasons that account for this 'fundamental shift' in criminological thinking in the following box.

Martinson's (1974) questioning of the efficacy of rehabilitation ideal in his infamous 'Nothing Works' paper brought in its wake a series of papers that challenged the orthodoxy that rehabilitation techniques, practised by the 'caring professions' of social workers and probation officers, could reduce crime. By extension, the gloom about rehabilitation spread to the welfare system with which it was associated. In the aftermath, the justice model of punishment in the form of 'just deserts' came to replace the rehabilitation model of punishment.

The revision of the idea that welfare provision and punishment were distinct and separate entities coincided with the growth in influence of academics, who sought to conceptualise welfare institutions and practices as part and parcel of the state's social control apparatus. The twofold impact was: (a) to lose sight of the principles of altruism and mutual help that were the bedrock of the welfare state; and (b) to conflate welfare and penality into the penal welfare state, and thereby to undermine the value of studying welfare as a 'variable in its own right'.

The 'failure' of the welfare state to fulfil its promise to prevent rising crime raised doubts about its expansion, and even retention. This decline in faith in the welfare state was seized upon by the New Right, who sought to portray the welfare state as the cause rather than the solution. Charles Murray, in his thesis on the 'underclass', promoted the idea that welfare created dependency and illegitimacy that were causally linked to crime and delinquency. His view, which influenced government thinking on both sides of the Atlantic, was that a less generous welfare state was the answer.

Personal welfare services were increasingly found wanting by academics and practitioners for their inability to meet the needs of vulnerable and marginalised people, whom it was their intention to help. Studies found that those that most benefitted from welfare provision were not the disadvantaged, but rather the educated and privileged, who least needed it. The unintended consequence of this critique was not better resourcing and a better targeting of resources, but rather a further decline in the belief in the efficacy of state provision of services to meet social needs.

Source: Downes and Hansen (2006a)

The net result of the decline in optimism about the welfare and crime and punishment nexus has meant that the pendulum has swung away from welfare-based solutions. As Downes and Hansen explain:

We are now at a period where 'welfare aims', ideals and institutions are increasingly and unduly marginalized as key variables in criminal justice policy and practice. The pendulum, as pendulums tend to do, has swung too far away from the view that welfare can or, indeed, should have any real purchase on the character of crime and punishment.

(Downes and Hansen, 2006a: 134)

The demise of the social democratic state and the rise of the neoliberal state: the importance of political ideology

Central to explanations for the decline in the welfare ideal are the social, economic and political transformations associated with changes to the political economy that have occurred over the last three decades. As Reiner reminds us:

> Political economy – whether a society is organised on neo-liberal or social democratic lines – helps explain much of the trends and patterns in crime and punishment.

(Renier, 2007: 20)

The erosion of the social democratic welfare state and the emergence of a 'hybrid' political economy that is increasingly influenced by the social and economic tenets of neoliberalism is one of key developments of the last 30 years (Downes and Hansen, 2006a). The policy of the 'rolling back' of the welfare state, which is a key feature of neoliberalism, began under the Conservative administration of Margaret Thatcher in the 1980s (and is a central pillar of the contemporary Coalition government's austerity programme). Heavily influenced by New Right thinkers and their lobbyists in both the UK and the USA, Thatcher embraced the principles of neoliberalism, characterised by an unfettered market economy, increased individualised purchasing power and self-reliance. In so doing, she reversed the post-war political compromise between capital and labour that had created the social market economy (Ryan, 2005). The resultant post-industrial social and economic insecurities associated with this ideologically driven reconfigured political economy are neatly summed up by Young (2007), who states:

> the post war settlement with high employment, stable family structures, and consensual values underpinned by the safety net of the welfare state has been replaced by a world of structural unemployment, economic precariousness, and systematic cutting of welfare provisions, and the growing instability of family life and interpersonal relations.

(Young, 2007: 59)

Neoliberalism is predicated on a relationship between the state and the citizen in which the state 'retreats' from the direct, centralised provision of social welfare that socialises risk (and as stated above is blamed for fostering dependency). In its place, new arrangements that individualise risk and risk management are created. These arrangements lay stress upon the self-activating capacities of the autonomous individual, alongside the enterprise of the market to provide the services and goods. The state, freed from direct provision, operates at 'a distance' overseeing, managing and 'steering' the activities of 'new' providers through the imposition of a range of performance management measures, such as service level agreements, contract, targets, audits and inspections that constitute 'regulating privatisation' (Crawford, 2006; Crawford and Lewis, 2007). In order to accomplish the transformation of society to one that was more individualistic, competitive and self-governing, Thatcher enacted legislation that changed almost all aspects of social welfare provision: consumption, choice, competition and self-sufficiency became the driving forces (Ryan, 2005). As McMahon points out:

> Life was transformed by the elevation of 'choice' as the motor-force of service delivery. At an individual level many welfare services were turned into quasi-markets for 'consumers'. Services previously provided by the state began to be contracted out. At one stroke not only did the profit calculation begin to govern but employment pathways were fragmented. At the level of the welfare state there was a huge shift away from an ethos of universal social insurance and a collective guaranteed minimum towards personal and family obligation.
>
> All that was solid about the post war welfare consensus – from lifelong employment to the welfare safety net – had been actively unravelled and seemed to have melted into air.
>
> (MacMahon, 2007: 24)

The transformation of the political economy landscape from the broadly social democratic to neoliberal, and in particular New Labour's retreat from the social democratic pathway laid out by the Atlee, Wilson and Callaghan governments, brought with it ideological changes that led to new modes of understanding crime and punishment, and a revision of the state's relationship to its citizens. It ushered in a raft of new pragmatic solutions, simultaneously establishing new models of the person to be governed, new causation models of poverty, deviancy and crime, and new modes of intervention; it also reconfigured the social contract that defines the rights, duties and responsibilities that are exchanged between the state and the citizen (see also Chapter 2). While New Labour maintained that the task of the welfare state was to tackle opportunity barriers, it no longer believed that the welfare state should function to extend opportunities for 'selflessness, to enhance social solidarity or deliver equality of outcome'. Essentially, the welfare state should function to complement, rather than conflict with, wider economic imperatives (Page, 2007: 19).

The demise of the social democratic welfare state and the rise of the neoliberal welfare state signalled the rejection of the structural determinism perspective on which the social causes model of crime is predicated, and the concomitant privileging of social policy solutions (the left hand of the state), and heralded its replacement with the individual deficit model of crime, which lays the emphasis on actor agency, holds the individual responsible for his or her economic and social misfortunes, and privileges penal solutions (the right hand of the state)

(Rose, 2000; Wacquant, 2001). As Downes, quoting Junger-Tas, commenting on the 'diminishing responsibility of the state' for the welfare of its populace, states:

> [The emphasis lies with] individual responsibility, causes of criminal behaviour are seen as no longer lying in the criminal's social background, life situation and circumstances of the offence, but in the moral fault of the actor resulting in acts of freewill for which he is purely responsible.
>
> (Junger-Tas, 1998: 19, cited in Downes, 2001: 68)

For Garland (2001), the new criminology of the neoliberal market economy is encapsulated in the two competing models: the *criminology of the self* and the *criminology of the other*. In the criminology of the self, crime is normalised and routinised: it is an everyday problem to be managed through strategies of individual 'remoralisation' and 'responsibilisation', coupled with the modification of situations and opportunity structures (crime prevention measures). In the criminology of the other, crime is depicted in melodramatic terms. It is viewed as catastrophic, framed in the language of warfare and social defence. Individuals are intrinsically 'evil' or wicked people, beyond rehabilitation, and require more than punishment. They are subjected to punitive segregation, exclusion and 'penal marking' (i.e. extended punishment in the community). They constitute a danger and/or threat to society, have no call on fellow feeling, and defy all attempts at rational comprehension or criminological understanding.

The rise of the penal state

As stated above, one of the key themes covered by the literature on neoliberalism is the rise of the penal state in which penal provisions are given precedence over social provisions (Hudson, 1993). Downes and Hansen, in their analysis of the welfare state and penal state relationship, state that the contraction of the welfare state (a key feature of the neoliberal welfare state) has been accompanied by the expansion of the penal state (2006a). Drawing our attention to the dramatic rise in prison populations in western countries (including the UK) over the last 30 years, they state:

> the fields of crime and punishment can run counter to those of welfare. Budgets for the former have often waxed as those of the latter have waned. Forms of blanket crime prevention coverage proliferate, as in the expansion of electronic surveillance and adolescent curfews, whilst universal provision of welfare is displaced by selective provision or none at all.
>
> (Downes and Hansen, 2006a: 136)

In their comparative study of welfare spending and imprisonment across 18 countries, Downes and Hansen demonstrate that countries which spend a greater proportion of their gross domestic product (GDP) on welfare have lower imprisonment rates. They placed the UK fourth (in the top quarter) in the league table of those with the highest imprisonment rates (behind the USA, Portugal and New Zealand in that order). The percentage of GDP spent on welfare was 20.8 per cent, and the imprisonment rate was 124 per 100,000 of the population. In the bottom quarter of countries were the social democratic Scandinavian countries that have resisted the European trend towards the neoliberal model of a less generous welfare state. These included Denmark, Sweden and Finland, that respectively spent 29.8 per cent, 31 per cent and 26.5 per cent of their GDP on welfare, and were found to have imprisonment rates of 63, 60 and 54 per 100,000, respectively.

Highlighting key differences between the inclusive (generous) social democratic welfare state and the exclusive (less generous) neoliberal welfare state, Downes and Hansen make the point that inclusive regimes place the emphasis on the social causes of marginality; insure citizens against income loss and protect them from poverty and low pay; enhance social harmony, and create a sense of equality and security; and seek to reduce social and economic inequalities and adopt less harsh crime and punishment policies. By contrast, exclusive regimes lay responsibility for social problems on the socially marginalised; view unemployed/ offenders as undeserving; and adopt a harsh stance on crime and favour imprisonment. They tolerate greater inequality among their citizens, and have higher levels of social problems, as well as generating a greater sense of injustice and unfairness. Consequently, they are less socially cohesive and stable. While the social democratic model of the welfare state is underpinned by the principle of universalism with social provision defined by need, the neoliberal model is underpinned by the notion of the citizen's responsibility, and access to assistance is conditional on the adherence to state-defined behavioural norms and mores.

Social exclusion

Downes and Hansen's arguments are developed by those (e.g. Young and Matthews, 2003; Squires, 2006) who provide a critical evaluation of the social exclusion agenda of Tony Blair (New Labour Prime Minister, 1997–2007). As Young and Matthews (2003) point out, central to New Labour's 1997 'tough on the causes of crime' electoral pledge was its social inclusion agenda, an agenda based on the notion that social exclusion is a series of linked social problems and is the 'genesis of crime'. It is clear that Blair acknowledged that social exclusion was the consequence of global social and economic transformations (laying the blame on the decline of manufacturing, the rise of knowledge-based industries and the demands of a flexible workforce), and that his social inclusion agenda included measures that 'derive from the welfarist tradition' (e.g. Sure Start and New Deals) (Downes and Hansen 2006b: 2). However, critics argue that the provision of welfare services to ameliorate the effects of globalisation were increasingly replaced by measures focused on manipulating the conduct of the individual.

Discipline and the New Labour social inclusion agenda

Young and Matthews differentiate between weak and strong forms of social inclusion. The weak form of social inclusion focuses on the consequences of marginality: individuals, families and communities at risk. Crime is attributed to the individualised dysfunction and the criminogenic tendencies of those who are marginalised. The strong form of social inclusion focuses on the structural causes of exclusion and promotes measures necessary for 'the realization of full citizenship economically, socially and politically' (Young and Matthews, 2003: 3). Faced with a choice between a strong version of social inclusion and its weaker counterpart, Blair and his ministers opted for the weaker version, placing the emphasis on the agency of the actor rather than on structurally induced inequality. As a consequence, social welfare 'tough on the causes of crime' initiatives became superseded by law and order 'tough on crime' measures. One manifestation of this privileging of crime control solutions was the unprecedented level of criminal justice policy activity during the period of the Blair administration, which culminated in an excess of 50 new Acts of parliament dealing with crime, disorder, policing and criminal justice being placed on the statute book (Solomon *et al.*, 2007).

Young and Matthews argue that New Labour's weaker form of social inclusion found its expression in a citizenship agenda that stressed the centrality of employment and self-governance, and was exemplified by the policy of imposing discipline and duties on disadvantaged communities that failed to meet the citizenship test. Embracing the criminology of the other, economic forces (the causes of crime) were relegated to 'simple context', and anti-social members were subject to stigmatising, punitive segregation (Squires, 2006). Welfare support was not determined by need, but instead became conditional on beneficiaries accepting the help available to become self-sufficient and work ready (Young and Matthews, 2003). The welfare state was no longer to be regarded as a 'permanent place of refuge or sanctuary from the vicissitudes of the market, but rather as a staging post for catching one's breath before returning to the economic fray' (Bochel *et al.*, 2009: 158).

The criminalisation of poverty: punishing the poor

The decline in the left hand of state solutions to public concerns and the contraction of the welfare state has led some to argue that poverty has become a crime. From this perspective, the concomitant rise in the right hand of state solutions constitutes the *criminalisation of poverty*: the process by which advanced societies use the penal system as an instrument for managing the social insecurity and social dysjunctions associated with neoliberal policies of economic deregulation, in particular the deskilling of labour, mass joblessness and precarious employment. In this analysis, social policy and penal policy are not separated and distinct domains of political action; rather, they act in tandem to regulate those on the lowest tiers of the social ladder. The 'invisible hand of the market and the iron fist of the state' combine in what amounts to the 'punishment of the poor' (Wacquant, 2001).

The *punishment of the poor* in the UK is demonstrated in the blurring of criminal justice and social policy through the creation of a shadowy secondary regulatory system where the focus is not restricted to crime, but also extends to the incivilities associated with 'a sizeable underclass, cut off from the main body of society, spatially located in the sink estates of the inner city and the outer suburbs, lacking the moral norms and values of the wider society' (Young and Matthews, 2003: 4). Linking the 'reform of the welfare system and the criminal justice agenda around dysfunctional families, anti-social behaviour in children and early intervention to rescue the ill-disciplined "feral children" in the peripheral housing estates and poor inner cities' (Rodger, 2012: 413), New Labour introduced a range of measures that coupled social rights with newly defined responsibilities. As 'conditionality' replaced need at the heart of the welfare system, the nuisance behaviour of neighbours and children was deemed to breach the revised social contract between the state and its citizens, and was subject to punitive sanctions (Young and Matthews, 2003; Rodger, 2012). As Young and Matthews point out:

> Undergirding Blair's argument is the distinctly New Labour credo of rights and responsibilities. People have the right to security, job opportunities, a stable community; against this they have responsibilities to act honestly, not violate the rights of other citizens and actively participate in the workforce.
> (Young and Matthews, 2003: 6)

With work at the heart of its social inclusion agenda, New Labour's vision was to bring the 'workless class back into society and into useful work' through the combination of new deals to encourage and support those seeking work, and benefit sanctions for those unwilling to take up work opportunities. Simultaneously, the government embarked upon 'civilizing offensives' that focused on managing the behaviour of those who 'violate the rights of other citizens' (Young and Matthews, 2003: 7–8). As part of its civic renewal agenda, New Labour promoted communitarian notions of duties and responsibilities as 'the basis for value commitments and social order': appeals to 'community' were 'appropriated as the focus of moral renewal' (Crawford and Lewis, 2007: 3). Spurred on by a vision of eradicating the misery inflicted on communities by anti-social and nuisance behaviour, New Labour coupled policy strategies that contained aspects of social support (such as 'voluntary' pre-crime interventions by social services and youth offending teams for families at risk) with the civil sanctions of ASBOs and Parenting Orders for those unwilling or unable to take up the assistance offered. Blurring the legal boundaries between undesirable and criminal behaviour, these orders, which could be granted by the courts on the lower levels of evidential proof ascribed to civil proceedings ('the balance of probabilities' rather than 'beyond reasonable doubt'), attracted criminal law penalties if not adhered to, effectively criminalising the behaviour of 'everyday life' (Squires, 2006).

Dispersal of discipline: net-widening and mesh thinning

For Rodger, the use of civil orders to regulate behaviour is consistent with Cohen's (1985) concept of the 'dispersal of discipline'. In Cohen's *Visions of Social Control*, the dispersal of discipline is accomplished by the dual process of 'net-widening', which subjects new groups to the state's regulatory functions, and 'mesh-thinning', which restricts the means by which groups subject to state regulation can extricate themselves from this. The new orders, in particular the ASBO, Rodger argues, constitute 'net-widening' in the sense that new categories of people whose behaviour had previously been tolerated or regulated informally by family, work and community, avoiding the state's gaze, came under the surveillance and control of criminal justice system legislation and policy action; and 'mesh narrowing', in the sense that the 'blurring of the boundaries between the formal and informal agencies of social support and those of social control results in there being no means of escape through the dense "fishing net" of joined-up initiatives, schemes and surveillance for the "tiddlers"' (Rodger, 2012: 416). The application of criminal sanctions for failing to comply with the new orders criminalised behaviour that was less serious in character, and constituted sub-crime or pre-crime (Rodger, 2012).

However, notwithstanding the persuasiveness of Rodger's arguments and the near universal agreement among criminologists that anti-social behaviour (ASB) constitutes a lower-order category of behaviour, dissenting voices can be found. Indeed, Brown (2004), drawing attention to the findings of a 2002 Home Office Research Study, is among those who cast doubt on assumptions that ASB constitutes minor behavioural infractions (such as neighbourhood disputes). She provides evidence to support the claim that ASBOs were specifically introduced to address persistent behaviour that, despite being in isolation too trivial for the criminal law, accumulatively met the threshold for inclusion. She states that those who were made subject to ASBOs frequently had previous convictions, with the mean number being 13. She argues that:

> half of cases involved a long history of convictions. All ASBO and repossession cases involved serious and repeated incidents over a long period, of various combinations of loud music, shouting and swearing, fighting, verbal abuse, banging doors, barking and fouling by dogs, and damage to common areas. In most cases, it involved the defendant and visitors, and often disputes with visitors, other family members, or ex-partners. All cases involved problems with several neighbours. In many cases, the problem was solved by the perpetrator being imprisoned for reasons other than breach of ASBO. In most cases, dozens of police call-outs had been made and these formed one of the main sources of evidence relied upon by local authorities. Not surprisingly, the research found that anti-social behaviour cases were in contrast to the nature of neighbour disputes found in mediation services, and were unlikely to be resolved by mediation alone.
>
> (Brown, 2004: 208)

In her study, the majority of cases subject to ASBOs had complex social problems such as mental health problems or alcoholism. They also included families with children who had histories of social work involvement, and individuals with learning disabilities. The cases were not new to the system, but rather constituted those groups and individuals who had been failed by the welfare agencies. From Brown's observations, ASBOs were, in response to neighbour demands, applied to individuals who had been in the welfare net, but had slipped through. With this in mind, she argues that these measures should be understood not in terms of net-widening, but instead as essentially mesh-thinning, providing new levels of surveillance for individuals who have eluded the less intrusive controls of the welfare agencies.

Where are we now? The Coalition government and the punitive welfare state

The focus on work, which was at the heart of social inclusion vision, has gained momentum under the Coalition. Under the guise of 'austerity', the Coalition has introduced a range of 'work incentivisation' initiatives (increasingly outsourced to target-driven private contractors), which take as their inspiration the US workfare movement: the substitution of 'welfare dependency' with 'work dependency'. This replacement of the welfare state with a workfare state has been achieved through the re-orientation of the welfare system to create a flexible, controllable workforce that is responsive to market needs and willing to work for the minimum wage. The overriding aim of the Coalition is to achieve 'a society populated by enterprising and educated citizens who are responsible for themselves and their families and eager to engage in productive work for Britain plc' (Rodger, 2012: 414).

Enforced through an expansion of punitive sanctions, more traditionally associated with the ethos of the criminal justice system, workfare schemes exploit the populist appeal of divisive rhetoric that pits 'strivers' against 'skivers'. Through the workfare discourse, those not engaged in productive work (those who are disabled, single parents and those more traditionally viewed as unemployed) are constructed as the new 'other': work-shy pariahs, the 'stay-in-bed layabout whose curtains are closed when [their] . . . neighbours drag themselves off to work at the crack of dawn' (Stewart, 2012: 40). Those unwilling or unable to cooperate with back to work preparation programmes, or not deemed to be trying hard enough to find work, are subject to a draconian withdrawal of benefits. This focus on enforcement and 'incentivisation' through fear has led some to argue that the Coalition has ushered in the 'punitive welfare state' – the latest variant of the penalisation of the poor (Rodger, 2012).

Case study: Criminalisation of poverty and ASBOs

This case study illustrates the blurring of boundaries between the previously distinct policy realms of social policy and criminal justice policy. It explores the way in which the crime prevention agenda changed the priorities of previously welfare-oriented services and transformed them from agencies that sought to meet social need into partners in crime control. It traces how lobbyists both within and outside local government exerted pressure on the government to enact new legislation and policy initiatives.

Tackling ASB, a broad, imprecise and subjective umbrella term applied to a range of non-criminal activities and incivilities that were deemed to cause harassment, alarm or distress, was at the heart of New Labour's social contract (Solomon *et al.*, 2007). ASBOs, which formed part of New Labour's flagship Crime and Disorder Act 1998, are viewed by some as a clear example of the 'criminalisation of social policy'. With its aim of imposing 5,000 new orders per year (a target that was never achieved), the policy of tackling problematic behaviour through court action (which gained momentum during New Labour's period in office) raised concerns that criminal justice measures (as opposed to social welfare measures) were being applied to solve the behavioural manifestations of social and economic problems, rather than addressing the underlying causes and motivations (Squires, 2006).

ASBOs are subject to considerable criticism for: the erosion of traditional notions of justice; their all-embracing and subjective basis; their criminalisation of non-criminal conduct; their deliberate blurring of civil and criminal law; and the neutralisation of the important rights and due process safeguards of traditional criminal law. ASBO proceedings allow the admission of hearsay evidence, including uncorroborated police reports and information shared among partner agencies, or even unsubstantiated complaints from neighbours. The order is a civil order, lasting for a minimum of two years but with no maximum; breach is a criminal offence triable by the Magistrates' or Crown Court. Tough sanctions imposed if the orders are not complied with represent a significant jump up the sentencing tariff and signify an important overlapping of civil and criminal legality (Squires, 2006):

> Section 1 of the Crime and Disorder Act 1998 provides: If without reasonable excuse a person does anything which he is prohibited from doing by an anti-social behaviour order, he shall be liable (a) on summary conviction, to imprisonment for a term not exceeding six months or to a fine not exceeding the statutory maximum or to both; or (b) on conviction on indictment, to imprisonment for a term not exceeding five years or to a fine, or to both.
>
> (Sentencing Guidelines Council, 2008: 2)

How and why did ASB become a central concern of government?

Burney (2003) traces the origins of ASBOs to the mid-1990s, and the 'handful of horror stories' from Labour constituencies that focused public attention on neighbourhoods 'blighted and terrorised' by individuals and families whose behaviour fell outside the law. The issue was taken up by a group of councillors and housing managers, mainly from deprived council estates, who, faced with a growing case load of complaints from tenants about the activities of their neighbours, joined forces with some big housing associations to form the Social Landlords' Crime and Nuisance Group. They constituted an influential policy network with a shared perspective on the causes and solution of the problem who sought to use their combined power to assert pressure on the incoming government. With a well-defined vision of the policy measures that would address the 'problem', which crucially resonated with New Labour's emergent citizenship agenda, they were successful in achieving their objectives of introducing measures that permitted civil action to be taken against neighbourhood nuisance, and were instrumental in the establishment of the non-tenure-specific ASBO.

For Squires, there are four underlying developments that shaped the New Labour policy agenda. It was these developments which meant that the lobby-ists were effectively pushing at an open door, as the following box describes.

A paradigm shift in criminal justice policy thinking associated with the emergence of Kelling and Wilson's (1982) 'broken windows' perspective in crime prevention that shaped a definition of urban 'incivilities' for which a specific social group, namely the poor and marginal, were largely seen as responsible. Underpinned by New Right criminological realism, there was an increasing focus on strategies to encourage communities to accept responsibility for the actions of its members, and to support and encourage residents to become more assertive in promoting community norms.

The growing recognition that crime, disorder and harassment problems were spatially located on deprived social housing estates. Influenced by Left realism in criminology, there was a growing concern with social exclusion and victimization. Especially within deprived and excluded communities, chronic rates of crime, disorder, violence and victimization were deemed to compound the intolerable experiences and disrupted life chances of residents.

The rediscovery of the notion that youthful or adolescent ASB was an indicator of a persistent criminal career. Casting doubt on the conventional wisdom of liberal youth justice policies that young people would 'grow up out of crime', the new focus held that the chances of so doing were greatly reduced for young delinquents in excluded communities. Nuisance, delinquent, disorderly and 'anti-social' behaviours were both a symptom of underlying problems and a warning light of worse criminality to come. This focus on the threat posed by anti-social young people found expression in the language of demonisation in the tabloids: 'mindless thugs', 'lager-fuelled yobs', 'feral children'.

Source: Squires (2006: 148–9)

The criminalisation of social policy

Squires argues that:

> enforcement activity aimed at tackling 'anti-social behaviour' is one
> of the clearest instances of a process of criminalization occurring
> within and across social policy programmes.
>
> (Squires, 2006: 154)

The erosion of traditional welfare functions and the dispersal of responsibilities for crime control from the traditional criminal justice agencies
(police court and prisons) to agencies, organisations and individuals (both
public and private) that operate outside the criminal justice system form part
of what Garland calls the 'responsibilisation' agenda. A central feature of
this process was the establishment of Crime and Disorder Reduction Partnerships under the 1998 Crime and Disorder Act, which provided the statutory platform for placing an obligation on local authorities and the police, in
partnership with other agencies, to: produce an audit of local crime and
disorder problems; consult locally on the basis of the audit; produce a
strategy for tackling issues identified in the audit; and monitor and evaluate
progress on the implementation (Newburn and Jones, 2002). The Act effectively co-opted local authority agencies such as housing, transport, education, planning and social services and voluntary groups into the field of
crime control, and in so doing ushered in organisational changes to ensure
the fulfilment of new priorities in 'strategic planning, inter-agency
co-operation and shared decision-making' (Garland, 2001: 125).

These new priorities signified the merging of the previously distinct
policy realms of social policy and criminal justice policy. Social needs such
as poverty and homelessness, once the exclusive domain of social welfare,
were redefined in terms of their contribution to crime. They were constructed
as a 'problem for penology, criminal law and policing and . . . crime prevention and community safety' (Hughes, 2002: 3) to be managed by criminal
justice agencies or their 'new partners in crime' (and disorder). As Squires
points out:

> [The crime and disorder agenda] went beyond a simple recognition
> that crime and disorder policy objectives might be achieved by a
> variety of ways and means to suggest that the maintenance of social
> order and control may have superseded the more familiar objectives
> of housing, education, youth, health, career and welfare service
> agencies.
>
> (Squires, 2006: 154)

This re-orientation of public service provision was achieved by both
the imposition of statutory obligations and the emergence of a range of

competitive, centrally funded, target-driven programmes and initiatives that were aimed at crime prevention. In relation to the youth service in England and Wales, new funding arrangements brought about the contraction of universal service provision, and its replacement with a 'potentially divisive and selective service working to crime prevention targets rather than youth citizenship and inclusion' (Squires, 2006: 154).

The emergence of ASB as the central motif of public policy under New Labour, and its decision to focus its attention primarily on enforcement powers to deal with ASB problems, resulted in the creation of a series of legislative additions to the 1998 Act. The far-reaching range and scope of these measures included the introduction of: interim ASBOs and ASBOs on conviction; acceptable behaviour contracts; Dispersal Orders; fines for parents whose children misbehave; parenting contracts; and powers to close premises used for drugs (or 'crack houses'), and for owners to tackle noise nuisance, graffiti, fly-tipping, fireworks and airguns (Hodgkinson and Tilley, 2007). This ensured that an ever-widening circle of actors was requisitioned into the process from previously distinct and separate realms of health and social welfare policy. With the ASBO increasingly presented by central government as the 'magic bullet' solution to ASB, social needs to be met by social welfare providers became reconfigured as risks to be managed. The allocation of resources to marginalised communities became less concerned with the objectives of the alleviation of poverty and disadvantage (the cornerstones of the post-war welfare state), and more concerned with social control objectives of the management of the behaviour of its citizens (Bennett, 2008). Precedence was given to 'behaviour, morality, character and choices, rather than needs or social circumstances' (Squires, 2006: 157). As Brown explains:

> ASB is purely about behaviour. Motivation and intention are largely irrelevant [which] explains why ASB control is unconcerned about mental health problems, learning difficulties, addictions, domestic violence and other potential problems that are common features of ASB cases.
>
> (Brown, 2004: 207)

Key points summary

This chapter traces the changes to welfare and criminal justice policies and approaches that have been adopted since the post-1945 era. It argues the following:

• The post-war welfare state, which was based on social democratic principles and emphasised equality and the social causes of crime, has been eroded, and has been replaced by a neoliberal model of the welfare state that has transformed our understanding of crime and the criminal.

- The social contract between the state and the citizen has undergone a series of changes, and this has brought in its wake a shift in the balance between welfare and penal provision. Previous boundaries between the two have become blurred and increasingly permeable.
- New Labour was elected in 1997 on a manifesto of change that promised to redress the social consequences of the previous Conservative administration and held out the prospect of a revitalisation of social policy to reduce the social exclusion that was associated with crime. However, faced with rising crime, the model of social inclusion that was adopted focused primarily on the conduct of the excluded and ushered in a series of measures that widened the scope of the penal state's gaze to include 'non-criminal' and 'sub-criminal behaviours'.

Critical thinking discussion topics

1   What are the distinctive features of the study of criminal justice policy that situates it within wider aspects of public policy?
2   To what extent has the changed political landscape transformed beliefs about crime, its causes and its solutions?
3   What are the differences between a generous welfare state model and a less generous welfare state, and how do they affect the prison population?
4   What is meant by the penalisation of poverty, and how convincing are the arguments that the Coalition government has created a punitive welfare state?
5   What does this quote from Dorling (2008) tells us about his views on the relationship of wider public policy to crime?:

> Behind the man with the knife is the man who sold him the knife, the man who did not give him a job, the man who decided that his school did not need funding, the man who closed down the branch plant where he could have worked, the man who decided to reduce benefit levels so that a black economy grew, all the way back to the woman who only noticed 'those inner cities' some six years after the summer of 1981, and the people who voted to keep her in office ... Those who perpetrated the social violence that was done to the lives of young men starting some 20 years ago are the prime suspects for most of the murders in Britain.
>
> (Dorling, 2008: 42)

6   Who were the key stakeholders in the development of ASBOs? How far does the collaboration of different interested parties constitute an example of networking theory?

Seminar task

Identify a contemporary 'social problem' (e.g. school non-attendance, loitering youths, drug misuse, squatting) and consider the differences in modes of government intervention that would characterise a 'left hand of the state' as opposed to a 'right hand of the state' approach. What are the implications for the 'offender', the victim and the wider public?

Recommended further reading

Downes, D. and Hansen, K. (2006a) 'Welfare and punishment in comparative perspective'. In S. Armstrong and L. McAra (eds) *Perspectives on Punishment: The Contours of Control*. Oxford: Oxford University Press.

Roberts, R. and McMahon, W. (eds) (2007) *Social Justice and Criminal Justice*. London: Centre for Criminal Justice Studies.

Rodger, J.J. (2012) ' "Regulating the poor": observations on the structural coupling of welfare, criminal justice and the voluntary sector in a "Big Society" '. *Social Policy and Administration*, 46(4): 413–31.

Squires, P. (2006) 'New Labour and the politics of antisocial behaviour critical social policy'. *Critical Social Policy*, 26(1): 144–68.

References

Alcock, C., Daly, G. and Griggs, E. (2008) *Introducing Social Policy* (2nd edn). London: Longman.

Becker, H. (1963) *Outsiders: Studies in Sociology of Deviance*. New York: Free Press.

Bennett, J. (2008) *The Social Costs of Dangerousness: Prison and the Dangerous Classes*. London: Centre for Criminal Justice Studies. Retrieved from http://www.crimeand-justice.org.uk/dangerousness.html (accessed 10 May 2013).

Bochel, H., Bochel, C., Page, R. and Sykes, R. (2009) *Social Policy: Themes, Issues and Debates*. London: Longman.

Brown, A. (2004) 'Anti-social behaviour, crime control and social control'. *Howard Journal of Criminal Justice*, 43(2): 203–11.

Burney, E. (2003) 'Talking tough, acting coy: what happened to the Anti–Social Behaviour Order?' *Howard Journal of Criminal Justice*, 41(5): 469–84.

Cabinet Office (2011) *Open Public Services*. London: Cabinet Office.

Cohen, S. (1985) *Visions of Social Control*. Oxford: Blackwell.

Crawford, A. (2006) 'Networked governance and the post-regulatory state?: steering, rowing and anchoring the provision of policing and security'. *Theoretical Criminology*, 10(4): 449–79.

Crawford, A. and Lewis, S. (2007) 'Global processes, national trends and local justice: the effects of neo-liberalism on youth justice in England and Wales' [translated from French]. In F. Bailleau and Y. Cartuyvels (eds) *Les Evolutions de la Justice Penale des Mineurs en Europe: Entre Modèle Welfare et Inflexions Neo-liberales*. Paris: L'Harmattan.

Dorling, D. (2008) 'Prime suspect: murder in Britain'. In D. Dorling, D. Gordon, P. Hillyard, C. Pantazis, S. Pemberton and S. Tombs (eds) *Criminal Obsessions: What Matters More, Crime or Harm* (2nd edn). London: Centre for Crime and Justice Studies.

Downes, D. (2001) 'The *"macho" penal* economy: mass incarceration in the United States – a European perspective'. *Punishment and Society*, 3(1): 61–80.

Downes, D. and Hansen, K. (2006a) 'Welfare and punishment in comparative perspective'. In S. Armstrong and L. McAra (eds) *Perspectives on Punishment: The Contours of Control*. Oxford: Oxford University Press.

Downes, D. and Hansen, K. (2006b) *Welfare and Punishment: The Relationship Between Welfare Spending and Imprisonment*. London: Crime and Society Foundation.

Garland, D. (2001) *Culture of Control*. Oxford: Oxford University Press.

Garland, D. (2012) *Punishment and Modern Society: A Study in Social Theory*. Chicago: University of Chicago Press.

Hill, M. (2013) *The Public Policy Process* (6th edn). Harlow: Pearson.

Hill, M. and Bramley, G. (1986) *Analysing Social Policy*. Oxford: Blackwell.

Hobbs, D., Hadfield, P., Lister, S. and Winslow, S. (2003) *Bouncers: Violence, Governance and the Night Time Economy*. Oxford: Oxford University Press.

Hodgkinson, S. and Tilley, N. (2007) 'Policing anti-social behaviour: constraints, dilemmas and opportunities'. *Howard Journal of Criminal Justice*, 46(4): 385–400.

Hudson, B. (1993) *Penal and Social Justice*. London: Macmillan.

Hughes, G. (2002) 'The shifting sands of crime prevention and community safety'. In G. Hughes, E. McLaughlin and J. Muncie (eds) *Crime Prevention and Community Safety: New Directions*. London: Sage.

Jenkins, W.I. (1978) *Policy Analysis: A Political and Organizational Perspective*. New York: St. Martin's Press.

Kelling, G. and Wilson, J. (1982) 'Broken windows'. *Atlantic* (March).

McMahon, W. (2007) 'New Labour – social transformation and social order'. In R. Roberts and W. McMahon (eds) *Social Justice and Criminal Justice*. London: Centre for Criminal Justice Studies. Retrieved from http://www.crimeandjustice.org.uk/sites/crimeandjustice.org.uk/files/socialjusticecriminaljusticeweb.pdf (accessed November 2013).

Martinson, R. (1974) 'What works? – Questions and answers about prison reform'. *Public Interest*, 35(1): 22–54.

Mills, C. Wright (1959) *The Sociological Imagination*. New York: Oxford University Press.

Newburn, T. and Jones, T. (2002) *Consultation by Crime and Disorder Partnerships*. London: Home Office.

Page, R.M. (2007). 'Without a song in their heart: New Labour, the welfare state and the retreat from democratic socialism'. *Journal of Social Policy*, 36(1): 19–37.

Pitts, J. (2008) *Reluctant Gangsters: The Changing Face of Youth Crime*. Cullompton: Willan.

Ramesh, R. (2013, May 27) 'Bedroom tax "will force tens of thousands on to streets" '. *Guardian*.

Reiner, R. (2007) 'Neoliberalism, crime and justice'. In R. Roberts and W. McMahon (eds) *Social Justice and Criminal Justice*. London: Centre for Criminal Justice Studies. Retrieved from http://www.crimeandjustice.org.uk/sites/crimeandjustice.org.uk/files/socialjusticecriminaljusticeweb.pdf (accessed November 2013).

Rodger, J.J. (2012) ' "Regulating the poor": observations on the structural coupling of welfare, criminal justice and the voluntary sector in a "Big Society" '. *Social Policy and Administration*, 46(4): 413–31.

Rose, N. (2000) 'Government and control'. In D. Garland and R. Sparks (eds) *Criminology and Social Theory*. Oxford: Oxford University Press.

Ryan, M. (2005) 'Engaging with punitive attitudes towards crime and punishment. Some strategic lessons from England and Wales'. In J. Pratt, D. Brown, M. Brown, S. Wallsworth and W. Morrison (eds) *The New Punitiveness: Trends, Theories, Perspectives*. Cullompton: Willan.

Sentencing Guidelines Council (2008) Breach of an Anti-Social Behaviour Order. [Online]. Retrieved from http://sentencingcouncil.judiciary.gov.uk/docs/web_Breach_of_an_Anti-Social_behaviour_order.pdf (accessed 1 March 2013).

Simon, J. (2007) *Governing Through Crime: How the War on Crime Transformed American Democracy and Created a Culture of Fear*. Oxford: Oxford University Press.

Social Exclusion Unit (2002) *Reducing Re-offending by Ex-prisoners*. London: Cabinet Office.

Solomon, E., Eades, C., Garside, R. and Rutherford, M. (2007) *Ten Years of Criminal Justice Under Labour: An Independent Audit*. London: Centre for Criminal Justice Studies.

Squires, P. (2006) 'New Labour and the politics of antisocial behaviour critical social policy'. *Critical Social Policy*, 26(1): 144–68.

Stewart, H. (2012, December 9) 'Autumn statement: compassionate Conservatism is now officially dead'. *Observer*.

Wacquant, L. (2001) 'The penalisation of poverty and the rise of neo-liberalism'. *European Journal on Criminal Policy and Research*, 9(4): 401–12.

Young, J. (2007) *The Vertigo of Late Modernity*. London: Sage.

Young, J. and Matthews, R. (2003) 'New Labour, crime control and social exclusion'. In R. Matthews and J. Young (eds) *The New Politics of Crime and Punishment*. Cullompton: Willan.

4 The criminal justice policy-making process – the formal and informal process

Chapter summary

This chapter examines how principles and ideas are transformed into formal policy in the UK. Its starting point is the notion of 'policy from below', and the important role that various pressure groups play in lobbying both the media and politicians in order to promote their position on preferred policy. The rise of the think tank is considered as well, and is appraised in terms of neutrality, partisanship and influence within the political sphere. Politicians, political power and ideology are also discussed, as is political commitment to crime policy, and the drive to 'join up' public policy in the associated areas that have affected crime in recent years. In addition, the chapter critically examines the role of government departments (principally the Home Office and the Ministry of Justice), and the significant role of the Civil Service, more specifically the Civil Service 'mandarins' in developing and augmenting policy outputs. The focus of the chapter also includes the path of social policy through parliament, and summarises how crime policy has been 'harnessed' by politicians over the past 50 years.

This chapter looks at:

- the historical and social development of pressure groups and think tanks, and their importance to contemporary crime policy-making;
- the reactive nature of modern politics, and the use of political power in the development of crime policy imperatives;
- an analysis of relevant government departments and their policy arenas;
- the public appetite for crime policy outputs, and the dramatic 'flashpoints' that have stimulated this appetite in recent years;
- the role of the Civil Service and specifically Civil Service mandarins in the political and policy process;
- the effect of significant social change on crime policy politics, requiring the need to be tough on crime and its causes;
- the consequences of the global recession for crime policy-making in Britain.

Case study: Social change, social policy and the procedural path of the Hunting Act 2004

The case study will introduce you to some of the key debates concerning the difficulty of transforming informal policy into law. The subject for this analysis is the progression of the various hunting Bills through parliament under Tony Blair's successive Labour governments between 1997 and 2004. The fierce debate surrounding the proposed hunting ban included issues of social class, social change, public disorder, animal welfare, public opinion and potential economic harm. Of further interest was the fact that both sides of the debate were supported by powerful pressure groups, which ensured that media and public focus was retained throughout. The case study also illustrates the tangle of parliamentary procedures that led to the case 'ping-ponging' between the House of Commons and the House of Lords for seven years.

The crime policy commodity: from pressure groups to collectives

The pivotal role of so-called 'pressure groups' in British policy-making is a historical one. The pressure groups that exist today are the descendants of the medieval religious guilds and brotherhoods that looked after the welfare of their members and publicised their particular culture. In time, these religious guilds developed into trade-oriented organisations, and by the time that Britain was empire-building in the eighteenth century, the tactic of recruiting and lobbying members of parliament and those able to influence policy was well established.

In the period that followed the Industrial Revolution in the early nineteenth century, the concept of the 'pressure group' that we recognise today was forming. Groups came together to discuss, publicise, petition and lobby against slavery, for education, for healthcare, for workers' rights. Several groups formed and consolidated during this period are still highly active and influential today, including the Royal Society for the Prevention of Cruelty to Animals (RSPCA), founded in 1824, the British Medical Association (BMA), formed in 1832, the Trades Union Congress, formed in 1868, and the National Union of Teachers, formed in 1870. The trades unions in particular have been highly influential within the political sphere, particularly when we consider that the Labour Party was founded as a political division of the Labour movement in 1906.

Pressure groups and crime policy from below

This initial impetus has led to an enormous raft of pressure groups in the UK utilising public opinion to influence or form public policy. Broadly, these include 'sectional' (interest) groups and 'promotional' groups. Sectional groups represent sector interest in terms of their members, and include the modern incarnation of the trade unions (e.g. UNISON, UNITE and the Universities and Colleges Union), business organisations (e.g. the Confederation of British Industry, the Federation of Small Businesses and the International Labour Organization) and professional bodies (e.g. the BMA, the British Dental Association and the Bar Standards Board). All of these sectional groups hold a great deal of influence in the political sphere, as the interests of their memberships are often closely allied to political public policy debates. Similarly, the level of expertise and experience among the members in many sectional groups ensures that opinions are readily sought by governments as part of the policy-making process.

Promotional groups, on the other hand, tend to focus on single causes, often allied to social problems such as poverty, environmental issues or indeed crime. Thus, the sphere of influence (and sometimes controversy) of promotional groups can encompass questions of society, culture, law, religion, health, housing and welfare. Most promotional groups operate as charities, and are funded via membership subscription, donation and occasionally public (government) grant, although the current economic climate has seen much of this type of funding cut. Some major promotional groups, particularly those with an international focus (such as Oxfam, Save the Children and Amnesty International), are highly influential in terms of their interest sector, and consequently are responsive and instrumental in policy change. A primary tool of contemporary pressure groups is the use and manipulation of the media to accelerate pet causes, or the 'acceleration of drama' as Jewkes suggests while discussing some of the smaller, more radical organisations operating in Britain:

> It is usually organisations that fall outside mainstream consensus politics which best understand this theory of acceleration. Groups with a radical political agenda are well practised in the art of manipulating the media and will frequently 'create' a story through the use of controversial but stage managed techniques, knowing that it will make 'good copy'. Greenpeace, the Animal Liberation Front, pro- and anti-foxhunting groups, 'Fathers 4 Justice' and anti-globalization, anti-capitalism movements are examples of pressure groups which have been extremely successful in garnering media attention and ensuring attention grabbing headlines.
>
> (Jewkes, 2011: 30)

An important factor here is the insider/outsider thesis, which demonstrates that pressure groups are subject to differing levels of access, influence and ultimately status within the political sphere. Although the insider model is subject to challenge by those who argue that ideal types create a false dichotomy which obscures the wide variations of relationships of interest groups to the executive decision-makers (Page, 1999), the concept that not all groups have the same influence as others, that specific groups enjoy privileged access to ministers, and that this in turn affects the strategies that they adopt provides a useful distinction when analysing the fluctuating nature of the power and influence afforded to the plethora of pressure groups that form part of the political landscape. As Page states:

As they used to say about the Ritz, the process of consultation between groups and government is 'open to everyone'. Government consults on matters large and small; the process has even become more immediately apparent over the past few years through the practice of posting consultation documents on the Internet. Yet, although the process of seeking the views of interested parties is supposed to be open, one important strand of thinking about pressure-group politics in Britain believes that only a minority of groups are 'insiders' and truly count in the process of decision-making. The 'insider' group is the one with privileged access to the executive; it is routinely consulted, and its views have a much better chance of affecting policy-making than those of the 'outsider' group. Its insider status may come from, among other things, its industrial or market strength or its ideological proximity to government.

(Page, 1999: 205–6)

With a favoured status among the legislature and the executive, insider groups characteristically argue their case quietly through facts and calm argument. In contrast, outsider groups, excluded from the corridors of power, adopt strategies of trying to impose their viewpoint on policy-making through mass media, raising petitions and/or organising demonstrations. The aim of these strategies is to mobilise public support by raising public awareness. While outsider groups may complain of being routinely ignored, the characteristics of insider groups include frequent contacts with ministers and preferred status in terms of formal consultation.

The rise of the think tank

Offset from these established models of pressure groups (sectional and promotional) is the notion of the 'think tank' – a development that seeks to depoliticise the ethos behind the pressure group, by ostensibly removing some of the pressure! Think tanks consist of a selected body of experts brought together to express ideas, research or generate advocacy on a particular social issue or social problem. Such organisations are seen as influential in the shaping of contemporary public policy, and possess an established historical foundation in the UK through the work of such organisations as the Council on Foreign Relations and Chatham House, which were both founded in 1919 in the immediate aftermath of the First World War. Think tanks should not be viewed as informal, as they influence government thinking, which in turn influences the manner in which we are governed, according to Richards and Smith:

'Governance' is a descriptive label that is used to highlight the changing nature of the policy process in recent decades. In particular, it sensitizes us to the ever-increasing variety of terrains and actors involved in the making of policy. Thus, governance demands that we consider all the actors and locations beyond the 'core executive' involved in the policy making process.

(Richards and Smith, 2002: 2)

The majority of current think tank organisations consciously adopt and express a 'centre' or 'non-partisan' position in terms of political allegiance; examples include the Centre for Strategic Research and Analysis and the Institute for the Study of Civil Society. Political affiliations can, however, sometimes be clearer, as with the Adam Smith Institute and the Institute of Economic Affairs, both striving to appear centre right, and the Bow Group, whose past Chairs have included former Conservative Home Secretary Michael Howard, and former Chancellors of the Exchequer Geoffrey Howe and Norman Lamont.

The use of think tanks in mainstream politics at the expense of pressure groups has grown enormously since the election of Tony Blair's New Labour government in 1997, with a drive towards the middle ground in politics and policy. In order to locate this elusive middle ground, Blair's Labour Party sought to distance itself from the libertarian credentials of many of its traditional pressure group partners, in favour of organisations like the Institute for Public and Policy Research, a centre left organisation producing policy-related research into issues of social justice, democratic reform and social inequality, and Demos, a 'public interest' consultancy.

Since the election of the Conservative–Liberal Coalition in 2010, the use of the think tank system has continued, including the advocacy and policy research of the influential Centre for Policy Studies (CPS), an organisation with historical links to the Conservative Party, and possessing a broadly neoliberalist focus on free market economy, monetarism and social responsibility. Recent policy research produced by the CPS has included controversial critical reports on monetary policy, which have directly influenced Treasury strategy and the public stance of the Chancellor of the Exchequer. Of further Conservative influence is the European Foundation, the leading Euro-sceptic think tank under the banner of 'yes to European trade, no to European government'.

Downes and Morgan (2002) provide a compelling reason for some of the movement from the counsel of independent pressure groups to the more partisan think tanks in recent years, by highlighting the media success of the former in terms of the criminal justice sector, in the early 1990s:

> The sheer proliferation of pressure groups in the law and order field is striking, but less salient than the impressive professionalization of the larger organisations. A good many do not merely campaign, they provide extensive services and undertake evaluative research. This makes them a formidable counter to Home Office senior advisors, who increasingly, as we have seen, seek representation from them when it comes to undertaking major stock-takes. Their challenge, if the government pursues policies of which they disapprove, is high profile: some of the leading spokespersons gather as much media attention, and are more widely known, as junior Home Office ministers. NACRO's Paul Cavadino, for example, achieved such prominence, and became such a *bête noire* for Conservative Home Secretary Michael Howard in the mid-1990s, that NACRO decided it was politic to give him a more backroom role for a while. This example illustrates a broader trend.
>
> (Downes and Morgan, 2002: 304)

Pressure groups and crime policy

The crime policy sector has a number of influential pressure groups that operate on both a national and an international basis. The eldest among these is the Howard League for Penal Reform, which is able to trace its establishment back to 1866 as the (John) Howard Association. The work of the Howard League focuses on prison reform, under the banner of less crime, safer communities and fewer people in prison. This translates to research and publicity into prison regimes, diversion, non-custodial sanctions and sentencing reform. The National Association for the Care and Resettlement of Offenders (NACRO), founded in 1966, also operates within the penal sphere and focuses on crime reduction through working with offenders in resettlement and rehabilitation.

Criminal justice groups can also be smaller in size, but draw attention to specific problems facing the sector. Of these, INQUEST, founded in 1981, is a highly active pressure group, specialising in the research and investigation of deaths in custody. Their work encompasses deaths in police stations, prisons, detention centres and secure hospitals, and offers support to bereaved people and specialist advice for lawyers, agencies and the media. INQUEST also undertakes research to monitor custodial death rates and produces data to highlight patterns and trends, while lobbying to reform the Inquest system in the UK. Additional specialist groups can be found offering advocacy and support for families with loved ones in prison (Action for Prisoners' Families), those affected by drug addiction (DrugScope) and young offenders (the Campaign for Youth Justice).

Other established pressure groups within the sector lobby on matters of law and order. These include JUSTICE (the British section of the International Commission of Jurists), founded in 1957, an organisation with an illustrious history in human rights and social justice activism. JUSTICE lobbies and researches in terms of law reform, legal intervention and legal education with respect to the UK legal system. Similarly, the Legal Action Group, founded in 1972, concerns itself with the administration of justice in terms of equal justice for all, including legal aid provision, social welfare and immigration and asylum. Liberty, founded as the National Council for Civil Liberties in 1934, campaigns on legal matters of civil liberties and human rights, and aims both to protect existing rights and stimulate a 'human rights' culture within British society. Liberty's history over the past 80 years has seen its involvement in many landmark campaigns on human rights, including the fight for women's rights, gay rights, an end to racial discrimination, the investigation of the surveillance practices of the security services and a number of miscarriage of justice cases. Most recently, it has offered legal and lobbying support for the autistic computer hacker Gary McKinnon against his extradition to America to face trial.

Human rights protection is also the foundation for important pressure groups based in the UK but operating internationally; foremost of these is Amnesty International, which campaigns for the rule of international law and against the use of torture. Founded in 1961, the organisation won a Nobel Peace Prize in 1977, and currently boasts over three million members worldwide. A more recent formation in this area is the charity Reprieve, founded in 1999 by the charismatic death-row lawyer and human rights activist, Clive Stafford-Smith. The organisa-tion is committed to promoting the rule of law and right to fair trial worldwide, and fighting against the erosion of human rights in extreme cases.

With an ever-shrinking planet and dwindling resources, the work of inter-national pressure groups such as Amnesty International and Reprieve appears ever more visible and necessary. A globalised media ensures that globalised violence is part of the domestic news agenda daily, recent shocking examples including Libya, Burma, Mali and Syria. As Muncie *et al.* argue:

> Repressive violence, normally perpetuated by states or political groups, can involve a vast variety of human or civil rights violations. In Libya, Gambia and India, for example, human rights activists have been arrested by their respective governments; and those promoting democracy and free speech in Iran, Georgia and Kosovo have reportedly been imprisoned by repressive governmental regimes.
>
> (Muncie *et al.*, 2010: 20)

In terms of the contemporary domestic landscape, a trend has seen many UK-based pressure groups formed into sector collectives via the amalgamation of smaller cohorts. The most prominent of these, with regard to crime policy, is the Criminal Justice Alliance (CJA) (formerly the Penal Affairs Consortium), founded in 1989 and now comprising a coalition of 70 organisations from the voluntary sector, research institutions, staff associations and trade unions. Broadly, the scope of the CJA includes analysis in terms of the prison population, sentencing, remand procedures, overcrowding, safety in custody and re-offending patterns. As Downes and Morgan point out with regard to the CJA's former incarnation:

> the Penal Affairs Consortium [now renamed the CJA], a lobbying collective which comprised thirteen organisations when it was formed in 1989 and now comprises forty, ranging from Prison Governors' and the Prison Officers' Associations to NACRO, the Prison Reform Trust, the Howard League, and Liberty – a previously unthinkable combination.
>
> (Downes and Morgan, 2002: 304)

When considering the amalgamated pressure of a collective such as the CJA, it is a useful exercise to examine the breadth and scope of the organisations that comprise its spiralling membership. At the time of writing, these include *inter alia* Barnardos, the Centre for Crime and Justice Studies, the Centre for Mental Health, the Children's Society, DrugsScope, INQUEST, JUSTICE, NACRO, Penal Reform International, the Police Foundation, the Prince's Trust, the Prison Officers' Association, the Prison Reform Trust, Prisoners Abroad, the Prisoners' Advice Service, the Prisoners' Education Trust, Release, the Restorative Justice Council, Unlock, Victim Support, Women in Prison, Working Chance and YoungMinds. Such large-scale consolidation provides a visible media presence and a loud collective voice for both the 'senior' and 'junior' partners of the criminal justice lobby. However, that is not to say that government departments are bound to listen to, or indeed agree with, the message delivered.

Policy vision to policy output

Contemporary politics can be described as *reactive* in many ways, in that 'doing' contemporary politics often involves a prompt reaction to rapid social changes (perpetually driven by intense media coverage), a reaction to opposition parties and pressure groups, a reaction to the party faithful and the prevailing reactive liability ideology – which often involves blaming the previous incumbents for policy oversight and error. When looking at how policy vision becomes output, an understanding of a particular state's political ideology in practice is key, as it is inextricably linked to the concept of power.

In the UK, the prevailing ideology is that of the elected representative within a parliamentary democracy, which allows elected members of parliament (MPs) to represent the interests of those who elected them, their constituents. Thus, the dominant political party has the most elected MPs and forms the government of the day (or, as currently, comes to power via a Coalition) – votes equal power. The crime policy output of the party in power is likely to be governed by a number of factors, which have in recent years included taking a 'traditional' tack (calls for family values, back to basics and so on), adopting a laissez-faire approach akin to what has been termed actuarial criminology (and linked to privatisation) (Feeley and Simon, 1994), right realism with an emphasis on responding to risk and involving the private sector (Wilson, 1983) or indeed attempts to find a way of combining all of these ideologies with the rehabilitative ideals of the past.

Politicians, ideology, personality and power

At the head of the dominant political party is the Prime Minister and his or her Cabinet. Despite the best efforts of the persuasive satirists of television programmes such as *Yes Minister* and *The Thick of It* to suggest otherwise, the Prime Minister and the Cabinet have a profound effect on shaping the criminal policy of the day. With leadership comes responsibility and accountability for policy and commitment to it, and as Margaret Thatcher, a predecessor and mentor of the current Prime Minster, David Cameron, succinctly put it, 'the party leader cannot dictate to senior colleagues; the rest of the government and parliamentary party need to feel committed to the manifesto's proposals' (Thatcher, 1993: 281). In other words, political policy commitment goes way beyond toeing the party line. The very essence of policy is that it belongs to a particular party or group who wish to see through a particular course of action: strong policy suggests clarity and obligation. Hence, it has also not been lost on successive Prime Ministers and their senior advisors over the past 40 years that the stance on crime is a key variable in garnering popularity, getting elected and remaining in power. As Easton and Piper argue, this area of policy is 'inherently' political:

Debates on law and order and their corollary, crime and punishment, have dominated British politics since the 1970s. Moreover, in a deeper sense the crime question is inherently political in that questions of crime, law, and order raise fundamental questions about the relationship between the state and the citizen, and the problem of how society can be held together, in the face of internal social divisions and the fragmentation of individuals' self-interest.

(Easton and Piper, 2012: 9)

Thus, the office of Prime Minister when considering crime policy is very much that of a figurehead, as when it comes to crime and national security, the public view is that it is an important enough subject to transcend party politics. With this backdrop, the selection (and ultimately dismissal) by the Prime Minister of key Cabinet ministers to support and render credible his crime credentials is of great consequence.

The current Coalition Cabinet comprises 22 senior ministers, of whom 17 are drawn from the Conservative Party, and five from the Liberal Party. The two offices of state that impact most obviously on criminal justice policy are currently filled by Conservative MPs, with Theresa May as Home Secretary and Chris Grayling as Secretary of State for Justice and Lord Chancellor. The office of Home Secretary encompasses a number of controversial areas, including national security, citizenship, immigration and policing. Up until 2005, the Home Secretary was also responsible for the prison system and the probation service in England and Wales, but these areas are now under the auspices of the Ministry of Justice, and are consequently the remit of the current Secretary of State for Justice and Lord Chancellor, Chris Grayling.

A further Cabinet office that is of great consequence to crime policy is that of the Chancellor of the Exchequer, the current incumbent being George Osbourne, another Conservative MP. It is the responsibility of the Chancellor of the Exchequer to control fiscal policy, allocate public funds from the Treasury and set financial limits for the various government departments. The cost of law, order, crime and punishment has been seen as a challenging burden to consecutive governments, and in the midst of the current economic downturn funding is very much a social fiscal balancing act. As Easton and Piper state:

These economic pressures are even more important now in the current economic climate of recession and cost effectiveness is a crucial consideration in current penal policy. So governments must respond to the public's demand to reduce crime and to make society safe, while reducing economic burdens on the public purse.

(Easton and Piper, 2012: 12)

Furthermore, in recent years, there has been a move to 'join up' public policy in areas that affect crime in an indirect, as well as a direct, manner. A legacy of 13 years of Labour criminal justice policy up to 2010 was the establishment of the multi-agency approach to crime policy. Based on social inclusion, the foundations of this policy are still visible, and when considering how the pieces of the crime policy jigsaw fit together, it is necessary to understand that a number of complementary governmental offices, and the policy that emanates from them, impinge significantly on the overall crime picture.

Key among these are policy areas that have implications for the built environment, public health and education. Crowther argues that, in the early 2000s, seven government departments were seen as having parts to play when considering crime policy: the Home Office, the Department for Education and Skills, the Department of Health, the Department for Work and Pensions, the Department for Environment, Food and Rural Affairs, the Department for Transport and the Department for Trade and Industry. As Crowther suggests, this was an example of collaborative welfarism and the pooling of expertise in an attempt to address a seemingly insurmountable social problem – that of controlling the root causes of crime: 'Each of the agencies working within the criminal justice system is now required to work with other agencies belonging to the welfare state to address and reduce crime, create safe communities and create a more inclusive society' (Crowther, 2007: 246).

Essential to this drive was the statutory framework instigated by the Crime and Disorder Act 1998, which established regional 'Crime and Disorder Reduction Partnerships' (CDRPs) with direct input from the police and local authorities. These publicly accountable partnerships 'joined up' or brought together senior representatives from several key sectors at a localised level including the police, the probation service, local government, social services, education, transport, the Magistracy and the voluntary sector. The aim was to allow local experts and partners to tackle local problems in terms of anti-social behaviour and crime, including street crime, burglary and racially motivated offending. These CDRPs were overseen by a centralised Crime Reduction Task Force, which would translate the national policy agenda, provide guidance and set targets. This regional and national apparatus was linked directly to wider social welfare policy affecting public housing, health and education.

In terms of policy crossover, these three variables were highlighted in contributing directly to social inequality, social strain and ultimately criminal behaviour. Public housing policy includes the serious social issues of homelessness, and poor design, build quality and maintenance of the built environment, which encourages anti-social behaviour. This has in turn led to some housing estates being labelled 'no go' areas by local residents and police, and seen by many potential employers as modern rookeries (Hawtin and Kettle, 2000). Similarly, public health policy includes a startling number of points of convergence with that of crime, which must include mental health and community care provision, drug and alcohol dependency and abuse, and the affected health of people living with domestic violence or sexual abuse, or under constant fear and anxiety due to the level of crime within their particular community (Ham, 2004). Finally, education policy has long been seen as a tool of inclusion or exclusion, with poor educational attendance, engagement and achievement often statistically evident within the most vulnerable groups. Such groups include young offenders, children in care, children in relative poverty (with disadvantaged parents, single parents or parents holding low socio-economic status) and those from particular ethnic minorities (particularly African-Caribbean communities).

The point to take from the development of the evident 'joined up thinking' in social policy in tackling crime as a social problem over the past two decades is that no government department is an island, and that whether the drive emanates from the Home Office, the Ministry of Justice or the Treasury, contemporary crime policy and the statistics that flow from it are affected by a multitude of departments and agencies, and augmented by the multiple personalities therein, both individual and corporate.

The Home Office and the Ministry of Justice

The two principal government ministries that affect criminal policy in the most direct sense are best described as gargantuan in size, focus and scope. Both the Home Office and its younger sibling the Ministry of Justice are based at the heart of government in central London. At a macro level, both departments are seen to deal with law and the justice system, and have ultimate responsibility and account-ability for the agencies under their respective controls. Although size evidently matters when considering such dramatic contemporary examples, it is worth considering at this point the characteristics of modern bureaucracies provided by Max Weber, which still ring true in terms of personnel, hierarchy and jurisdiction (influence and power), according to Weber. Modern officialdom functions in the manner described in the following box.

There is the principle of official jurisdictional areas, which are generally ordered by rules, that is, by laws or administrative regulations:
    This means:

1   The regular activities required for the purposes of the bureaucratically governed structure are assigned as official duties.
2   The authority to give commands required for the discharge of these duties is distributed in a stable way and is strictly delimited by rules concerning the coercive means, physical, sacerdotal or otherwise, which may be placed at the disposal of officials.
3   Methodical provision is made for the regular and continuous fulfilment of these duties and for the exercise of the corresponding rights; only persons who qualify under general rules are employed.

In the sphere of the state these three elements constitute a bureaucratic agency, in the sphere of the private economy they constitute a bureaucratic enterprise. Bureaucracy, thus understood, is fully developed in political and ecclesiastical communities only in the modern state, and in the private economy only in the most advanced institutions of capitalism.

Source: Weber (2006: 49)

Both departments still function in the manner that Weber describes, in that both the Home Office and the Ministry of Justice are assigned official roles and duties by the state; both work with the government in power at a particular time but not necessarily 'for' it; and the nature of social change dictates that the character of the duties discharged, and indeed the persons discharging them, are likely to change and develop over time. In practice, this means that the Home Office and Ministry of Justice are best described as multilayered responsive institutions, which are likely to further grow and diversify (alongside society) rather than diminish.

Public appetite and central government crime policy

The multiplicity and complexity of roles assigned to the Home Office and the Ministry of Justice and their exponential growth as departments over the past three decades can be directly linked to the seemingly constant flow of public concerns during this period. These concerns commenced with a series of serious miscarriages of justice and police misconduct cases during the 1980s, which flowed into the highly visible prison riots and rooftop protests of the early 1990s. By the mid-1990s, the British public had been forced to digest the graphic depictions of the murder of James Bulger by two older children, and the unprovoked racial murder of 18-year-old Stephen Lawrence, the latter resulting in the Macpherson Report 1999, which described the Metropolitan police as 'institutionally racist'. In the year of the millennium, the murder of seven-year-old Sarah Payne by Roy Whiting, a previously convicted paedophile, resurrected recent public fears over child safety, and when this was quickly followed by the murder of two 10-year-old girls in the small Cambridgeshire village of Soham in 2002, public mood had reached fever pitch (Cohen, 2002). Tragically, the two victims in the Soham case, Holly Wells and Jessica Chapman, had known their killer Ian Huntley, a local man working as a school caretaker despite a history of sexual offending.

During the same period, the rise of Islamic terrorism post 9/11 was brought home to the British public by a series of coordinated suicide bomber attacks on the London public transport system on 7 July 2005, which left 52 people dead and over 700 injured. This in turn fired discussions on both large-scale legal and illegal immigration into the UK, which had culminated in inner city riots in Bradford during 2001 and Birmingham in 2005, harking back to memories of earlier race riots in Brixton, Greater London, and across the UK during the early and mid-1980s. In recent years, concern over large-scale immigration and the apparent 'disappearance of borders' as a consequence of globalisation has extended to migrant workers from countries in Eastern Europe as they have joined the European Union (EU).

In 2011, anxiety over control of the media and public privacy surfaced during what became known as the 'phone hacking scandal', principally involving journalists from Rupert Murdoch's powerful global News International organisation with 'targets' that included the families of murder victims and soldiers killed on active service, alongside their traditional political and celebrity quarry. Downes and Morgan describe the illegality and basis of the outcry in the following terms:

> At stake was the increasing anxiety that key institutions of the state, the police, the Crown Prosecution Service, and Parliament itself, are unable effectively to withstand the power of the Murdoch empire, a trans-national media corporation whose writ has purportedly played a major role in deciding elections since that of Margaret Thatcher in 1979.
>
> (Downes and Morgan, 2012: 200)

Later in 2011, the public eye became focused on a series of public disturbances that started in Tottenham, London, during early August, and became known as the 'London riots' 2011. As the unrest quickly spread across the capital and into other large British cities, including Bristol, Birmingham, Liverpool and Manchester, it presented the spectacle of problem youth once more, with most of the perpetrators depicted as children and older adolescents united in what the media described as a 'shopping spree with violence'. Concerns over media power, specifically celebrity culture, returned during 2012 with revelations revealed following a television documentary on the famous British media personality Jimmy Savile (who had died aged 84 in October 2011), linking him to a series of sex attacks on young people that spanned four decades. The police operation that followed, named Operation Yewtree, has to date opened in excess of 400 lines of enquiry, investigating abuse by celebrities (many household names), from the 1950s to the present day.

Finally, at the time of writing, two suspects accused of the brutal public murder of a British soldier, Drummer (Private) Lee Rigby in Woolwich, London, on 22 May 2013, are awaiting trial in Belmarsh high-security prison. Video footage of one of the accused, Michael Adebolajo, blood soaked in the direct aftermath of the attack and shown widely on television, led to the public disclosure that both Adebolajo and his co-accused Michael Adebowale were vocal converts to radical Islam, and that both men had previously been known to the security services as individuals of interest. The Rigby case and its reprisals has brought the work of the Home Office (in terms of policing, national security and immigration policy), and that of the Ministry of Justice (in terms of operation of the criminal justice system), into sharp focus once more. This focus includes the role of over 100,000 employees who work day to day in these policy generative departments alongside elected politicians.

The Civil Service and mandarins

The primary role of Her Majesty's Civil Service in the UK is to facilitate the government of the day in its policy-making process and policy implementation. Civil servants can best be described as career officials. Like ministers, civil servants are servants of the Crown, but as they are in post for the term of their career, they are not affected by the outcome of general elections; therefore, the position of the Civil Service can best be described as a politically neutral permanent bureaucracy. The title of 'crown servant' confers a 'duty' element to the role, which is well explained by Weber:

> That the office is a 'vocation' finds expression, first, in the requirement of a prescribed course of training, which demands the entire working capacity for a long period of time, and in generally prescribed special examinations as pre-requisites for employment. Furthermore, it finds expression in that the position of the official is in the nature of a 'duty'.
>
> (Weber, 2006: 51)

Section 5(5) of the Constitutional Reform and Governance Act 2010 placed the Civil Service on a statutory footing and answerable to a code of practice, the 'Civil Service Code'. The code itself was first formulated in 1996 and contains a number of provisions regarding the character of the Civil Service and its performance. It states that Civil Service appointments should be made on merit and in open competition, and that subsequent duties should be discharged with integrity, honesty, objectivity and impartiality. The values are described in detail in the following terms: *integrity* is putting the obligations of public service above your own personal interests; *honesty* is being truthful and open; *objectivity* is basing your advice and decisions on a rigorous analysis of the evidence; and *impartiality* is acting solely according to the merits of the case and serving equally well governments of different political persuasions. Added to this list can be *secrecy*, as all civil servants sign, and are thus bound by, the constrictions of the Official Secrets Act 1989.

The Civil Service currently employs around 489,000 people, most of whom are based in London. At the very top of this hierarchy are around 1,000 senior civil servants, sometimes called 'mandarins.' The term 'mandarin' (from the Portuguese word 'mandarim', often translated as 'minister') was the name given to senior bureaucrats in imperial China. In the current context, the term (often used in a slang or satirical context) refers to an experienced civil servant who has attained high office and wields a large amount of power. In practice, the most senior person in each department is called the Permanent Secretary (a grade 1 post). Reporting to the Permanent Secretary in an 'open structure role' are his or her deputies, with these posts graded at Director General (grade 2) level, Director (grade 3) and Deputy Director (at grade 4, Deputy Director grades ranging from 4 to 7). Civil Service senior grading continues to Deputy Director (grade 7), before moving on to Senior and Higher Executive Officer grades, followed by Executive Officer, Administrative Officer and Administrative Assistant levels.

Within this extensive hierarchy, the mandarins indeed possess a great deal of power, as each holds a significant field of responsibility within a department. The Permanent Secretary in particular is expected to offer direct support to the government minister, and is accountable to parliament for the performance of his or her department. The role also encompasses that of 'accounting officer' in that the Permanent Secretary is responsible for the allocation (expenditure) of public funds. As Weber has alluded to above, the power in the mandarin system lies in the experience and longevity attached to the post, in that a Permanent

Secretary, as essentially a permanent employee of the Crown, should be able to garner departmental support, and draw on decades of first-hand knowledge and diplomatic know-how to approach a problem of policy or negotiation. A minister, on the other hand, may stay in office for a governmental term at best, or quite possibly a matter of months depending on public profile and prevailing public and peer opinion (which includes the much used option of 'reshuffle'). Thus, the conclusion in this important area of policy-making must be that many of the key decisions made in government policy direction are to be made, or directly influenced, by relatively anonymous unelected permanent officials.

From parliamentary debate to black letter law

Government policy is alive to social change and the public opinion that modern politicians hold dear. Thus, when conflict, anxiety or moral panic becomes evident, governments will consider a policy change or policy intervention that confers new rights or limits existing ones. As we have previously seen, modern government is able to draw on an enormous bank of ideas and opinions when it comes to policy, from the public via the traditional media and social media, from pressure groups and think tanks, from politicians and the enormous bureaucratic departments that support them.

The procedural machinery in the UK that takes an initial policy idea and transforms it into law has three components – the *executive*, the *judiciary* and the *legislature*. The work of these three components is governed by the political doctrine of 'separation of powers', which seeks to ensure that the three arms of government operate with independence from one another. As Britain does not possess a codified constitution, and parts of the executive and legislative functions are shared, a more accurate description would be an amalgam of powers, rather than a separation (Dicey, 2013).

The *executive* includes all government departments and 'authorities', local and central, and the unelected bureaucrats and administrators of the Civil Service.

The *judiciary* is concerned with dispute resolution and the machinations of public and private law in the court system. As the UK is a member state of the EU, the Judiciary must also interpret European Law, and in certain cases, notably the Human Rights Act 1998, ensure compliance with it.

The *legislature* in the UK is parliament. Parliament comprises a lower House, the House of Commons (elected), and an upper House, the House of Lords (appointed) and the Sovereign (currently Queen Elizabeth II), whose 'Royal Assent' is required for draft laws formulated in parliament (known as 'Bills') to become law. The work of parliament includes debate, acting as a 'check' on government and government departments, instigating public policy and passing legislation.

Source: Dicey (2013)

The earliest formal stage of the 'idea to law' process is the development of a 'Green Paper' on a particular policy subject. Green Papers are consultation documents produced by the government to instigate discussion both inside and outside parliament, and to garner feedback and opinion. If feedback is positive and the policy has support (or the policy area is seen as essential for public health, national security, etc.) the government may then produce a White Paper. This provides detailed information of the policy proposal and what the government intends to do, thus allowing for further debate and feedback prior to placing the proposal before parliament as a Bill.

For a Bill to progress to law, it will start its path in the House of Commons or the House of Lords in one of two ways: as a Private Members' Bill (a time-restricted practice for opposition MPs often used to instigate debate on an area of morality, controversy or public anxiety) or as a government Bill (primarily used as a vehicle for government policy for ministers). In both cases, the procedure is the same: the Bill has its 'first reading' where it is printed, and the title of the proposal is read out to the House of Commons. The Bill then moves to a 'second reading' where policy objectives are read out and debated in the House, and a vote is taken on whether to proceed with the proposal. If the vote is successful, the Bill then moves to the 'committee stage' where a standing committee (comprising between 16 and 50 MPs, or in certain cases the entire House) examines the proposal in detail and amends it if necessary. The Bill then moves to the 'report stage', where it is printed (with any amendments), reported to the House and voted upon. The final stage is the 'third reading', where the Bill is once again scrutinised, and amended if necessary, before being voted on once more, and passed on to the House of Lords.

At this stage, the Lords will examine the Bill and pass it back to the originating House for further amendment if necessary; this toing and froing between the Houses is normal and can occur several times until there is agreement, the process runs out of time (due to protracted procedure or what is known as 'filibustering' – strategic time-wasting by opponents) or the Parliament Acts of 1911 and 1949 are used (primarily to place a time limit on the House of Lords). Once the two Houses are in agreement over the content and validity of a Bill, it is forwarded to the Sovereign for 'Royal Assent', which in contemporary British politics is seen as an administrative formality rather than an examination. What then started out as a Bill becomes a Statute, the primary legislation of the UK, and moreover a policy device to emancipate or restrict.

Towards the harnessing of crime policy

A consequence of the buoyant state paternalism that proliferated following the Second World War was a policy interest in public safety and security alongside welfare. Throughout the 1960s, a period of unprecedented social change and rising crime rates, political calls commenced for a return to the law and order stability of earlier times – and the notion of party political crime policy was born. A decade later, crime policy was seen as fair game, an electoral battleground for public support, with law and order a key theme used against the beleaguered

James Callaghan-led Labour government by the Margaret Thatcher-led Conservatives in the run up to the 1979 election.

Reflections on crime policy and the development of the blame game

Following the Conservative election victory in 1979, consecutive Conservative governments over the next 18 years mobilised law and order as both a motif and a weapon to attack their opponents, proudly declaring themselves the 'party of law and order'. Later, reflecting on this policy, Thatcher stated:

> Law and order is a social service. Crime and the fear which the threat of crime induces can paralyse whole communities, keep lonely and vulnerable elderly people shut up in their homes, scar young lives and raise to cult status the swaggering violent bully who achieves predatory control over the streets. I suspect that there would be more support and less criticism than today's political leaders imagine for a large shift of resources from Social Security benefits to law and order – as long as rhetoric about getting tough on crime was matched by practice.
>
> (Thatcher, 1995)

The political backdrop to this rhetoric throughout the 1980s and early 1990s was an all-out attack on the Labour opposition as the party of disorder and permissiveness, in tandem with a significant increase in policing and criminal justice spending. As Barton and Johns make clear, in responding to the crime problem, the state is able to utilise three principal devices:

> the reality is that in WLDs [western liberal democracies] the state is restricted to three core vehicles on which all policy will be based. These are: intervention based on legal regulation . . . intervention based on the distribution of resources . . . interventions designed to promote normative change.
>
> (Barton and Johns, 2013: 17)

All three vehicles described were widely used and successfully applied to the 'crime problem' in various forms during this period – a stance described by Downes and Morgan as a 'bravura performance' (2012: 185). This performance included a widely criticised programme of privatisation across the criminal justice system (described in detail in Chapter 7), which encompassed escort duties being removed from police and prison officers to fully fledged private prisons, a policy that Christie described in the following terms:

> Compared to most other industries, the crime control industry is in a most privileged position. There is no lack of raw material: crime seems to be in endless supply. Endless are also the demands for the service, as well as the willingness to pay for what is seen as security. And the unusual industrial questions of contamination do not appear. On the contrary, this is an industry seen

as cleaning up, removing unwanted elements from the social system . . . Only rarely will those working for or in any industry say that now, just now, the size is about right. Now we are big enough, we are well established, we do not want any further growth. An urge for expansion is built into industrial thinking.

(Christie, 2000: 13)

New Labour, new focus

With mimicry widely regarded as the highest form of flattery, the 'New' Labour opposition began by the mid-1990s to overtake the increasingly beleaguered Conservatives as the party with the energy to tackle the crime problem. Driven forward by former Shadow Home Secretary Tony Blair's pirated US mantra to be 'tough on crime, tough on the causes of crime', Labour won a land-slide victory at the 1997 election, the left enthusiastically embracing the right's realism in crime policy (see Wilson and Kelling, 1982; Wilson, 1985, 1991). Party political manoeuvring on crime policy rhetoric waned preceding the 2001 and 2005 general elections, with a greater focus for all three main parties on the economy, public services and Britain's place in Europe. Crime policy for the Blair governments during this period focused on continual support for the police, changes in sentencing that reflected 'seriousness', the tackling of anti-social behaviour and the increased threat of terrorism after 9/11 in an increasingly multi-cultural Britain.

By the 2010 general election, the economy was eclipsing all other manifesto issues; in the eye of the worst financial storm in almost a century, fighting crime was afforded the status of a sideshow. However, the Conservative Party Manifesto provided insight to a number of familiar tried and tested themes:

We will fight back against the crime and anti-social behaviour that blights our communities. We will take steps to reduce the causes of crime, like poverty and broken families. We will put the criminal justice system on the side of responsible citizens, take tougher measures against knife criminals, and crack down on the binge-drinking that leads to violence. We will cut paperwork to get police out on the street and give people democratic control over local policing. We will introduce honesty in sentencing and pay voluntary and private providers to reduce re-offending.

(Conservative Party, 2010: 55)

With no single party winning an overall majority on 6 May 2010, the Liberal Party accepted an invitation by the Conservatives to form a Coalition government. The former criminal QC, Kenneth Clarke, was to be the Coalition's first Secretary of State for Justice and Lord Chancellor, with a mandate for sweeping reforms. With large cuts to public expenditure across the board and the backdrop of a Home Office budget cut of 23 per cent, the Coalition's first crime policy proposal was the election of regional Police and Crime Commissioners, tasked to deter-mine police priorities and cut bureaucracy.

The Green Paper that followed in December 2010, *Breaking the Cycle* (Ministry of Justice, 2010), outlined the shape of crime policy for the Coalition term, which included 'firming up' in a number of areas, including the increased use of deportation and more onerous work programmes in prison, alongside 'Pathfinder' projects to tackle youth offending. The need for 'justice' in criminal justice was emphasised, with a drive towards the utilisation of private companies to provide treatment and rehabilitative services, underpinned by the use of restorative justice. Proposals for policing would focus on the smart use of technology, and the sharing of information including hospital records, with police terms and conditions of employment to undergo review. Furthermore, the Freedom of Information Act would be extended, while whole-sale reform or repeal of the Human Rights Act would be considered to include a debate on replacement with a Bill of Rights. Immigration also provided a populist focal point with the creation of a 'beefed up' border police force, a revision of the number of non-EU migrants into the UK, and a major review of the asylum system.

The return of the 'Nasty Party'

In March 2012, a detailed report entitled *Critical Reflections: Social and Criminal Justice in the First Year of Coalition Government* was published via the independent Centre for Crime and Justice Studies, London. The report, edited by Arianna Silvestri (2012), included *inter alia* a section on the 'Return of the Nasty Party' by Professor Robert Reiner (Reiner, 2012). Contained within is a thorough review that pinpoints promises and policy narratives focusing throughout on the social backdrop and Coalition 'security blanket' of the austerity legacy and global recession. In policing, a review of police remuneration and conditions of service was undertaken (part one being published in March 2011, with the final version published in January 2012); this recommended £1 billion of 'savings' with restrictions on paid working hours and overtime. Unsurprisingly, the response from the Association of Chief Police Officers was highly critical, with one research report suggesting that the proposed changed would leave most police officers £4,000 a year worse off (Winsor, 2011). A significant change was also proposed for the probation service, which would see the service competing with private companies and voluntary organisations in certain traditional areas of practice. The court system was also targeted, with an announcement in December 2010 that 42 County Courts and 93 Magistrate's Courts faced closure, a decision that, in many cases, would affect the ability of both litigants and counsel to travel to a local court.

Behind all of this rapid change was a blanket policy to implement 'accountability' and 'transparency', and cut through 'red tape'. This was to be done by encouraging 'localism' in terms of policing and social responsibility (the politicisation of policing), greater access to Home Office and Ministry of Justice crime data (much of which was incomplete or ambiguous, and ultimately unusable) and the restructuring or disbanding of 316 non-departmental bodies (also known as 'quangos'), the most far-reaching of which would see the replacement of the Serious Organised Crime Agency (the previously much vaunted 'British FBI') with a National Crime Agency.

Much of the impetus behind such a radical change in criminal justice during the first term for the Coalition was administrative and driven by cost-cutting, and thus deregulation in sense and purpose, leaving Reiner to reflect:

> It was sadly predictable that the Coalition's liberal ambitions would be frustrated in practice by increasing crime and disorder flowing from the financial cuts and downturn. What was less predictable was the speed and the savagery with which David Cameron squashed Kenneth Clarke's reforms, buckling under to tabloid fury . . . The growth of demonstrations and protests against the Coalition's cuts and the unjust tax burden placed on the relatively poor by the legal tax avoidance of the rich, spearheaded by heroic groups such as UK Uncut, and the harsh policing tactics they have been met with, indicate clearly the order problems posed by neoliberal economic policy. So too do the riots of 2011.
>
> (Reiner, 2012: 29–30)

At the time of writing (August 2013), wide-scale opposition is continuing across the criminal justice sector against further Coalition plans for a U turn on the building of private prisons, the dramatic limiting of legal aid and the introduction of price-competitive tendering for law firms undertaking criminal defence work (limiting a defendant's right to choose their lawyer). Changes, such as these in criminal defence provision, would see a policy move towards an American-style public defender system with legal services provided by a government-approved panel. On reflection, a policy area that was initially seen as a sideshow by the incoming Coalition government in 2010 has proved as controversial an arena as it ever was, and will be seen as a no holds barred battleground in the run up to the 2015 general election in the UK.

Case study: Social change, social policy and the procedural path of the Hunting Act 2004

This case study illustrates the inherent difficulties attached to transforming informal policy, even when it appears on the surface to be popular public policy, into formal policy as law. Hunting in the UK carries important cultural significance, and scrutiny of the path of what would become a 'series' of Bills through parliament allows us to consider *inter alia* issues of representation and efficacy, alongside the role of powerful pressure groups as collaborators and instigators of social change.

Social change and hunting in the UK

Hunting with hounds in the UK is seen as a controversial issue. The sport involves the tracking and the chase of a fox (or deer) over distance, usually by a pack of specially trained fox hounds or scent hounds accompanied by riders on horseback, with the quarry being killed by the pack at the climax of the chase. As a blood sport, hunting of this type had been popular in rural communities since the sixteenth century, especially among the aristocracy and their retainers. By the seventeenth century, several organised 'hunts' existed in Britain, meeting regularly to pursue fox and hare. The very act of hunting can be seen as of enduring cultural importance in many western societies, with links to elitism and class structure. English fox hunting in particular has ritualistic connotations that provide distinct images of the aristocracy and the countryside. Howe (1981) argues that these images of the aristocracy and rural society generally are important symbols that place modern society in historical perspective. Indeed, over the past century, the class structures that have been part of hunting since its organised inception have been viewed by many as class divides, with hunters often seen as relics of a class system that no longer exists.

Much of the opposition towards hunting in the UK comes from those concerned with animal cruelty. Animal rights activism has a proud history in the UK that has existed for almost the same length of time as organised hunting. Laws were passed to protect animal welfare during the Protectorate Government of Oliver Cromwell in the seventeenth century, and Cromwell himself was an opponent of blood sports and hunting, seeing their practice as elitist and unnecessarily cruel. This led to the passing of Britain's first 'hunting ban' in 1653, an attempt at social policy that lasted for just seven years until 1660, when it was revoked by the returning monarchy. During the nineteenth century, a series of attempts was made to control various forms of hunting and blood sports, including parliamentary Bills opposing bull baiting in 1800 and 1802, which both failed, and were cited respectively as being 'anti-working class' and likely to 'destroy the character of rural England'. A significant turning point came in 1822 when an Act was passed 'To Prevent the Cruel and Improper Treatment of Cattle' (following a Bill proposed by Richard Martin in 1821), which carried the weight of the criminal law. Two years later, Martin collaborated with a group of like-minded individuals in forming a pressure group to lobby for the protection of animals; this pressure group would become the RSPCA.

In recent decades, animal rights has consistently occupied the news agenda, with images of hunting in the UK often depicting physical clashes and tense stand-offs between hunters and their opponents. Many such activists belong to the Hunt Saboteurs Association, an organisation formed in 1963 to actively oppose blood sports that now operates across Europe and North America. The Hunt Saboteurs Association operates by way of using various techniques to disrupt hunt meetings, allowing the pursued quarry to escape. Opposition to hunting in the UK has also frequently been expressed by the League Against Cruel Sports (LACS), a pressure group formed in 1924 that at its inception opposed fox hunting and the ritualistic practice of 'blooding' children attending hunts (a 'rite of passage' involving smearing the blood of the killed animal on the child's face). This powerful lobby with traditional links to the Labour Party has led to a number of attempts to ban fox hunting and hunting with hounds, with two Private Members' Bills requesting a ban put before parliament in 1949 (the first withdrawn, the second defeated at the 'second reading' stage), and a further proposal that ran out of time in 1970. Throughout the 1990s, a series of attempts was made to get the subject back on the political agenda; with Private Members' Bills to make hunting with dogs illegal rejected in 1992, 1993 and 1995.

In May 1997, the Labour Party won the general election following almost 20 years of Conservative government. The new government realised the need to 'honour' manifesto promises, or at the very least be seen to respect them, by means of formal debate in parliament. A key part of what was a compelling Labour manifesto had been the promise of higher standards of animal welfare (with the anti-vivisection animal rights 'terrorism' and the 'veal protests' at UK ports of the early 1990s fresh in the memory), and the assurance of greater protection for wildlife. Greater protection for wildlife would extend to a free vote in parliament on whether the traditional practice of hunting with hounds (primarily fox hunting, hare coursing and stag hunting) still had a place in the UK at the turn of the millennium.

Parliamentary 'ping-pong' and the development of the Hunting Act 2004

Within six months of the Labour Party coming to power in 1997, Labour MP Michael Foster published a Private Members' Bill requesting the banning of hunting with hounds, but was denied adequate parliamentary time for the proposal, and the subject was temporarily dropped from the political agenda. However, in early 1998, Foster's Bill passed the 'second reading' stage in the House of Commons, and in early March a quarter of a million hunting supporters converged on London to protest against it. This march had been organised by the pro-hunting Countryside Alliance (CA), a powerful pressure group that believed any possible ban would have disastrous consequences for the rural economy in Britain. The march led to sporadic violence and anger on the streets of London, with small elements of the CA support clashing with animal rights activists. The effect of these scenes, playing out in news broadcasts, was to place the policy area firmly within the public consciousness.

Later that month, as before, the Foster Bill ran out of time in parliament. However, Michael Foster remained determined to see the issue through and was delighted to have gained the support of his Prime Minister Tony Blair, who went on to vow that hunting with hounds would be made illegal during Labour's first term of office. The resolve shown by Blair in making this statement was immediately tempered by a press revelation that the Labour Party had recently received a £100,000 donation from an anti-hunting pressure group to support a ban. Amid concerns over the financial cost associated with an out and out ban, Lord Burns, a senior former Treasury civil servant, was commissioned in November 1999 by the government to chair a research inquiry into the consequences for the rural economy of the proposed ban on hunting with dogs.

In early 2000, a Bill to ban hunting with dogs in Scotland was proposed to the Scottish parliament by Michael Watson MSP, and, watching closely, the Labour Government announced that it would offer support to a similar backbench Bill at Westminster. With this in mind, the Labour Party set about lobbying its MPs, stating that the ban should be seen as an important issue for potential Labour voters, urging solidarity in supporting the proposal. The government further stated that any proposal put before the House would include a series of options offering no change (the status quo), stricter regulation, local referenda or a complete ban. In June 2000, the Burns Inquiry reported to parliament that around 8,000 jobs would be lost if the hunting ban was successful; the report also passed on its recommendations on 'animal cruelty' in terms of the 'humane credentials' of hunting with hounds.

In early 2001, all hunting activity in the UK was suspended due to the widespread outbreak of foot and mouth disease, and on the last day of February scenes of desolation in the countryside accompanied the media announcement that MPs in the House of Commons had voted for an outright ban on hunting by the significant majority of 179. Concerns for the safety of MPs were expressed in March 2001 when the names of two pro-hunting Labour MPs were found on 'hit lists' following a police raid on an anti-hunt organisation, adding fuel to an already controversial issue. A month later, the Hunting Bill was passed to the House of Lords, only to be rejected by the enormous majority of 249. This stoic and ultimately strategic opposition in the Lords ensured that the passage of the Bill through parliament would run out of time due to the pending general election, and thus fail to progress to law during Labour's first term as promised.

By 2002, the Labour Party was celebrating its second term of office and placed the subject of the hunting ban back on the political agenda as the Scottish parliament banned hunting with dogs in Scotland, only to face immediate court challenges by pro-hunting pressure groups. Thus, the original Bill in the House of Commons was amended, and MPs and Lords were asked to vote on a choice of a simple 'no' to the ban, a licensing system for fox hunting or a 'yes' to the ban. The Commons voted for the ban by a majority of 211 (Prime Minister Blair abstaining), with the Lords favouring licensing by a majority of 307. With the Commons and the Lords seemingly poles apart on the issue, veteran Labour Party MP Gerald Kaufmann issued a threat to withdraw the Labour Party whip should the will of the Commons be further rejected by the Lords. Following this statement, Kaufman was placated by the Rural Affairs Minister Alun Michael, who threatened the use of the Parliament Act 1911 to force the issue into policy if the parliamentary ping-pong continued.

Sensing that legislation was growing nearer, several pro-hunting and rural economy pressure groups came together under the umbrella of the 'Liberty and Livelihood' slogan. Once again, an enormous crowd marching under this slogan, estimated at around 450,000, converged on London to vocally condemn the proposed ban. Late in 2002, Alun Michael MP placed another revised Hunting Bill before parliament in an amended form that contained appeasement for the Lords by allowing some licensed and regulated fox hunting to continue, but banning the hunting of stags and hares. The main purpose of this significant amendment was to head off any further filibustering and time-consuming opposition in the House of Lords.

In June 2003, under much backbench pressure, the government amended the Bill once more, returning to an outright ban, and in the House of Commons it passed the motion by a majority of 208 after several hours of heated debate. By October that year, the Bill was before the House of Lords at the 'committee stage' and the proposal of a complete ban was revoked, with other parts of the Bill amended by the Lords in an attempt to force a licensing system for hunting. By this stage, the Bill had become a 'political football' and was returned to the Commons, only to be sent back to the Lords with the ban proposal in place. As was the case in 2001, this repeated toing and froing between the two Houses on this issue eventually ensured that the matter ran out of parliamentary time.

With government resolve and patience tested, an announcement was made in September 2004 that a further 'free vote' on the issue would once again be put to parliament, requesting a complete ban on hunting. Consequently, a new 'olive branch' was offered by the Labour Government to its opposition (primarily in the Lords) via the tabling of a new policy proposal to ensure that, should the ban be successful, it would not become law for two years, allowing the rural economy time to adjust and to recover. A further issue that led to the olive branch being proffered at this juncture was concern over visible mass protests in London and intense media activity and lobbying from pro-hunting pressure groups in the direct run up to the general election in 2005, with the Country Landowners' Association pledging to fight the policy in 'every court in the land' and bring 'true civil disobedience' to bear on the government should a ban be enforced.

On 16 September 2004, the House of Commons voted again for the banning of hunting inside the Chamber, while a large-scale pro-hunting demonstration was taking place outside in Parliament Square. This protest escalated into violence, and a tense stand-off with the police occurred, during which time a group of five pro-hunting demonstrators broke into the House of Commons and directly confronted MPs. Having cleared the Commons following this drama, the Bill was once again presented to the House of Lords and, as in all previous attempts, was soundly rejected, this time by a majority of 250. On 18 November 2004, with the backdrop of a clearly frustrated government, the Speaker of the House of Commons, Michael Martin, invoked the provisions of the Parliament Act 1911 for only the seventh time in history, and the Hunting Bill was finally passed for Royal Assent, coming into force as the Hunting Act 2004 on 18 February 2005.

Reflections on the Hunting Act 2004

The path of what was to become the Hunting Act 2004 offers a rare insight into the wide range of trials and tribulations and the functions and foibles of the UK parliament, in an attempt to develop social policy in an area that would at first sight seem highly popular with the British electorate and its political representatives. In practice, the issue under scrutiny drew out deep issues linked to social class, social change and culture. Significantly, both sides of the debate were able to draw on powerful pressure groups and politicians to fight their respective corners, primarily the Labour MPs in the House of Commons and the LACS for the ban, and the Conservative Peers (alongside a large contingent of their Liberal and Labour Party colleagues) in the Lords and the CA against the ban. This led to something of a public relations 'arms race' both inside and outside parliament while the Bill ping-ponged between the Commons and the Lords. The eventual passing of the Hunting Act 2004 is particularly notable in that it required invoking the rarely used Parliament Act 1911 to finally steer it through parliament and into policy, after being soundly defeated in the House of Lords every time it appeared there.

During the campaign, the pressure groups on either side utilised all the tools at their disposal in taking up the fight, with campaign strategy frequently being drawn along social class lines. The stance of the CA was particularly interesting, with media focus on loss of tradition and the erosion of British culture, alongside the apparently 'doom-laden' economic implications for the rural economy. The latter was of clear concern to the politicians, and led to government action in the instigation of the inquiry chaired by Lord Burns, a highly experienced and accomplished former senior civil servant. The resulting report, *Hunting With Dogs, Final Report* (Burns, 2000), provided interesting reading and made the important distinction that while some jobs within the hunting sphere merely served the rural economy, others were dependent upon it. This distinction can be illustrated via the report's views on the effect of the ban on the horse industry:

> It is impossible to predict with any certainty what would happen in practice. What we can say with some confidence is that, even on a worst case scenario, not all jobs presently dependent on hunting would be lost. In particular, we believe that only a small proportion of the horse owners would immediately seek to get rid of their horses if a ban was introduced. It is much more likely that many would take up equestrian activities, reduce the use of their horses or not buy new horses when the time came to replace them.
>
> (Burns Report, 2000)

Consequently, the higher end of Burns' estimate was that 8,000 jobs were dependent on hunting, but from this number only around 700 were directly fixed to it, information that would prove crucial to politicians on the fence, particularly Labour politicians tuned to resisting any call for widespread job losses. Indeed, a research briefing paper for the Northern Ireland Assembly on the effects of the hunting ban undertaken in 2010 suggests that Burns was correct in his estimations, stating that: 'The evidence from BETA on the numbers of horses and riders in the UK, suggests that the horse industry did not drop into decline since the ban, that other factors clearly kept it on the increase' (2010: 6).

There is considerably more difficulty in attempting to quantify the social and cultural changes brought about by the ban. Hunting has continued with former hunts engaged in drag hunting and trail hunting (both utilising artificial lures and scents), with the number of individual participants actually increasing. The number of organised hunts, however, has shown a decrease in number, although this decrease suggests a drop of only around 10 per cent. Furthermore, despite the suggestion by the LACS of widespread law-breaking, annual conviction rates under the Hunting Act have been consistently low since the ban. The stance of the CA and its allies in the Master of Foxhounds Association and Foundation over the past decade has been to continue to lobby for the ban to be overturned, seeing it as 'bad law' and a waste of police resources, while highlighting continued harassment and disruption from animal rights activists. The stance of the LACS has been to maintain counterpressure against the CA by continuing to directly lobby MPs and highlight the cruelty attached to the practice of hunting, and to monitor hunts directly. These actions have intensified, following the promise from Prime Minister David Cameron in May 2010 delivered in his first policy programme that: 'We will bring forward a motion on a free vote enabling the House of Commons to express its view on the repeal of the Hunting Act' (HM Government, 2010). This approach has led to accusations of elitism, and the reappearance of traditional alliances and sensibilities, and of hunting being seen as a campaign case for many Conservatives.

In terms of policy analysis, the question of banning hunting had been considered by parliament with Bills tabled over a dozen times between 1949 and 2004, and being rejected. This was despite intense lobbying by animal rights pressure groups, apparent public support and scenes of violence and public disorder, from supporters on both sides, regularly being shown by the media. Furthermore, support from the then Prime Minister Tony Blair, the majority of the elected representatives in the House of Commons and a persuasive inquiry from the Civil Service were not enough to see the Bill pass to law, primarily due to the strategic actions of the unelected House of Lords, which included filibustering. The Hunting Act 2004, and the enduring debate on its validity, stand as an example of the difficulty in transforming informal principles into formal policy.

Key points summary

This chapter explores a number of the key debates concerning the formal and informal processes utilised in criminal justice policy-making in England and Wales. It argues that:

- Criminal justice pressure groups have played a pivotal role in the formation of criminal justice policies, and possess expertise that is both sought and shunned by media and politicians depending on the nature of the social problem under scrutiny. Pressure groups differ in focus and power, and those which fall outside the mainstream are more likely to resort to radical means to promote their policy messages.
- In recent years, pressure groups have, in many cases, been replaced as sources of information (and ultimately policy) by politicians in favour of think tanks. Think tanks accordingly are often seen as partisan and supportive rather than fully independent.
- Contemporary politics is still reliant on political personality for much of its policy drive and initiative, with capable leadership seen as essential for public belief in crime policy outputs.
- While the traditional 'crime-oriented' government departments – the Home Office and the Ministry of Justice – can still be identified as crucial to the formation and direction of crime policy in the UK, there appears to be a growing focus on the need for 'joined up' policy to tackle crime. Such joined up policy includes and encompasses departments that deal with key welfare issues, such as housing, health and education, which are seen to influence social strain and criminal offending.
- Alongside the actions of politicians (who tend to be generalists), the non-elected 'career politicians' within the Civil Service (who tend to be experts) should be seen as highly influential and central to the formation, direction and implementation of government policy.
- Contemporary politics has witnessed the harnessing of crime policy as an electoral 'tool' by politicians, and the appearance of what can be termed the 'blame game' in party politics This, combined with the current global recession, has led to what Reiner has referred to as 'the return of the Nasty Party' in British politics, and moreover British criminal policy.

Critical thinking discussion topics

1   What are the distinctive features of criminal justice pressure groups?
2   How and why have think tanks 'replaced' pressure groups in the British political landscape?
3   Richards and Smith (2002) argue that, in modern society, 'governance demands that we consider all the actors and locations beyond the "core executive" involved in the policy making process'. Who are the actors that 'govern' crime policy beyond the core executive in the UK?

4   Is individual political personality still important in the crime policy-making process in the twenty-first century?
5   To what extent is the public appetite for central government crime policy an insatiable one? Give reasons for your answer.

Seminar task

You are a group of senior civil servants working for the Home Office. You are asked by the charismatic Home Secretary to undertake research into a controversial policy proposal on the feasibility and implications of placing CCTV cameras in the boardrooms and offices of all banks in the City of London. You are informed that the government feels that, in light of the recent banking crisis, there is a need to monitor potential malpractice and 'get tough' on the causes of white collar crime. Advise the minister on the following:

1   the questions that will form the basis for the research report;
2   the type of opposition that the minister should expect to face on the proposals, both inside and outside parliament.

Recommended further reading

Barton, A. and Johns, N. (2013) *The Policy-Making Process in the Criminal Justice System.* London: Routledge.

Christie, N. (2000) *Crime Control as Industry: Towards Gulags, Western Style* (3rd edn). London: Routledge.

Easton, S. and Piper, C. (2012) *Sentencing and Punishment: The Quest for Justice* (3rd edn). Oxford: Oxford University Press.

Richards, D. and Smith, M. (2002) *Governance and Public Policy in the United Kingdom.* Oxford: Oxford University Press.

Silvestri, A. (ed.) (2012) *Critical Reflections: Social and Criminal Justice in the First Year of Coalition Government.* London: Centre for Crime and Justice Studies.

References

Barton, A. and Johns, N. (2013) *The Policy-Making Process in the Criminal Justice System.* London: Routledge.

Burns, T. (2000) *Inquiry into Hunting with Dogs, Final Report* (Burns Report). London: Stationery Office.

Christie, N. (2000) *Crime Control as Industry: Towards Gulags, Western Style* (3rd edn). London: Routledge.

Cohen, S. (2002) *Folk Devils and Moral Panics* (3rd edn). London: Routledge.

Conservative Party (2010) *Invitation to Join the Government of Britain: The Conservative Party Manifesto 2010.* London: Conservative Party.

Crowther, C. (2007) *An Introduction to Criminology and Criminal Justice.* Basingstoke: Palgrave Macmillan.

Dicey, A.V. (2013) 'The law of the constitution'. In J.W.F. Allison (ed.) *The Law of the Constitution*. Oxford: Oxford University Press.

Downes, D. and Morgan, R. (2002) 'The skeletons in the cupboard: the politics of law and order at the turn of the millennium'. In M. Maguire, R. Morgan and R. Reiner (eds) *The Oxford Handbook of Criminology* (3rd edn). Oxford: Oxford University Press.

Downes, D. and Morgan, R. (2012) 'Overtaking on the Left? The politics of law and order in the "Big Society" '. In M. Maguire, R. Morgan and R. Reiner (eds) *The Oxford Handbook of Criminology* (5th edn). Oxford: Oxford University Press.

Easton, S. and Piper, C. (2012) *Sentencing and Punishment: The Quest for Justice* (3rd edn). Oxford: Oxford University Press.

Feeley, M. and Simon, J. (1994) 'Actuarial justice: the emerging new criminal law'. In D. Nelken (ed.) *The Futures of Criminology*. London: Sage.

Ham, C. (2004) *Health Policy in Britain: The Politics and Organisation of the NHS* (5th edn). Basingstoke: Macmillan.

Hawtin, M. and Kettle, J. (2000) 'Housing and social exclusion'. In J. Percy-Smith (ed.) *Policy Responses to Social Exclusion: Towards Inclusion*. Milton Keynes: Open University Press.

HM Government (2010) *The Coalition: Our Programme for Government*. London: HM Government.

Howe, J. (1981) 'Fox hunting as ritual'. *American Ethnologist*, 8: 278–300.

Jewkes, Y. (2011) *Media and Crime* (2nd edn). London: Sage.

Ministry of Justice (2010) *Breaking the Cycle: Effective Punishment, Rehabilitation and Sentencing of Offenders*. London: Stationery Office.

Muncie, J., Talbot, D. and Walters, R. (eds) (2010) *Crime: Local and Global*. Cullompton: Willan.

Northern Ireland Assembly (2010) *The Fox Hunting Ban in Britain*. Briefing Paper 123/10, Belfast: NIA.

Page, E. (1999) 'The insider outsider distinction: an empirical investigation'. *British Journal of Politics and International Relations*, 1(2): 205–14.

Reiner, R. (2012) 'The return of the Nasty Party'. In A. Silvestri (ed.) *Critical Reflections: Social and Criminal Justice in the First Year of Coalition Government*. London: Centre for Crime and Justice Studies.

Richards, D. and Smith, M. (2002) *Governance and Public Policy in the United Kingdom*. Oxford: Oxford University Press.

Silvestri, A. (ed.) (2012) *Critical Reflections: Social and Criminal Justice in the First Year of Coalition Government*. London: Centre for Crime and Justice Studies.

Thatcher, M. (1993) *The Downing Street Years*. London: Harper Collins.

Thatcher, M. (1995) *The Path to Power*. London: Harper Collins.

Weber, M. (2006) 'Bureaucracy'. In A. Sharma and A. Gupta (eds) *The Anthropology of the State: A Reader*. Oxford: Blackwell Publishing.

Wilson, J.Q. (1983) *Thinking About Crime*. New York: Basic Books.

Wilson, J.Q. (1991) *On Character: Essays by James Q. Wilson*. Washington DC: AEI Press.

Wilson, J.Q. and Hernstein, R. (1985) *Crime and Human Nature: The Definitive Study of Causes of Crime*. New York: Simon & Schuster.

Wilson, J.Q. and Kelling, G. (1982) 'Broken windows'. *Atlantic Monthly*, 249(3): 29–38.

Winsor, T. (2011) *Independent Review of Police Officer and Staff Remuneration and Conditions*. London: Stationery Office.

5   The expert and research-led criminal justice policy-making

Chapter summary

In recent years, there has been considerable academic debate about the relationship between research expertise and public policy-making. Originating in the field of health policy, the idea that policy should be underpinned by research evidence spread to other policy areas, and formed part of the 'what works' movement adopted by the New Labour administration. However, in October 2009, in defiance of its own commitment to produce policy that would reflect research-based evidence, the Home Secretary forced Professor David Nutt, the government's appointed scientific advisor on the misuse of drugs, to resign after he made public research findings that ran counter to the government's policy on drugs (Tran, 2009). The controversial 'sacking' was a very public example of government refusal to reverse its policy-making, despite being presented with 'a formidable body of evidence that could make a strong case' in favour of a change of direction (Currie, 2007: 117). With this case in mind, this chapter traces the rise and fall of evidenced-based policy-making (EBP) as a primary influence on policy-making, and serves as a timely reminder that governments are ever mindful of how their actions will be interpreted by the media, the electorate and vested interests.

This chapter looks at:

- the development of the research-led policy-making movement, and its influence on New Labour penal policy-making;
- the movement's trajectory, examining how a project that was initially embraced by criminal justice academics and practitioners as a radical departure from the defeatism of 'nothing works' and 'prison works' policy-making fell into disrepute as practical politics took precedence;
- how what counts as 'evidence' is distorted (suppressed or denied) and presented to the public by government and sympathetic media in a manner that fits political imperatives;
- how politicians can choose from a range of sources of 'expert' evidence, providing examples of how evidence counter to the political agenda is contested (and rejected) by politicians;
- contemporary debates about the role of academics in undertaking policy-oriented research, discussing the literature on 'public criminology'.

Case studies: Hope's burglary study and Nutt's drug misuse report

In the cases, you will be given concrete examples of how research evidence that failed to produce results which served government policy imperatives was suppressed, distorted and/or rejected. The studies serve to highlight the degree to which, despite the rhetoric and activity, there has been a perceptible reduction in the status and influence of research evidence. In reading the case studies, you should consider the implications for future criminological research.

The emergence of EBP

If 'nothing works' to rehabilitate the offender was a reflection of the academic and political mood of 1970s and 1980s criminal justice policy-making, and heralded the 'just deserts' and public protection agenda (Nutley and Davies, 2004), and 'prison works' was the populist response of the Conservative government seeking to appease a public hell bent on retribution following the vitriolic press coverage of the murder of James Bulger (Baker, 1996; Berry *et al.* 2012), one of the key characteristics of New Labour public policy-making in the late 1990s was the 'what works' movement, which signalled the rediscovery of EBP. EBP – 'an approach that helps people make well-informed decisions about policies, programmes and projects by putting the best available evidence from research at the heart of policy development and implementation' (Davies, 2004: 3) – offered the prospect of an impartial search for policy solutions, unsullied by politically determined ideological preferences or quick-fix populism.

Research-driven policy-making has a long history. Its high points include: Chadwick's report on the state of sanitation in London in 1842 that prompted the provision of clean water pipes and the creation of London's sewage network; Rowntree's 1860s poverty survey; Booth's studies of working-class life and work in London; and the Beveridge report in the 1940s (Dean, 2012). The recent resurgence of research-driven policy-making can be traced to 1999, the year in which New Labour published the *Modernising Government* White Paper (Cabinet Office, 1999), setting out its commitment to policy based on sound research evidence; established a number of new units (including the Social Exclusion Unit, the Women's Unit and the Performance and Innovation Unit); and announced plans to embark on a crime reduction programme that would be informed by evidence gained from research. Acknowledging the decline in deference to authority, and focusing on the need for greater public accountability, the White Paper stated:

> People are becoming more demanding, whether as consumers of goods and services in the market place, as citizens or as businesses affected by the policies and services which government provides. To meet these demands, government must be willing constantly to re-evaluate what it is doing so as

to produce policies that really deal with problems; that are forward-looking and shaped by the evidence rather than a response to short-term pressures; that tackle causes not symptoms; that are measured by results rather than activity; that are flexible and innovative rather than closed and bureaucratic; and that promote compliance rather than avoidance or fraud. To meet people's rising expectations, policy making must also be a process of continuous learning and improvement.

(Cabinet Office, 1999)

New Labour's promise to re-invigorate criminal justice policy through the establishment of a new partnership between policy and research (Morgan and Hough, 2008) was at its outset met with enthusiasm by academics and practitioners alike. The wide acceptance of the ethos that policy-making and practice should be 'evidence based' was not difficult to understand. After all, as Hamersley asks: 'who would want policy or practice not based on evidence?' (2005: 85). EBP offered the tantalising vision of rational policy-making premised on 'reasoned, evidenced criteria for decision-making and resource allocation' (Hope, 2004: 289), rather than political preferences or vote-catching slogans. For social scientists, who had been marginalised as a source of influence in the preceding decades, it held out the real possibility of academic knowledge about the roots of crime problems, and the crime-related harms experienced by poor and socially excluded communities, contributing towards the design and implementation of social policy (Hope, 2001, 2004).

While much of the literature focuses on the ideological appeal of EBP, there is little doubt that pragmatic considerations played their part in the early rush of optimism. For the probation service and other practitioners in the criminal justice system, whose sheer existence had been under threat by the law and order agenda pursued after 1993, EBP offered a lifeline. Mair (2004), in his compelling critique of 'what works' (as implemented by the probation service), argues that EBP was enthusiastically and, in the main, uncritically embraced as the panacea for all the service's problem. Consequently, there was little room for reflection or criticism: those whose response to the initiative was more measured or questioning were condemned by managers as 'Luddites' stuck in the past, working within a professional ideology of 'knowledge destruction' or at best 'bad common sense'. Mair states:

In the rush to embrace the tenets of What Works there has been surprisingly little academic or professional debate about the risks associated with it. What Works has been sold as the answer to all the problems of probation: it will prove its effectiveness as a credible sentence, it will lead to more funding, it will secure its future as a powerful organisation within the criminal justice system. The message emanating from the National Probation Directorate has been that What Works is beyond criticism; there is no alternative to it.

(Mair, 2004: 2)

Similarly, for cash-strapped university administrators, who had seen the social sciences 'under-valued and under-funded' by the previous Conservative administration, the proliferation of new crime reduction programmes generated by the EBP agenda offered unprecedented new funding streams for academic institutions and research centres (Hope, 2005). In 1998, the newly elected government undertook a Comprehensive Spending Review, followed a year later by the launch of a £250 million Crime Reduction Programme (CRP), administered by the Home Office, with £25 million allocated to the evaluation of its first three years of implementation. This was supplemented by a wide range of other more targeted initiatives (the youth justice provisions in the 1988 Crime and Disorder Act, Drug Treatment and Testing Orders, Offending Behaviour Programmes in prisons and literacy and numeracy programmes within the probation service). All of these attracted generous evaluation budgets from their inception, and in the main were contracted out to non-Home Office research institutions (a reversal of the previous practice of in-house research). Responsive to the needs of the Treasury and the Home Office, the aim of the evaluation process was to identify programmes that were effective both in reducing crime and in terms of value for money. It was envisaged that this would be achieved by a phased roll out of programmes with evaluation built in to each phase to identify lessons that could be integrated into the design and delivery of the next phase. The overall aim of the process was 'an upward spiral of effectiveness'. To this end, an additional annual budget of £40 million was allocated (Hope, 2004; Morgan and Hough, 2008).

Competing models of the research and policy relationship

Young *et al.* (2002) argue that there are five models of the research and policy relationship: the *knowledge-driven model*, the *problem-solving model*, the *interactive model*, the *political/tactical model* and the *enlightenment model*.

The knowledge-driven model: assumes that research leads policy. The expert is 'on the top'. In its more extreme form, knowledge-driven (really expert-driven) policy exemplifies the abdication of political choice.

The problem-solving model: research follows policy, and policy issues shape research priorities. From the government's point of view, the expert is 'on tap', but not on top.

The interactive model: contrasts sharply with both of these in positing a much more subtle and complex series of relationships between decision-makers and researchers. It portrays research and policy as mutually influential, with the agenda for both research and policy decision shaped within 'policy communities' that contain a range of actors. In this model, it is recognised that (some) researchers will themselves be influential. The archetypes are academics or think tank policy analysts, whose grasp and understanding of a policy problem enables them to propose new solutions.

The political/tactical model: assumes that policy is the outcome of a political process. This model sees the research agenda as politically driven, with studies commissioned and/or used to support the position adopted by the government of the day, the relevant minister or perhaps the civil servants most closely concerned. Research is commissioned to establish a point, rather than in the spirit of disinterested enquiry.

The enlightenment model: portrays research as standing, if not aloof, then certainly a little distant from the hothouse of immediate policy concerns. Rather than research serving policy agendas in a direct fashion, the benefits are indirect. It is often addressed not to the decision problem itself, but to the context within which that decision will be taken, providing a frame for thinking about it. Research conducted within this model seeks to illuminate the landscape for decision-makers.

Source: Young *et al.* (2002: 216–17)

The loss of faith in New Labour's vision of EBP

As mentioned earlier, evidence-based practice and policy-making has its origins in medicine and health settings, and is predicated on very specific types of evidence production. Its aim was to prevent medical practitioners from doing harm, and to promote procedures and practices that would secure the best clinical outcomes for patients (Hammersley, 2005). While the efficacy of implementing EBP in health settings was not without its critiques (Packwood, 2002), early optimism about the appropriateness of rolling out the programme to all areas of public policy began to fade as the limitations that the government were to impose upon the process of knowledge-gathering and dissemination became apparent to researchers and practitioners. Although some surprising converts remained wedded to the initiative, one of the most noteworthy features of the CRP (synonymous with the EBP movement in relation to criminal justice policy) was the speed with which 'tensions and contradictions inherent in the differences in cultures, perceptions and time-frames of policy-makers and politicians, practitioners and academics, including differences in their under-standings of the nature, purposes and reliability of "research" itself' (Maguire, 2004: 232) manifested themselves in a souring of the relationship between the academic researchers and the New Labour administration. As Morgan and Hough explain: 'The Crime Reduction Programme had a fairly short and unhappy life' (2008: 56). In 2005, *Criminal Justice Matters* published a special edition on the 'Uses of Research'. In this edition, early advocates of the New Labour project emerged as some of its greatest critiques (Hope, 2005), with some of the project's more vehement opponents going as far as to call for its total boycott (Walters, 2005).

While there are a range of explanations for the loss of faith in EBP, with both sides of the funder–contractor relationship levelling accusations (see Morgan and Hough, 2008), one of the key problems to emerge was the fundamental 'incompatibility between the ideology of evidence-based practice and the natural inclination of the political process to want to secure best outcomes' (Hope, 2005: 4). Under political pressure for 'quick wins', an initiative that at its inception seemed to endorse the *expert-led model* of policy-making reverted, albeit in a more sophisticated guise, to the *political/tactical model*. Although academic researchers at the outset anticipated being afforded the intellectual freedom and openness implied in *the expert-led model* (a model of practice that would make it possible for researchers to produce and disseminate research findings that cast doubt on government claims of the success of its activities), the inclination of ministers to relate a 'good story', by seeking out evidence that validated its predilections, interventions and programmes, created an irreconcilable conflict of interests and agendas (Hope, 2004).

That said, there is little doubt that the challenges posed by the CRP evaluation strategy were immense. These included: the wide range and sheer number of disparate initiatives, frequently implemented at the same time in the same area; tight timetable deadlines; political pressure for 'quick wins'; overly optimistic expectations of agencies' capacity to simultaneously implement new programmes and produce data for the researchers; and an inclination by agencies, struggling with implementation issues, to avoid drawing attention to themselves by 'dragging their heels'. A dilemma was created by evaluators' feedback to their policy-making paymasters, operating in New Labour's 'can do' environment, of endemic implementation problems and inconclusive evidence of 'what works' (Morgan and Hough, 2008).

This dilemma, critics claim, was in part resolved by ministers selecting evidence on the basis of its compatibility with prevailing political objectives (Hope, 2004). The government's endorsement of research that supported its political commitments and ideological preferences, and its simultaneous dismissal of data that cast doubt on the effectiveness of its CRP initiative, served as a depressing but timely reminder that 'the influence of criminological ideas and knowledge on public policy [is] always . . . contingent upon the degree to which they are in tune with the broader political ideas, or ideologies of those in power' (Tierney, 2010: 330). Indeed, it is a widely held view that the EBP experiment merely served as confirmation that ideology, political expediency and economic theory, rather than academic evidence, drives policy (Packwood, 2002).

For Hope, one of EBP's most vitriolic critics, the project was illusory. Academic research 'evidence' did not inform policy, but rather provided a veneer of scientific objectivity to legitimate political actions. The political usefulness of the research undertaken was restricted to its capacity to deliver 'preferred outcomes' (Hope, 2004, 2005), and to 'rubber stamp' political actions. Walters, summing up the political function of research evidence, states:

> Home Office criminology has a very clear purpose: to meet the 'needs' of ministers and members of Parliament. It is politically-driven criminology, one that provides policy salient information for politically relevant crime and criminal justice issues. It is motivated by outcomes that are of immediate

benefit to existing political demands – it is *embedded criminology* ... It is clear that the Home Office is only interested in rubber stamping the political priorities of the government of the day.

(Walters 2005: 6; italics added)

The prevalence of the *political/tactical model* of EBP manifested itself in a number of government tactics. These included the designation by government of what counted as research and what counted as evidence. The Home Office exerted control over the process by means of the granting or refusal of funding, and through its oversight of the way in which research findings were presented and disseminated (Hope, 2005). Evidence that differed from politician orthodoxy was routinely denied, distorted or selectively presented (Hope, 2004). Indeed, critics identify numerous examples of interventions by ministers and their civil servants, intended to subvert the publication of findings from Home Office-funded research that 'ruffle policy assumptions or programmes' (Morgan and Hough, 2008: 64). Subversion was achieved by either suppressing the information altogether, or delaying the dissemination of findings. On some occasions, research funded under the CRP initiative was embargoed and consequently went unpublished. On other occasions, research was subject to long delays, and/or in some cases was subsequently published elsewhere. These points are illustrated in the case studies (see later).

The evidence base of EBP

For critics of the restrictions placed on independent, academic enquiry, the EBP initiative signalled the establishment of a new relationship between politics and science that afforded civil servants and their political masters considerable influence over what counted as science, who counted as experts and whose methodologies and 'truth claims' were given precedence.

What counts as evidence?

As any student of criminology knows, crime is not a simple problem. There are a wide range of theories of criminal behaviour from biological positivism to postmodernism, each of which provides distinct modes of understanding and offers different policy solutions. Equally, there are a plethora of domestic and international studies employing different methods of enquiry and producing different findings and recommendations. This leaves policy-makers, academics and practitioners grappling with a series of fundamental questions about the status of different types of research evidence, as against other sources of information, including the personal experience of users, policy-makers and professional practitioners; about the role of evidence versus the role of judgement in decision-making; about how the relevance of research evidence should be defined; and about how methodological soundness should be determined (Hammersley, 2005). As Nutley and Davies remind us:

policy makers and practitioners have available a large body, of sometimes conflicting, research evidence relating to the causes of criminal behaviour and the effectiveness of various prescriptions for dealing with it.

(Nutley and Davies, 2004: 93)

For critics of the EBP movement, there are numerous examples of policy-making that, despite claims by politicians to the contrary, flies in the face of sound academic research evidence and/or is based on a flimsy, limited or unreliable body of evidence (Kendall, 2008). This has led some criminologists to conclude that a great deal of criminal justice policy-making is made 'in spite of, rather than because of, criminological research' (Morgan and Hough, 2008: 64). Examples of this include Anti-Social Behaviour Orders (see Chapter 3), which, despite the lack of evidence about their effectiveness in either reducing or preventing anti-social behaviour among the target population of unruly youths and 'neighbours from hell', and considerable concerns about net-widening and human rights, were vigorously promoted by New Labour (Burney, 2009). A similar example includes the UK adoption of American-style mandatory sentences such as 'three strikes and you're out' (see Chapter 7), which, despite providing a catchy sound bite, were devoid of an evidence base, providing neither an effective crime prevention measure nor a deterrent (Tonry, 2010).

Who are the experts? The creation of a research market

One of the key features of the EBP initiative was the 'narrowing of the range of [academic] knowledge that [was] admitted as policy-relevant results' (Morgan and Hough, 2008: 60). This reduction in the range and scope of 'acceptable' academic evidence was accompanied by an expansion of expert governance networks beyond the traditional political and academic range of bodies through the attribution of research evidence status to knowledge produced by a hybrid range of bodies such as think tanks, commercial organisations, inspection regimes and auditing agencies (Hope, 2004; Hammersley, 2005). The EBP initiative in effect created a market in research, which provided *experts on tap*.

The newly expanded knowledge pool was made up of a hybrid body of public-oriented research 'experts', who had established close working links and exchanged personnel. These new 'experts', while granted the status of more tradi-tional researchers, differed significantly in the 'constitution, working practices and institutional relationships from those traditions governing the universities, the civil service and party politics' and the Home Office (Hope, 2004: 289). The advantage to politicians of the establishment of this expanded pool of experts to call upon was that it provided them with considerable scope to choose their preferred experts, and thereby to manipulate and/or cherry pick the evidence that they presented to the public. For some of the most cynical commentators, the establishment of a wide pool of potential *experts on tap* to choose from created a situation whereby programmes could be decided in advance on the basis of the selection of expert representatives (included in the evidence production process) who could be relied upon to produce the desired research outputs (Beck, 1992). To sum up this perspective, expert evidence in EBP could be deemed to mean whatever ministers chose it to mean.

What research is commissioned and how commissioned research evidence is used

In their comprehensive overview of the politics of research, Morgan and Hough claim that what is considered 'criminological research – what . . . does or does not get commissioned (and how ultimately that work is used) is necessarily a political project and process' (2008: 46). In this process of establishing the efficacy of criminological research, funding plays a crucial role both in determining the research emphasis (what is researched), and establishing the acceptable research methodology (how the research is conducted). The net result of the government's unwillingness to give up the reins of its power over the EBP initiative was the privileging of administrative research projects aimed at controlling, rather than correcting, offending behaviour that fitted with its emerging law and order policy direction. Despite its electoral pledge to 'fight crime and the causes of crime', the primary focus of New Labour's EBP research became the more effective targeting and management of offenders; effective strategies to tackle underlying social exclusion were a subsidiary consideration (Morgan and Hough, 2008). As a consequence, EBP did not represent the high point of a genuine scholarly search for causal explanations and solutions that academics and practitioners had envisaged, but rather formed part of a 'new technology of governance' (Hope, 2004).

For some critics, it was the Home Office's creation of a selective hierarchy of acceptable research methods, imposing restraints on researcher autonomy, that led to a loss of academic faith (Gelsthorpe and Sharpe, 2005). The hierarchy of research methods established by the Home Office elevated randomised controlled trials alongside systematic reviews and meta-analyses (key aspects of medical research, particularly in relation to pharmaceutical trials) to the top rungs (Bennett and Holloway, 2010), with research using other methods, such as case studies, relegated to lower rungs in the hierarchy of credibility (Packwood, 2002). Any criminological knowledge produced that failed to meet the gold standard imposed by the Home Office was effectively invalidated.

One explanation for the establishment of a 'threshold' of acceptable method-ologies, which privileged quantitative and statistical data collection methods, was the desire of Research, Development and Statistics (RDS) managers at the Home Office to provide definitive evidence of 'what works' (as more often than not the evaluations produced inconclusive results) in the face of pressure from the Treasury to provide 'hard' evidence to justify the allocation of resources to new initiatives. The net result of this was the predominance of one-off studies that met the methodological 'gold standard' set by the RDS, and the simultaneous discounting of studies that, despite providing significant knowledge about crime, scored low on the hierarchy of preferred methodology. The research process imposed by the Home Office, the privileging of one-off studies, resulted in a failure by civil servants and ministers to recognise that knowledge about 'what works' was more than the sum of its individual parts. Morgan and Hough argue:

> Theoretical studies and insightful descriptive research have proved of immense value, and generally have a longer shelf-life than many high-quality evaluations. The value of the evidence base is to be found in its *cumulative* nature: individual studies may be tentative, but in combination, we actually know quite a lot about 'what works'.
>
> (Morgan and Hough, 2008: 59)

End note

Summing up the role played by the CRP in providing an evidence base for policy-making, Tonry observes:

> it was a debacle. Budgeted at £400 million over 10 years, it was abandoned within 3 years and illustrates almost every way in which a government program can go wrong (insufficient resources, heavy-handed central planning, failures of planning and implementation, and political interference).
>
> (Tonry, 2010: 788)

Public criminology

In recent years, the EBP 'debacle' in the UK has evolved into a more far-reaching series of academic discussions and debates about the role and fundamental purpose of criminological research. Influenced by developments within sociology, these debates have arisen within the 'context of . . . notions of public criminologies' (Tierney, 2010: 329). At the forefront of this is the question of the degree to which academic criminologists should or should not prioritise the production of findings that have as their objective the influencing of criminal justice policy. As Sim argues:

> [The] key question confronting contemporary criminology [is] . . . what role should criminologists play in intervening in the current baleful political situation where the symbolic representation of the atavistic criminal has been used, abused and manipulated by successive governments to legitimate the law and order clampdown that has apparently occurred in the last three decades?
>
> (Sim, 2011: 72)

In 2007, *Theoretical Criminology* published a special edition on the 'diverse perspectives on the academia and policy', which, triggered by concerns over the degree to which EBP had demonstrated that criminological knowledge had become extraneous to policy decision-making, sought both to:

outline a range of views that have been offered by academic criminologists on the discipline's public status and its relationship to public policy formation and intellectual practice, [and to] argue the need for a diversity of 'public criminologies' wherein explicit value is placed on moving policies in more progressive directions.

(Chancer and McLaughlin, 2007: 155–6)

Why don't criminologists have more influence over criminal justice policy?

Although the last three decades have witnessed an unprecedented expansion of the field of knowledge that constitutes criminology, opening it up to new voices and perspectives, this outpouring of criminological knowledge has paradoxically been accompanied by its marginalistion as a primary source of knowledge for criminal justice policy-making. From the many articles that have been written about this, two key sets of explanation have emerged: the first is sociological, and the second is data related.

Sociological explanations equate the gradual decline in public understanding of and engagement with academic criminological knowledge with wider social, economic and political changes in the last three decades (the advancement of neoliberalism, the politicisation of law and order policy, the emergence of the victim agenda, the high-crime society and new punitiveness). These developments have given rise to a wide range of new perspectives, views and truth claims, and have brought in their wake the fragmentation of the 'late modern criminology' into a multitude of new voices. This fragmentation has resulted in the collapse of the 'boundaries over who is authorized to speak about crime and on what terms' (Chancer and McLaughlin, 2007: 158), and has created a vacuum in which right realism and administrative criminology have been able to construct a policy base 'within the groove of an increasingly punitive criminal justice system' (p. 159).

The corrupted state of criminological scholarship that this gives rise to has manifested itself in 'political clientalism': the development of a commissioning process that favours research that fits the crime control agenda at the expense of critical perspectives on criminalisation and penality (see earlier). While some optimism is retained in relation to the influence that radical social movements can have on policy-making (e.g. feminism on the victims of domestic violence and rape), there is equally a recognition of a conservative backlash and unintended punitive consequences that can arise from these movements. These demonstrate that there is 'no easy relationship between policy recommendations, formulation, implementation and outcomes' (Chancer and McLaughlin, 2007: 160).

Data-oriented explanations locate the problem of policy influence in 'un-addressed structural weaknesses of the evidence base' (Chancer and McLaughlin, 2007: 160), which has resulted in a failure to produce findings that are convincing to policy-makers. From this perspective, it is the ideological and methodological preferences of contemporary British criminology that have led to the production of findings that lack 'the evidence-based knowledge on offences, offenders, victims and their interconnections that would allow it to guide policy' (p. 161). Currie, in his analysis of criminology's marginality to mainstream debates about crime and punishment, argues that the fault lies with 'the modern research university and the professional disciplines which increasingly drive the university's conception of itself' (2007: 186). He claims that modern academics, at the behest of their employing institutions, have become preoccupied with peer recognition. The structures and priorities that define the profession result in the production of research that is narrowly tailored to the publication imperatives of a few journals, and focuses on the generation of research findings related to established academic fields, as opposed to the analysis of the meaning or import of those findings. Publication in peer-reviewed journals is the 'yard stick for career advancement'; publications that seek to inform a wider audience are derogatorily dismissed as 'trade books'.

These debates are expanded upon by Loader and Sparks (2011) in their critical narrative of the discipline of criminology, which addresses the question of 'how, and whether, criminologists should engage with the world outside the confines of their discipline' (p. 710). Their objective is to enquire into:

> the relationship between criminology and democratic politics; its focal concern lies in figuring out how theory, research and reflection can best orient themselves towards the 'dire state' of modern politics and play their part in reaching towards a better politics of crime and its regulation.
>
> (Loader and Sparks, 2011: 736)

The following box sums up Loader and Sparks's observations in *Public Criminology*.

Successful failure paradox: as the popularity of criminology as a discipline has increased, so its policy relevance has declined. There has been a withdrawal from concerns with government and public life. The profession is absorbed in producing self-referential papers, rather than solving contemporary crime problems.

The responses of some academics to this dilemma are:

- *Passive tolerance:* criminology has fragmented into a series of discrete, disconnected fields of study. Criminologists pass each other 'like ships in the night', and have abandoned wider social issues and public concerns.
- *Takeover bid:* a 'legislator' seeks to bring the conduct of others into line with his or her preferred vision of the field. He or she attempts to impose on others a specific mode of enquiry on the grounds that this is the sole means by which criminology can produce data relevant to policy-makers.

- *Divorce:* the outcome of the failed endeavour by a 'frustrated legis-lator' who concludes that criminology cannot achieve what is neces-sary for relevance and legitimacy. Divorcees abandon the discipline, seeking new horizons and alliances.

Five modes of contemporary criminological engagement with public concerns have emerged:

- *Scientific expert:* emphasises dispassionate objectivity, methodological rigour, empirical discovery, detachment and relevance. Sees the task of criminology as being to produce valid, reliable and useful knowledge about crime, its distribution, causes and costs, and the situations in which it occurs, as well as interventions that lead to its reduction.
- *Policy advisor:* emphasises the importance of producing findings that inform political debate and action. Sees the tasks of criminology as providing evidence to parliamentary committees, sitting on commis-sions of inquiry and advising politicians.
- *Observer turned player:* emphasises the importance of working within government agencies. Sees the task of criminology as to become an 'insider' and to reject the lofty superiority of those who view this as 'supping with the devil'.
- *Social movement theorist/activist:* emphasises the importance of engaging in social/political movements for justice and the reduction of social harm that invigorate criminal justice practice and policy (e.g. environmental and domestic violence movements).
- *Lonely prophet:* emphasises the importance of 'big picture research' and grand theory creation. Sees the task of criminology as to connect with debates in the world of politics and science such as globalisation, governance and risk. Seeks to perform the 'civic duty' of alerting students, practitioners and the public to the perils of illiberal criminal justice policy-making.

Source: Loader and Sparks (2011)

What is to be done?

The key question posed by Currie for those criminologists who support the case for a public criminology and wish to see criminology re-invigorated through 'more vigorous, systematic and effective intervention in the world of social policy and social action' (2007: 176) is: 'what is to be done'? The solution offered by Loader and Sparks is the '*democratic under-labourer*': an individual who 'brings coherence to criminology's public role by combining intellectual curiosity and generosity on the one hand, with political humility, the knowing of one's limits and one's place, on the other' (2011: 132). This is in part achieved through the development of greater knowledge and understanding of political decision-making processes. Adopting the heat metaphor, they state:

> Criminology as a democratic under-labourer . . . has an internal relationship with a more deliberative politics of the criminal question . . . It is committed both to participating within, and to facilitating and extending, institutional spaces that supplement representative politics with inclusive public delibera-tion about crime and justice matters, whether locally, nationally, or in emer-gent transnational spaces. In this regard, the public value of democratic under-labouring lies not in 'cooling' down controversies about crime and social responses to it, but in playing its part in figuring out ways to bring the 'heat' within practices of democratic governance.
>
> (Loader and Sparks, 2011: 132)

For some criminologists, the current state of crime and punishment in the western world, which promotes 'tough justice' and prison expansion to deal with the impacts of a 'global destruction of communities and livelihoods', renders the case for the public presence of a vocal and influential criminology more urgent than ever (Currie, 2007: 176). Making the point that the criminal justice system would look very different if it were designed by criminologists, rather than right of centre politicians, Currie advocates a university-inspired programme of public education and public engagement. He argues that the lack of accessible academic knowledge about crime and punishment means that the public increasingly rely on distorted media accounts of crime. He claims:

> [The public] remain in the dark about much of what is most important about crime and justice; to the extent that they get any information on critical issues at all, it is likely to be from talk radio or television. Consequently, they are easily swayed to support policies we know have failed and will fail again; to buy into beliefs about crime and punishment that criminologists shattered long ago; and to reject most of the strategies that might be both more humane and more effective.
>
> (Currie, 2007: 179)

The solution, Currie argues, lies in reducing negative incentives that block the social impact of criminological work, and increasing positive opportunities to broaden that impact. Central to this is: rewarding academic activities that disseminate findings to audiences beyond the professions; convincing funders of the importance of the dissemination and analysis of research findings; estab-lishing institutions where new types of partnerships can be formed with 'policy makers, journalists, the general public, community leaders and non profit organi-sations' (Currie, 2007: 187); and the establishment of greater dialogue between disciplines.

Carrabine *et al.* (2009), who share Currie's vision of a criminology that engages with 'general ignorance around crime issues, moral indifference and uncivilised intolerance', and places the public at the centre of debates, make the case for the creation of 'empowerment-orientated criminology', a criminology that is underpinned by the pursuit of social justice and human rights (2009: 454). For Carrabine *et al.*, criminology is essentially a moral enterprise that has in its sights inequality, deprivation, injustice and the privileging of some offenders and some types of crimes (e.g. the crimes of the powerful), and has important contributions to make to discussions about citizenship entitlement and obligations. They stress that public criminology should be 'transparent', 'applied' in orientation, evidence-based and committed to empowerment, social justice and human rights (Carrabine *et al*, forthcoming).

Case study: Hope's burglary study

This case study illustrates the uses and status of 'scientific' evidence in politics. Specifically, it illustrates what can happen when responsibility for validating policy – that is, for establishing 'what works' – is placed in the hands of (social) science but the evidence produced is not, apparently, congenial to the particular 'network of governance' that is responsible for the policy.

As part of the government's crime reduction agenda, local government Crime and Disorder Reduction Partnerships were invited to bid for funding to central government as Strategic Development Projects (SDPs). A particular focus of these projects was burglary, with funding allocated to areas that had experienced rates of burglary that were twice the national average. SDPs were tasked with devising and delivering a range of different local burglary reduction initiatives (under the guidance of Home Office consultants), and received grants averaging £60,000. Evaluation of their successfulness (or otherwise) was awarded to a consortium of academics, including Professor Tim Hope.

During the course of the evaluation, the researchers noted that SDPs were failing to deliver the programmes in the way that had been laid out in the original design. The researchers attributed the problems of delivering programmes in the way intended to a range of strategic and operational problems. The implementation problems identified included: delays in implementation; differences in the level of resource allocation, and of measures implemented; the simultaneous adoption of different measures creating new mixes and combinations; the abandonment or partial implementation of measures; modifications of measures; and/or the creation of new additional measures that lacked the clear aims and objectives outlined in the original specifications.

The ensuing academic research included the adoption of methods of data collection and analysis that the researchers claimed both served to accommodate the variations of implementation, and eliminated effects that could not be attributed to the projects. The findings produced suggested that, counter to government predictions, reductions in burglary rates attributable to SDP activity were only identifiable in a third of the 21 SDPs. Faced with the prospect of publicly acknowledging a less than outstanding endorsement of its actions, the government reacted by taking the unprecedented step of tasking the Home Office to undertake a re-analysis of the original data. The consequence of this review of the data was the production of two in-house 'positive' research reports by the Home Office that could be presented to the public as evidence of a 20 per cent reduction in domestic burglaries as a consequence of the programmes. In the press release that accompanied the publication of 'Findings 204', the minister stated that the reducing burglary initiative had produced 'a tremendous impact on burglary rates' and had 'identified effective anti-burglary strategies that could be shared with other areas'. In summing up the validity of the evidence presented in these in-house reports, Hope states:

> The analyses of the data presented in these reports differ fundamentally from our own, as do the inferences and interpretations made. A comparison of our own methods with these ... reveals ... the way in which political considerations penetrate methodological concerns in the new dispensation of 'evidence-based policymaking'.
>
> (Hope, 2004: 295)

For Hope, the Home Office findings constituted a subversion of the original research that was politically embarrassing, and provided ministers with a face-saving means by which they could pretend to the electorate that their policy initiatives were working.

Case study: Nutt and evidence-based drugs policy

This case study is illustrative of the draconian measures that governments adopt to suppress evidence that runs counter to their policy-making position.

In October 2009, following the publication of the Eve Saville Memorial Lecture, delivered earlier in the year, Professor David Nutt, the chairman of the Advisory Council on the Misuse of Drugs (ACMD), was effectively sacked by the Labour Home Secretary for accusing ministers of distorting scientific evidence on the harmfulness of cannabis, and misrepresenting its research findings into public opinion on its classification, in order to justify its policy of raising the classification of cannabis from class C to class B (Jones and Booth, 2009). In the paper, Nutt described the findings of a series of cannabis studies conducted by members of the ACMD, highlighting evidence, contrary to government orthodoxy, which he claimed proved that there was a weak causal link between cannabis use and psychotic illness, and that cannabis was less harmful than other drugs that were classified as class B (Nutt, 2009).

In the paper, which called for an evidence-based approach to drugs classification policy, Professor Nutt made the case for the establishment of a tripartite drug harm ranking system that ranked the risks that both legal and illegal drugs pose in terms of their physical, dependence and social harm. He also challenged the government's 'precautionary principle' policy, adopted to justify the Home Secretary's decision to reclassify cannabis from a class C to a class B drug. He argued that, by erring on the side of caution, politicians 'distort' and 'devalue' research evidence. Furthermore, commenting on the impact of this on public confidence in the government's willingness to make best use of scientific research, he stated:

> This leads us to a position where people really don't know what the evidence is. They see the classification, they hear about evidence and they get mixed messages. There's quite a lot of anecdotal evidence that public confidence in the scientific probity of government has been undermined in this kind of way.
>
> (Nutt, 2009: 8)

In his drug harm classification table, Nutt ranked alcohol as the fifth most harmful drug after heroin, cocaine, barbiturates and methadone, with tobacco ranked ninth. This was higher than cannabis, LSD and ecstasy, which were ranked at 11, 14 and 18 respectively. Taking issue with the conventional classification system for drugs, he claimed that the focus of successive governments on the harm that illegal drugs posed resulted in an 'isolated and arbitrary' debate about relative drug harm. Central to his paper was the cannabis debate, in particular reports (some of which he maintained were of dubious scientific quality) linking cannabis use to schizophrenia: reports that had attracted considerable, sensationalist media attention. Arguing the case for a 'concerted public health response . . . to drastically reduce its use' (Nutt, 2009: 4), Nutt made the following observations about the relative risks of experiencing a psychotic episode as a consequence of using cannabis:

> taking cannabis, particularly if you use a lot of it, will make you more prone to having psychotic experiences. That includes schizophrenia, but schizophrenia is a relatively rare condition so it's very hard to be sure about its causation. The analysis we came up with was that smokers of cannabis are about 2.6 times more likely to have a psychotic-like experience than non-smokers. To put that figure in proportion, you are 20 times more likely to get lung cancer if you smoke tobacco than if you don't. That's the sort of scaling of harms that I want people to understand. There is a relatively small risk for smoking cannabis and psychotic illness compared with quite a substantial risk for smoking tobacco and lung cancer.
>
> (Nutt, 2009: 4)

In relation to parliamentary debates about the classification of ecstasy, during which the ACMD recommended it be classified as a class B drug, Nutt cast doubt on the government's willingness to make policy based on evidence, arguing that although the ACMD had 'won the intellectual argument . . . we obviously didn't win the decision in terms of classification' (2009: 11). Among the recommendations made by Nutt were:

- stopping the 'artificial separation of alcohol and tobacco as non-drugs';
- the provision of 'more accurate and credible' information on drugs and the harms they cause;
- drug classification based on the best research evidence.

The persistent failure of governments to embrace a research-led approach to drugs is well documented. In 2010, Bennett and Holloway, in their study of the research policy link in relation to drugs, claimed that although UK governments do consult research, the main problem is the selectivity, interpretation and reporting of research results. They identified examples of bias in terms of research study selection, and the distortion and misrepresentation of findings. In conclusion, they argued that 'there are many factors that influence the generation of policy and it is unrealistic and perhaps disingenuous, to suggest in relation to drug policy, that evidence is its primary focus' (2010: 411).

Summing up the government's rejection of the findings of the scientific research that it had commissioned, Nutt makes the point that drug policy is a highly politicised electoral issue. Drug policy is shaped by the activities and pressure exerted by a range of organisations and institutions: international partners signed up to the United Nations' War on Drugs policy; commercial interests (e.g. the tobacco and alcohol industry); public opinion (or what politicians think is the public's opinion); and the news media (Nutt, 2009), which stifles rational debate, focusing instead on sensationalist, isolated cases. An example of this was the (mis)reporting of the death of Leah Betts in 1995. Despite the fact that the coroner attributed the death to 'water intoxication' caused by excessive water intake, it was attributed to her taking ecstasy at her birthday party. In the media frenzy that followed her death, highly emotive billboards were posted depicting Leah in intensive care with the misleading, inaccurate caption: 'Sorted. Just one ecstasy tablet killed Leah Betts' (BBC News, 2005).

Final thought

From studying the cases of both Hope and Nutt, it is clear that even when governments commission research, the relationship between the knowledge generated and government policy-making is neither straightforward nor predictable. Politicians are constantly balancing competing interests and pressures, and have to consider how their actions will play themselves out with different audiences.

This is particularly important when their actions risk flying in the face of conventional wisdom. Acknowledging the complex relationship between research and policy-making, Tombs offers this helpful overview:

> it is clear that there are many different kinds of relationship between criminological knowledge and its political/policy uses. The influence of knowledge on policy is always problematic, indirect, multi-partial, deeply layered and mediated by various processes, not the least of which is political.
>
> (Tombs, 2011: 729)

Key points summary

This chapter traces the development of EBP and the influence that the expert has upon political decision-making. It argues that:

- A key feature of the early stages of New Labour administration was the research-led policy-making initiative. This initiative, which signalled the reversal of populist policy-making that had become the hallmark of the later years of the Conservative government and was embedded in 'prison works', saw the rise of the 'what works' movement and offered the possibility of policy-making that was grounded, rational and based on empirical evidence.
- The change in direction was broadly welcomed by practitioners, academics and penal reformers, who had seen their sphere of influence eroded, and recognised the potential to re-establish their credentials. In terms of criminal justice policy-making, the initiative manifested itself in the £250 million CRP that offered unprecedented levels of funding to cash-strapped research bodies to undertake evaluations of government-led programmes in order to identify 'best practice'.
- The early years of the scheme brought with them a flurry of research activity. However, despite its early promise, the initiative became marred in academic controversy as government (the funding source) sought to restrict academic freedom by shaping both the data production process and the use of the data produced. This development generated considerable academic debate and raised important issues about the knowledge–policy relationship. It also exposed the rise of a research market, and the emergence of a range of new (non-university-based) research bodies that could provide 'data to order'. Academic support for the initiative fell away as an increasing number of examples of data generated by university researchers that were distorted, denied or suppressed became apparent.
- The chapter finished with a discussion of the key themes and debates about the future of academic research and policy-making. It explored a range of explanations for the failure of academics to influence criminal justice policy-making, and argued that university systems of reward and notions of academic excellence have contributed to the process.

Critical thinking discussion topics

1   What are the distinctive features of the evidence-led initiative?
2   How did the government seek to regulate the evidence produced as part of the CRP?
3   What are the competing models of the research and policy relationship? Which one(s) have acquired precedence in recent years? Back your arguments up with examples.
4   What does Tombs mean by her claim that 'the influence of knowledge on policy is always problematic, indirect, multi-partial, deeply layered and mediated by various processes, not the least of which is political'? What evidence is there to support or contest this?
5   Do you agree or disagree with the arguments made by Currie and others that criminologists should engage with public policy-making?
6   This chapter has traced the way in which the traditional expert has declined in influence. With this in mind, you should consider the following: What was the source of power of that group? Whose interests does this loss of power to shape the policy debate serve? What theory of the policy-making process best explains this phenomenon?

Seminar task

Identify an aspect of recent criminal justice policy (e.g. drug policy, tougher prison regimes, the 'automatic' imprisonment of those found guilty of riot-related offences) and consider the differences in government policy that would characterise evidence-led policy-making. What are the implications for the 'offender', the victim and the wider public?

Recommended further reading

Davies, H., Nutley, S. and Smith, P. (eds) (2004) *What Works? Evidence- based Policy and Practice in Public Services.* Bristol: Policy Press.
King, R. and Wincup, E. (eds) (2008) *Doing Research in Crime and Justice* (2nd edn). Oxford: Oxford University Press.
Loader, I. and Sparks, R. (2011) *Public Criminology.* Oxford: Routledge.

References

Baker, E. (1996) 'From "making bad people worse" to "prison works": sentencing policy in the 1990s'. *Criminal Law Forum*, 7(3): 639–71.
BBC News (2005, 16 November) The Legacy of Tragic Leah. [Online]. Retrieved from http://news.bbc.co.uk/1/hi/uk/4440438.stm (accessed 10 October 2013).
Beck, U. (1992) *Risk Society.* London: Sage.
Bennett, T. and Holloway, K. (2010) 'Is UK drug policy evidence based?' *International Journal of Drug Policy*, 21(5): 411–17.

Berry, M., Tiripelli, G., Docherty, S. and Macpherson, C. (2012) 'Media coverage and public understanding of sentencing policy in relation to crimes against children'. *Criminology and Criminal Justice*, 12(5): 567–91.

Burney, E. (2009) *Making People Behave: Anti-social Behaviour, Politics and Policy* (2nd edn). Cullompton: Willan.

Cabinet Office (1999) *Modernising Government*. London: HMSO. Retrieved from http://www.archive.official-documents.co.uk/document/cm43/4310/4310.htm (accessed 3 November 2012).

Carrabine, E., Cox, P., Lee, M., Plummer, K. and South, N. (2009) *Criminology: A Sociological Introduction* (2nd edn). Abingdon: Routledge.

Carrabine, E., Cox, P., South, N., Hobbs, D., Fussey, P. and Theil, D. (forthcoming) *Criminology: A Sociological Introduction* (3rd edn). Abingdon: Routledge.

Chancer, L. and McLaughlin, E. (2007) 'Public criminologies: diverse perspectives on academia and policy'. *Theoretical Criminology*, 11(2): 155–73.

Currie, E. (2007) 'Against marginality: arguments for a public criminology'. *Theoretical Criminology*, 11(2): 175–90.

Davies, P. (2004) 'Is Evidence-based Government Possible?' Paper presented at the 4th Campbell Collaboration Colloquium, Washington DC. Retrieved from http://www.sfi.dk/graphics/campbell/dokumenter/artikler/is_evidence-based_government_possible.pdf (accessed 6 November 2012).

Dean, M. (2012) *Democracy Under Attack: How the Media Distort Policy and Politics*. Bristol: Policy Press.

Gelsthorpe, L. and Sharpe, G. (2005) 'Criminological research: typologies versus hierarchies'. *Criminal Justice Matters*, (62): 8–43.

Hammersley, M. (2005) 'Is the evidence-based practice movement doing more good than harm? Reflections on Iain Chalmers' case for research-based policy making and practice'. *Evidence and Policy*, 1(1): 85–100.

Hope, T. (2001) 'The road taken: evaluation, replication and crime reduction'. In G. Hughes, E. McLaughlin and J. Muncie (eds) *Crime Prevention and Community Safety*. London: Sage.

Hope, T. (2004) 'Pretend it works: evidence and governance in evaluation of the Research Burglary Initiative'. *Criminology and Criminal Justice*, 4(3): 287–308.

Hope, T. (2005) 'Things can only get better'. *Criminal Justice Matters*, (62): 4–39.

Jones, S. and Booth, R. (2009, November 1) 'David Nutt's sacking provokes mass revolt against Alan Johnson'. *Guardian*.

Kendall, K. (2008) 'Dangerous thinking: a critical history of correctional cognitive behaviouralism'. In G. Mair (ed.) *What Matters in Probation*. Cullompton: Willan.

Loader, I. and Sparks, R. (2011) *Public Criminology*. Abingdon: Routledge.

Maguire, M. (2004) 'The Crime Reduction Programme in England and Wales: Reflections on the vision and the reality'. *Criminology and Criminal Justice*, 4(3): 213–37.

Mair, G. (2004) 'The origins of What Works in England and Wales: a house built on sand'. In G. Mair (ed.) *What Matters in Probation*. Cullompton: Willan.

Morgan, R. and Hough, M. (2008) 'The politics of criminological research'. In R. King and E. Wincup (eds) *Doing Research in Crime and Justice* (2nd edn). Oxford: Oxford University Press.

Nutley, S. and Davies, H. (2004) 'Criminal justice: using evidence to reduce crime'. In H. Davies, S. Nutley and P. Smith (eds) *What Works? Evidence-based Policy and Practice in Public Services*. Bristol: Policy Press.

Nutt, D. (2009) *Estimating Drug Harms: A Risky Business.* Briefing Paper No. 9. Centre for Criminal Justice Studies. Retrieved from http://www.crimeandjustice.org.uk/archived_publications.html (accessed 5 November 2012).

Packwood, A. (2002) 'Evidence-based policy: rhetoric and reality'. *Social Policy and Society*, 1(3): 267–72.

Sim, J. (2011) 'Who needs criminology to know which way the wind blows?' In I. Loader and R. Sparks (eds) 'A symposium of reviews of public criminology'. *British Journal of Criminology*, 51(4): 707–38.

Tierney, J. (2010) *Criminology: Theory and Context* (3rd edn). Harlow: Pearson.

Tombs, J. (2011) 'Which public? Whose criminology?' In I. Loader and R. Sparks (eds) 'A symposium of reviews of public criminology'. *British Journal of Criminology*, 51(4): 707–38.

Tonry, M. (2010) '"Public criminology" and evidence-based policy'. *Criminology and Public Policy*, 9(4): 783–97.

Tran, M. (2009, October 30) 'Government drug advisor David Nutt sacked'. *Guardian*.

Walters, R. (2005) 'Boycott, resistance and the role of the deviant voice'. *Criminal Justice Matters*, (62): 6–7.

Young, K., Ashby, D., Boaz, A. and Grayson, L. (2002) 'Social science and the evidence-based policy movement'. *Social Policy and Society*, 1(3): 215–24.

6 The rise of the public voice, the victims' movement and the mass media

Chapter summary

In recent years, there has been considerable criminological debate among academics, practitioners and penal reformers about the role that the public should play in shaping criminal justice policy. Central to this are concerns that a punitive public, fed on distorted and sensationalist crime reports by the popular press, have been the driving force behind the penal excess that has characterised the last three decades of policy-making. Political parties, eager to secure electoral success, have sought to 'out-tough' each other on law and order, and in so doing have ushered in a new period of expressive, retributive justice. Pivotal to this development has been the rise of the victim as a major stakeholder in the criminal justice system, and the seeming privileging of those who claim to represent or speak on the victim's behalf.

This chapter, which develops themes covered in the previous chapter relating to the marginalisation of the academic expert, will guide you through the literature and encourage you to develop a more critical approach to the subject.

This chapter looks at:

- the politicisation of law and order, the demise of the bi-partisan consensus on penal policy, the decline of the Platonic guardians of penal policy and the reconfiguration of the penal axis;
- the rise of the public voice, with particular emphasis on populist penal policy and the democratisation debate; this includes the emergence of new forms of communication between the government and the public;
- the emergence of the politicised victim, and the role of the media in campaigning on behalf of victims;
- the vacuum created by the demise of the Platonic guardians as managers of information about crime, identifying new sources of public 'mis'information, for example the tabloid press and new genres of the media (such as the television programme *Crimewatch* and celebrity phone-ins).

Case study: The Sarah's Law campaign

The case study will introduce you to some of the key debates about the rise of the victim agenda, the dangerousness agenda and the role of the tabloid press. The case study will explore how and why the campaign appealed to the public, and will examine the impact that the campaign had on penal policy-making. When reading the case study, you should consider the implications for justice that the case poses for the offender, the victim and the public. You should also think about the problems that can arise when policy is made on the basis of exceptional high-profile cases.

The rise of the public voice and the decline of the expert: a historical overview

Although for most of the twentieth century overt expressions of vengeful sentiments, particularly by government officials, were a rarity, recent decades have seen a reversal of this, with politicians and the public alike embracing a new discourse of crime replete with condemnation and punishment. What purports to be the expression of public opinion increasingly takes precedence over professional judgement and expert advice in law and order policy-making. The seemingly changing face of post-war penal policy is associated with a reconfiguration in the field of criminal justice in which criminal justice experts and professional elites have been disenfranchised, and the rise of the public voice (or those who claim to speak on their behalf) has filled the void.

This reconfiguration of the penal axis is attributed to structural changes that have created a 'high-crime society', characterised by a 'new collective experience of crime and insecurity', alongside a concomitant rejection of previously unchallenged institutions (e.g. the Civil Service and the judiciary), whose ideas and policies have become associated with a failure to stem the tide of rising crime. The privileging of the new penal policy stakeholders, in particular the 'victim', has contributed towards the emergence of a populist penal policy-making strategy of public protection and victim-centeredness. In this process, discredited penal philosophies of expressive justice underpinned by a belief in the merits of the symbolic and communicative aspects of punishment have replaced the rational, formal and academic (Garland, 2001).

The decline of liberal elitism

The immediate post-war period of penal policy was characterised by a bi-partisan agreement that crime and punishment was not a party political issue. It was generally acknowledged that a distance should be maintained between crime and punishment and electoral politics. Crime and penal policy-making were seen as the preserve of traditional experts, and the newly emerging welfare state professionals (Garland, 2001). This was the heyday of the Platonic guardians (senior civil servants, academics and strategic practitioners) who, adopting the rational choice model of penal policy-making, reached decisions in a patient, deliberative and dispassionate manner. Driven by the 'civilisation project', their objective was the establishment and maintenance of a 'decent', 'humane' and 'constrained' system of justice that balanced the competing civil liberties of offenders and the public, and, in particular, managed 'public demands for vengeance . . . in an effective and civilized manner' (Loader, 2006: 564). Pivotal to this process was the directing and/or management of public opinion. While it was accepted that public opinion should neither be totally dismissed nor disregarded, the conventional wisdom was that 'untutored public sentiment towards crime is a dangerous thing', and that one of the key functions of the Civil Service was to channel it down 'appropriate paths, rather than give it government endorsement and expression' (Loader, 2006: 568).

The hegemony of the Platonic guardians was largely uncontested in the 'golden years' of the post-war welfare state. An entrenched top-down approach to policy-making flourished in a highly deferential political culture where the belief that the 'men from the Ministry' know best went largely unchallenged. The political elite had an almost free hand in policy-making: public opinion on penal matters was 'attended to, not in order to accommodate it, but rather to circumvent it' (Ryan, 2005: 140–1).

Despite this, five key 'moments' can be identified that called the legitimacy of liberal elitism into question. These moments were: *the crisis of the rehabilitative ideal* that developed as a consequence of growing dissent from policy orthodoxy on the part of critics both outside and within the Home Office; the *rise of the 'nothing works' agenda* and concerns about the effectiveness of rehabilitation measures in reducing re-offending; *the emergence of a split within the Home Office* as some sought to replace the treatment model with situational crime prevention (SCP) strategies; *the rise of New Right 'law and order' politics* and 'authoritarian populism' in the 1980s; and the *'populist punitive' turn* taken by penal politics since 1993. The cumulative effect of these developments was the demise of the influence of the expert, and the creation of a new axis of penal power in which the mass media (in particular the red-top tabloid press) filled the void, both directly through its overt and explicit lobbying and campaigning work on specific crime-related issues, and more subtly and indirectly through its shaping of public opinion (Garland, 2001; Ryan, 2005; Loader, 2006).

The politicisation of law and order: authoritarian populism

While the SCP movement and the demise of the rehabilitative ideal were a challenge to the rule of the Platonic guardians, it was the 1979 election, which saw Margaret Thatcher sweep into power, that precipitated the real decline of their influence (Loader, 2006). Thatcher's election on a law and order platform represented a 'very British moment of populism' that challenged the prevailing political hegemony. Appealing directly to the public's concerns about rising crime, she sought to shift the balance of power away from the 'elite ensemble of metropolitan opinion formers, who had so arrogantly ignored the people' in the past (Ryan, 2005: 141).

However, although it is undisputed that Thatcher's administration heralded a break with the post-war consensus of keeping politics out of criminal justice and penal policy-making, and established a new relationship between politicians and the public, this new direction in politics did not amount to a new period of 'bottom-up' policy-making. Despite her rhetorical claims, the Iron Lady's vision of politics never extended to true participatory democratisation. Essentially autocratic and authoritarian, she was reluctant to relinquish control by handing the reins of power to the people (Ryan, 2005). Although her landmark electoral victory was proof that she had gained considerable electoral advantage by mobilising public sentiments behind her political agenda (Bottoms, 1995), her version of populism was essentially top-down 'authoritarian populism', rather than 'bottom-up' (Hall, 1980). What is more, despite her best efforts to curb the powers of the liberal elite, particularly the Civil Service, which she had in her sights, her administration never fully wrenched power from the traditional bastions of criminal justice and penal policy-making. During this period, the Platonic guardians were able to maintain much of their power base by adapting to survive. In so doing, they successfully acted as a break on the government's more draconian ideas (Loader, 2006). Indeed, it should never be forgotten that it was under the Thatcher administration that statutory due process initiatives, in the form of the 1984 Police and Criminal Evidence Act, were introduced, which significantly curtailed the powers of the police in relation to the collection of criminal evidence (Zander, 2005).

The populist punitive turn

However, the final death knell to the 'nostrums of liberal elitism' was tolled in 1993, following the murder of James Bulger. The media frenzy and public outcry that followed the event signalled a decisive break with the values of the Platonic guardians. Responding to the public mood of the vengeance, the Major administration wedded itself to the populist 'prison works' mantra. At the same time, the Labour Party, seeking to distance itself from its electoral Achilles' heel of being perceived in the public imagination as 'soft on crime', was actively repositioning itself as the party of law and order – a position that it sought to reinforce once elected in 1997. As critics (Garland, 2001; Pratt, 2007) have pointed out, the mid-1990s onwards witnessed a sea change in penal policy towards new 'more punitive and populist forms of policy making' (Garside, 2007: 35). This new era of criminal justice policy was characterised by an unprecedented period of increasingly punitive legislative activity, driven, some argue, by sensationalist tabloid headlines (Ryan, 2005; Loader, 2006).

Exit the Platonic guardians and enter the public

As Ryan states:

> Politicians are required to engage with the public in a manner that a generation ago would have been unheard of in most Western democracies . . . the wider public nowadays refuses to be air brushed out of the policy making equation.
>
> (Ryan, 2005: 143)

The new democratisation?

The disenfranchisement of the expert and the concomitant rise of public voice(s) in penal policy-making are the subject of considerable debate. While some see this as a retrograde step, arguing that politicians merely tap into moral panics to produce punitive responses that placate the loudest voices (orchestrated by the tabloid press), others take a more positive line, arguing that the rise of the public voice should be welcomed as an indication of a new democratic shift: a reversal of the 'elitist' exclusivity of top-down policy-making (Ryan, 2005). From this perspective, the power to punish is no longer concentrated in the hands of the unelected officials operating behind closed doors, whose actions are accountable neither to the politicians nor to the public. The involvement of the public in the design and delivery of penal policies is consistent with positive, democratic processes, signalling the potential to pave the way for 'truly participative penal policy which need not necessarily be punitive' (Bell, 2007: 45).

Roberts *et al.* (2003), in their study of public opinion and penal populism, seek to differentiate between policy that is merely popular, responding to what is perceived by politicians to be punitive sentiments of the public, and that which is determined by genuine democratic processes. As there is a tendency in some criminological writing to conflate the two, there is a case to be made for their separation. Populist policy-making arises under any of three conditions:

- an excessive concern with attractiveness to the electorate;
- an intentional or negligent disregard of the effects of criminal justice policies;
- a tendency to make simplistic assumptions about the public, based on inappropriate methods, for example opinion polls.

In common with Bell and Ryan, Roberts *et al.* advocate policy-making, which has as its objective true public engagement. Although they argue that policy-making, which is based upon the dissemination of public information, and which recognises the importance of research evidence, can be consistent with consensual principles of sentencing, such as constraint and proportionality, they recognise that a key problem with the achievement of this is public misinformation about the reality of crime and punishment, and the prominence of misconceptions and distortions perpetrated by the mass media. The perpetuation of misinformation is compounded by politicians colluding in the mass media's rejection of 'good news stories', and their failure to promote evidence that would run counter to mass media representations (Roberts *et al.*, 2003).

Public participation and 'new technologies of communication'

Although it is understandable, in the light of the 'punitive turn' (see also below), that the political purposes to which public opinion are put remain controversial, what is undisputable is that (for better or worse) the public are having a greater say in government policy decision-making on both a formal and an informal basis. At a formal level, there is greater public consultation on policy proposals (see Chapter 4). At an informal level, the adoption of new technologies of communication, including new social media (blogs and Twitter), mean that: government information can be easily accessed by the public; ordinary people have the opportunity 'to make, report and comment on (crime) news' (Pratt, 2007: 80), and to converse directly with politicians; and politicians in turn can easily speak directly to the public to elicit their views. Talk-back radio is cited as one of the means that has 'accelerated ... moves towards mass participation in news making and opinion formation' (p. 81). Other developments that are attributed to the government's objective to increase public participation include the creation of Downing Street website and e-mail as part of Tony Blair's 'Big Conversation' (Ryan, 2003; Pratt, 2007); deputy Prime Minister Nick Clegg's weekly appearance on the radio taking live questions about government policy (Topping, 2013); and the recent launching by the government of an online questionnaire seeking the public's view on whether or not they support an increase in the maximum sentence that can be imposed on the owners of dangerous dogs that kill (Bowcott, 2013).

Democratisation or populism?

While public accountability, inherent in the democratisation perspective, provides the justifying principle for encouraging public participation debate, the view that public engagement merely serves as a means of attracting votes by ensuring the adoption of a policy that is popular is a widely held view (Garland, 2001; Roberts *et al.,* 2003; Pratt, 2005; Ryan, 2005). From this perspective, the significance of the demise of the Platonic guardians is that the 'concerns and anxieties of the general public are not only unabated, but seem to gather momentum' (Pratt, 2005: 266). Politicians 'no longer simply acknowledge the public mood or representations of this, but instead allow themselves to be led by it' (Pratt, 2005: 266). The outcome is populist penal policy-making: 'the pursuit of a set of penal policies to win votes rather than to reduce crime or to promote justice' (Roberts *et al.*, 2003: 5).

Related to the concept of penal populism is the more assiduous one of populist punitiveness. Although the concepts are conceptually and practically interdependent, there are subtle differences. Specifically, populist punitiveness is predicated on the belief that successive governments, seeking to appeal to the electorate, have acted on the premise that the public are punitive (Cullen *et al.*, 2000). Tough on crime policies, it is claimed, characterised by a greater use of imprisonment, disproportionate sentences and 'ostentatious and emotive' forms of punishments (Garland, 2001) give a risk-averse public what they want; to do otherwise, it is claimed, would be tantamount to electoral suicide.

Knee-jerk populism or political autonomy?

Opinions about the aetiology of the 'new punitiveness' are, however, divided between those who view policy as driven by the public from below and those who see policy as top-down, imposed on the public by self-serving politicians (Matthews, 2005).

From the bottom-up perspective, governments are no longer insulated from the public. The closer relationship between populist governments and the public (or those who claim to speak on their behalf) has created a situation whereby policy-making process is reduced to 'immediate responses to exceptional cases as they occur' (Pratt, 2007: 25–6). Politicians are 'hostages to fortune', reacting in a 'knee-jerk' manner to public pressure (Garside, 2007). By contrast, from the top-down perspective, politicians' actions reflect voluntarism, agency and choice.

Bottoms (1995), who first coined the term 'populist punitiveness', argues that while populist punitiveness corresponds with lived experiences of rising crime, and offers a rich stream that 'politicians seeking popularity can easily tap into' (Bottoms, 1995: 47), politicians ultimately retain autonomy and make choices between different policy options. Politicians are never divested of the capacity to renege on electoral promises once in power. Politicians seeking to gain political advantage at times of insecurity do so for their own purposes: their own predilections and concerns always take precedence. As Maruna and King (2004) note, if this were not so, capital punishment would have been re-introduced, and the US form of community notification of sex offenders would have found its way onto the statute book. Garside, summing up, states:

> populist punitiveness arises on the freely determining decisions of politicians. Playing the populist punitive card confers certain benefits on those politicians who seek to do so. But politicians are in no sense compelled to so play that card and can easily choose not to play it. Populist punitiveness is thus largely a form of political voluntarism, an act of will on the part of the politician.
>
> (Garside, 2007: 33)

So, are the public punitive?

Although the view that the public harbour increasingly punitive views, and that politicians of both the left and the right merely pander to these when making penal policy, features regularly in criminological texts, there are some noteworthy dissenting voices. Cullen *et al.* (2000) and Matthews (2005) are among those who seek to expose the 'myth of the punitive public', drawing our attention to studies of public attitudes which repeatedly show that respondents support multiple sentencing goals. There is a 'mixture of punishment, rehabilitation and public protection': retribution and rehabilitation co-exist alongside other sentencing options (Matthews, 2005: 191). Garland, summarising this perspective, states:

> It is often claimed that public punitiveness is a shallow, media-generated phenomenon. The claim tends to be that punitive policies do not originate in any groundswell of public demand; that the public are not truly committed to these policies; or that such commitment as does exist has been artificially aroused and excited by media images and campaigns that misrepresent both crime and public sentiment.
>
> (Garland, 2000: 353)

Central to the critique of the frequently repeated assumption that the public are universally highly punitive, and that punitive policies represent a true deference to public opinion, is the work of Hough and Roberts (1995, 1999). In their much quoted 1999 study of public opinion and public knowledge, Hough and Roberts first tested the respondents to assess their pre-existing knowledge and understanding of sentencing options and sentencing practice, and subsequently outlined the details of real crimes to test the degree to which participants' assessment of an appropriate sentence corresponded to those of actual sentencers. Their main findings were that when participants were given the full information on a case, their choice of sentencing options was not 'highly punitive'. A summary of their findings is given in the following box.

It would be wrong to characterise the British public as 'highly punitive', or as being consistently more punitive than sentencers. Although some respondents expressed extremely punitive attitudes, there were more whose attitudes were consistent with, or less punitive than actual sentencing practices.

Most people do not look exclusively to the court to prevent crime. Crime is not seen as purely a criminal justice matter, requiring criminal justice solutions, but as one that relates to wider social issues, such as family and environment, and unemployment.

Using opinion polls to measure levels of public punitiveness does not provide an accurate picture. Opinion polls tend to suggest that the public are clamouring for more severe sentences, despite the fact that the public are largely unaware of actual sentencing practices. When asked whether or not they thought sentences are too lenient, the public have atypical recidivist violent offenders in mind and express the view that sentences were too lenient. However, when presented with the details of a real case, and given information about the full range of sentences, respondents are less likely to endorse the use of prison.

The public are misinformed about crime and punishment. The public do not receive balanced information about sentencing practices in the news media, and the government does too little to address public misconceptions. The news media highlight cases of sentencing *mal*practices in which judges appear to pass lenient sentences for violent offences. In such cases, the media rarely explains the judges' reasons for the decision, or places the sentence in a statistical context. The dissatisfaction with judges that this creates continues unabated.

Demographic factors relate to the level of misinformation about sentencing patterns, and underestimates of actual sentencing patterns. Less educated members of the public and tabloid newspaper readers tend to provide large underestimates of actual sentences.

Source: Hough and Roberts (1999)

Hough and Roberts conclude that it is public ignorance and misconceptions about crime and punishment that are the central issues. They claim that the media construction of crime and punishment creates an emotional investment in crime narratives and punitive sentiments that express themselves in an electorate willing to vote for parties that spend their taxes on expanding the penal state.

The media

What role does the media play in crime and justice policy-making?

Although considerable weight is given to the argument that 'mass media is . . . critical in fuelling public sentiments and creating the conditions in which retribution and vengeance *can* more readily be expressed' (Matthews, 2005: 182), Berry *et al.* (2012) argue that the research evidence to support the claim that there is a direct link between the media and public attitudes towards the criminal justice system is non-conclusive. Problems include establishing directionality and isolating the influence of the media from wider social factors. At best, the relationship is one of co-relation, rather than causality. However, while the argument that caution needs to be maintained in the face of assumptions that media reporting contributes directly to specific social outcomes has its merit, there is a case to be made that the cumulative impact on public perception of media representations of crime should not be dismissed. As Peelo states:

> Even if it is not possible to assess the (direct) impact of reporting on each individual reader, newspapers are, nonetheless, powerful voices contributing to the public narratives within which societies make sense of crimes.
>
> (Peelo, 2006: 161)

The media as source of (mis)information

Although it is self-evident that it is not easy to establish the precise role that the media plays in forming public opinion, the way in which the tabloid press (in particular) presents crime and punishment, the selection and framing of stories, distorts the truth. Media representations of crime create the impression that crime is more violent and prevalent than it is, and that sentences are more lenient than they actually are (Hough and Roberts, 1995, 1999; Roberts *et al.*, 2003). Pivotal to this is the appetite for dramatic and sensationalist crime stories that the mass media satiates. As Young points out, 'bad news sells':

> As has been frequently noted, the media have an institutionalized focus on negative news – the crime rate going up sells newspapers and settles audiences in front of their television set watching programmes such as *Crime Watch*. The crime rate going down is, or it is so believed, less of a draw.
>
> (Young, 2003: 43)

The problem of the media's distortion of crime and punishment is compounded by a style of reporting that focuses on individual pathology explanations, rather than social circumstances (Iyengar, 1991). This individualisation of crime reinforces the dominant neoliberal model of crime and crime control, and steers the public towards modes of understanding that centre on 'right-hand state solutions' (Wacquant, 2001). Through the combination of real depictions of crime and fictional representations, the public are encouraged to view crime through the lens of the police and law enforcement responses to offending (Beckett and Sasson, 2000). This ensures that the law and order perspective on crime and punitive solutions remains dominant.

So, what factors shape the way in which crime is reported? Pratt provides the following overview of the changing face of mass media and popular representations of crime.

The effects of globalisation and media de-monopolisation, which have given rise to: a greater diversity of providers (e.g. cable and satellite networks); a greater competition for audiences; the emergence of instantly recognisable and understood explanations; and new and competing crime and punishment discourses that challenge the orthodoxies of the old elites.

The impact of sloganization: faced with an electorate that is advertising savvy and time poor, short-hand slogans provide an easy means of conveying policy imperatives. Communications are reduced to sound bites such as 'tough on crime, tough on the causes of crime'.

The simultaneous increase in quantity and decrease in quality of crime presentation, fuelled by a seemingly insatiable public appetite for sensational crime stories. This is demonstrated by the rise in the number of 'crime shows' (e.g. *Crimewatch*) and high-drama real crime depictions with simple narratives (frequently of police activities such as drug raids or car chases), and the decline in more factual documentaries.

A change in the reporting style of the popular press, with personalised stories replacing statistical analysis, and a greater focus on violent and sexual offences, the bizarre, the unusual and new crimes such as stalking and road rage that focus on the loss of personal safety. This new reporting style privileges the 'personal experience of ordinary people, particularly crime victims over expert abstractions'. The result is that commonsensical explanations of crime and punishments are 'given authority and prestige'.

New styles of reporting characterised by titillation, excitement and the ability to shock and frighten. Crime representations that focus on 'randomised, unpredictable and violent attacks invariably committed by strangers on ordinary people' receive the highest coverage and create the impression that crime is an ever-present risk. The popular press is increasingly seeking to take on a role in influencing policy-making and actively campaigning for harsher sentences. This is demonstrated by the *News of the*

World's Sarah's Law campaign; the 'outing' of paedophiles by the *News of the World* in its infamous 'name and shame' campaign; and tabloid press portrayals of prisons as 'holiday camps'.
The replacement of the investigative journalist with 'celebrity' presenters whose style of presentation glamorises, simplifies and exaggerates crime to 'capture audience attention' and push up audience ratings.

Source: Pratt (2007: Chapter 3)

The power to punish: enter the political spin doctor.
Who is manipulating whom?

It is frequently claimed that the press has become the primary source of crime knowledge (see Chapter 5). This has led critics to argue that the media has assumed the power to punish. However, while some argue that the structural coupling of the mass media system and the political system has had the effect of producing risk-averse policy-making, which is responsive to the demands of electoral success rather than good governance, others claim that politicians retain the power to punish, shape policy to meet their own political commitments and ideological considerations, and exert their power through the manipulation of the media. They cite the emergence of media-conscious politicians (see also earlier), and the rise of the political spin doctor as evidence that governments are at pains to ensure that the mass media promotes policies that suit their political agenda (Luhmann, 1989, 1990; Moeller, 2006).

Solomon (2006), in his analysis of the relationship between crime policy and the media, takes issue with media blaming accounts of punitive penal policies. While acknowledging that the popular media is sensationalist and focuses on the unexpected and on unpredictable events, he questions the degree to which the press can be held responsible for the punitive turn. He argues that news values that govern the behaviour of journalists are not politically neutral; rather, they are determined by the government's and politicians' agendas. Although newspapers define themselves on the basis of their political beliefs and readers buy newspapers that reflect their views and beliefs, media-savvy politicians employ spin doctors and public relations firms to exert pressure on journalists to produce stories that are in line with their political objectives. Since the onset of the political war over the law and order agenda, serious papers as well as the tabloids have been complicit in the regurgitation of tough on crime headline-grabbing sound bites that ministers have fed them. Political parties seeking to 'out-tough' each other, hyperactivity in the field of crime control and the high profile given to criticisms by politicians of the criminal justice system have had the effect of convincing the public that the system is not working, and that punitive policies are warranted.

Dean, a senior journalist by profession, responding to accusations that the press is responsible for the move towards more right of centre policies, provides an insider's analysis of media–government relationships. He chronicles the rise of 'the media machine' under the Blair administration, and identifies the centrality of the press in the body politic with the granting of powers to his media director to attend Cabinet meetings and instruct civil servants. The fact that Blair's first appointment on becoming party leader was a press director (Alastair Campbell), rather than a policy chief, is indicative, he argues, of the importance of the media machine to Blair. While previous governments sought to maintain a distance between themselves and the media, there was under Blair's administration a media-feeding frenzy, encapsulated by Campbell's infamous: 'If we do not feed them, they eat us' (Dean, 2012: 2).

In Dean's account, Blair's media machine not only 'wooed' the tabloid papers to achieve electoral success in 1997, but also took the campaign media machine to Number 10 once in power. This was mobilised to 'shape the narrative', with the presentation of policies afforded the same level of importance as policy creation. Positive spinning of government policy was accompanied by a robust system of rebuttal. The wide-ranging policy agenda embraced by Blair simultaneously provided an enormous challenge to those whose task it was to get the press on side, but also 'offered new opportunities for control' (Dean, 2012: 7). By a selective leaking of news to sympathetic reporters, specialist journalists could be wrong-footed, and 'good story' headlines could be assured. Dean states:

> Policies were never knowingly undersold. They were pre-announced, announced, post-announced and re-announced. Campbell's high command kept up a grid of media announcements, parcelling out releases to fit the government's narrative . . . . Campbell's unit . . . organised new convenient pre-packaged deals to television news teams that were eagerly snapped up even though they had little opportunity to check them out properly.
>
> (Dean, 2012: 7)

The press and the media maintain an interdependent, mutually beneficial symbiotic relationship. The press and politicians are essentially a double act, with the press playing the role of the willing stooge on criminal justice matters. As Dean argues:

> disentangling the labyrinth link between politicians and the press in the field of law and order is a difficult one. They live in a symbiotic relationship. With drugs, the tabloids act as the host and the politicians are the parasite. With law and order it is the other way around. The main fault for the rise of penal populism in the last two decades can be laid more firmly at the feet of politicians than the press, although tabloids have been eager accomplices.
>
> (Dean, 2012: 109–10)

The influence of the victim agenda

One of the most significant developments of the last three decades has been the emergence of the victim as a key stakeholder in the contemporary criminal justice system. Traditionally a minor player, side-lined in both policy-making and services delivery, the victim can no longer be ignored. As Garland (2001) points out, the victim's voice must be heard, victims' anger must be expressed and victims' fears must be addressed.

Initially a welfare-focused movement that has as its primary objective the enhancement of victim satisfaction through the improvement of services to victims, inside and outside the court setting, the power of organisations that claim to represent victims' interests (e.g. Victim Support) has grown expeditiously. Repositioning themselves as powerful pressure groups, victims' organisations have entered the mainstream of the body politic. In so doing, they have acquired 'insider' status, enjoying close links to key government ministers and civil servants, and establishing themselves as key figures in formal and informal consultation processes. Victims' interests are now considered at each stage of the criminal justice process, including prosecution, sentencing and release planning (Elias, 2011). In 2009, the centrality of victims' interests to government law and order policy-making was exemplified in the creation of Sara Payne (the mother of Sarah Payne, murdered by a registered paedophile) as the first ever Victims' Czar – a role that has its origins in the USA and is an example of criminal justice policy emulation (Winnett, 2009).

While the insertion of the 'victim' into the criminal justice process has been broadly welcomed by academics and practitioners, some argue that the politicisation of the victim has led to the victim agenda being hijacked by right of centre politicians who perceive that there is electoral advantage to be gained by using the victim to legitimate punitive sentencing. From this perspective, it is argued that, despite the best intentions of those involved in the victim movement, the victim who dominates political rhetoric and penal policy debate is an idealised, 'righteous figure', a sanctified figure whose memory must be honoured and would be sullied by expressions of interest in or concern for the welfare offender. The privileged victim who is the object of political attention, the one on display at political party conferences, is a highly politicised figure, a figure whose needs and interests can only be fulfilled through the pursuit of vengeance and retributive justice. The political imperative to be seen to be responsive to the victim is enshrined in policies of penal segregation (Garland, 2000, 2001). As Garland points out:

> The interests and feelings of the victims – actual victims, victims' families, potential victims, the projected figure of the victim – are routinely invoked in support of measures of punitive segregation ... A political logic has been established wherein being 'for' victims means automatically being tough on offenders. A zero-sum game is assumed wherein the offender's gain is the victim's loss.
>
> (Garland, 2001: 11)

The victim and media campaigns

Although victims of crime are predominantly located in lower socio-economic groups, in the media construction of the 'symbolic figure of the victim', it is only certain types of victims that are afforded victim attribution. Styles of media reporting favour highly personalised stories that the audience can relate to, and simple explanations that privilege some victims over others (e.g. young, white and middle-class victims are privileged over black and working-class victims). The iconic victim of media representations either signifies 'lost innocence', as in the cases of James Bulger, the Soham murder victims and Sarah Payne, or 'new-found heroism', as in the case of the 'have a go' hero Tony Martin (Armstrong and McAra, 2006). In mediated news stories, defenceless, innocent victims of crimes are juxtaposed against the demonic figure of the offender. The victim is no longer an unfortunate, atypical individual, but rather a representative figure whose experience is common and collective. Media images of the victim simultaneously instil empathy, and whip up anger, rage, retribution and hate speech directed at the perpetrator or groups that are perceived as the perpetrator class, for example Muslim individuals. The simple good/evil narrative that frames the publicised victim elicits visceral public emotions, and provides a space within which punitive sentiments can be expressed, and punitive policy solutions can be mobilised (Garland, 2000).

The 'suffering persona of the sanctified victim' that emerges from the pages of both the tabloid and the quality press is a valued commodity in the media/politics exchange: a persona that is stage managed to promote repressive legislation. A noteworthy example of this is the abolition of the presumption of *doli incapax* and the criminalisation of children with the effective reduction of the age of criminal responsibility from 14 to 10 years following the murder of James Bulger (Bandalli, 1998). One key aspect of the contemporary politics of the victim is the emergence of the victim celebrities, and the 'naming of criminal laws and penal measures for victims' (Garland, 2001: 143). Purporting to honour the victim, such measures are an effective means of deflecting competing voices. The positioning of the victim and the offender in an oppositional binary ensures that any compassion expressed for the offender, any promotion of offender rights, can be neutralised by emotive appeals to the victim's memory (Garland, 2001: 143). In a political climate in which the vilification of the offender (in the name of the victim) has become normalised, those who fail to acquiesce with offender 'othering' by challenging the dominant discourse or seeking to promote restraint and understanding are effectively 'silenced' (Mathiesen, 2004).

Examples of the creation of victim celebrities include Sarah Payne, whose murder provided the catalyst for the reform of paedophile monitoring in a campaign launched in her name, which attracted considerable public attention following its adoption by the *News of the World*, and the knife crime campaign launched in the name of Ben Kinsella, who was murdered in 2008, and gained media recognition following its promotion by his sister, Brooke, an actress who had appeared in a well-known soap opera, *EastEnders*. A distinguishing feature of these new single-issue victims' groups is the adoption of lobbying tactics, characteristically associated with 'outsider' groups, which are at odds with the more traditional 'insider' activities of mainstream victims' movements such as Victim Support (see above), and gain their momentum from direct appeals to the public through high-profile media coverage (Savage and Charman, 2010).

Notwithstanding the debates about the degree to which the media directly influences public policy (outlined earlier in the chapter), there is near universal agreement that the transformation of the justice agenda to one of dangerousness and public protection policy has been heavily influenced by the heightened public concerns about risk and dangerousness embodied in media presentations of the predatory, homicidal paedophile. A convincing argument is made that public concern has been fuelled by the sheer volume of press coverage, and the style of reporting that juxtaposes the stereotypical victim – the vulnerable, innocent child – against the non-familial, 'bad, mad or sad' monster (Kemshall, 2003).

Kitzinger (1999), in her analysis of the rise of the paedophile agenda, traces the aetiology of the problematisation of the released sex offender that became the focus of the Sarah's Law campaign. She argues that the origins of media attention to child sex abuse can be traced to the mid-1980s, and its 'discovery' by the television programme *Childwatch*. She notes that, since that broadcast, there has been a massive expansion in media coverage. Between 1985 and 1987, there was a fourfold increase in coverage in the *Times*. Similarly, in a computer search of newspaper articles on paedophiles, it was found that there were '712 articles in six leading British newspapers' in the first four months in 1998. This was an increase from '1,312 times in total in the 4 year period between 1992–1995' (Cobley, 2000: 2). Paedophiles feature as a regular topic for investigative documentaries, contributing towards the burgeoning of a lucrative industry in true-life survivor stories. In recent months, the graphic revelations about Jimmy Savile's past, and the unprecedented police activity that has accompanied it, have seen stories of newly identified paedophiles appearing most days in all media outlets.

Although there was little or no public interest in paedophiles prior to the 1990s, and few outside forensic psychiatry actually used the term, public attention from the mid-1990s began to focus on the risks and dangers posed by released paedophiles. The paedophile entered public discourse with the term 'pead' forming part of the common lexicon of school yard insults. In spite of the fact that media attention to the 'paedophiles in the community' problem initially followed the 'routine media practice whereby media agendas are traditionally set by politicians with high status profiles' (Kitzinger, 1999: 137) (in 1996 the then Home Secretary proposed to introduce measures to monitor sex offenders), control of the agenda by government officials declined, as 'media coverage and public debate shifted' with the joining up of the forces of the media and pressure groups in the wake of several high-profile cases (p. 147).

In 1998, Robert Oliver and Sydney Cooke, who were part of a paedophile ring that had abducted, buggered and killed 14-year-old Jason Swift, were released from prison, promoting lurid headlines about 'monsters in our midst' on the front pages of the tabloid press. The coverage provoked considerable public hostility in the form of a series of demonstrations and vigilante acts by locals as the police moved Cooke around the country in an attempt to reassure the public and defuse local unrest. In May 1988, the BBC reported that 'there was a near riot in the Knowle West area of Bristol and a series of protests in the Somerset towns of Yeovil and Bridgwater after it emerged that Cooke was being kept in a police station in the Avon and Somerset area' (BBC News, 1998).

Localised events covered by regional newspapers were picked up by the national media, and prompted headlines and editorials demanding that the government act. Highlighting the pivotal role of the regional press in the development of the paedophile agenda, Kitzinger comments:

> Protest spread rapidly from one area to another, and concern quickly escalated: the role of the local press in voicing these concerns was crucial. Although often ignored, when thinking about the media, the local press can play a key role . . . Indeed, many of the national stories about paedophiles began life on the front page of local papers and some protests were sparked by local press reports, rather than vice versa.
>
> (Kitzinger, 1999; p. 137 in Critcher, 2006)

It was against this background of heightened public sensibilities that the Sarah's Law campaign was launched in July 2000 after the abduction and murder of Sarah Payne by Roy Whiting, one of the country's first registered sex offenders under the 1997 Sex Offenders Act. The movement, which drew its inspiration from the USA policy of community notification of registered sex offenders, known as Megan's Law (Thomas, 2008), was oriented around a national newspaper campaign that sought to mobilise public opinion through emotional appeals to justice for an innocent child victim defiled by the depraved, evil 'other'.

End note

Although the role that the public and the mass media play in policy-making (particularly the new punitiveness) is contested, there is little disagreement that the mass media has been a potent force in exerting influence over one succinct aspect of law and order policy: the paedophile agenda.

Case study: The Sarah's Law campaign

This case study illustrates the way in which the tabloid press joined forces with a single-issue victim's group around the paedophile agenda to influence law and order policy.

Savage and Charman, in their overview of the 'Sarah's Law' campaign, explain how campaigning groups 'engage in the business of policy-shaping' (2010: 436). In their analysis of the campaign, activists were knocking on the open door of the Labour government that was 'very much steeped in the public protection ethos' (p. 437). Although the campaign was only partially successful in achieving its aim (as professional organisations, who feared vigilantism and offenders going underground, effectively resisted proposals for universal community notification), the outcome can be attributed to the way in which the movement abandoned traditional pressure group strategies, preferring a high-profile, media-focused, single-issue campaign.

Eight-year-old Sarah Payne went missing on 1 July 2000, prompting extensive national and international media coverage. Following the discovery of her daughter's body, Sara (a familiar figure from press conferences appealing for information) learnt about the weaknesses of the monitoring arrangements that had been placed on Whiting. She also found out about the success of the high-profile campaign in the USA waged by parents in the name of their daughter, Megan, following her murder by a convicted paedophile. When approached by journalists to sell her story, Sara Payne refused to do so, instead challenging the press to exert pressure on the government to enact a UK version of Megan's Law. Within 24 hours, Rebekah Wade, the newly appointed *News of the World* editor, was proposing a 'For Sarah' campaign. The campaign had the twin objectives of lobbying for a 'Sarah's Law', which would give parents the right to be informed of child sex offenders living in their area, and mounting a 'name and shame campaign' that would identify by name and location the most dangerous convicted sex offenders in the community.

Within a week, the *News of the World* launched its name and shame initiative with the publication of the names, but not addresses, of 49 convicted sex offenders. It also ran an editorial claiming that there was a convicted sex offender living within one mile of every Briton, organised petitions in support of Sarah's Law, and introduced the production and distribution of badges featuring Sarah with the slogan 'For Sarah'. The public response was unprecedented; public opinion polls indicated that there was widespread support for the policy initiative. Despite the fact that a number of vigilante attacks and disorderly demonstrations coincided with the campaign, the campaign continued apace.

Alert to the political advantage that could be gained by acting, the Home Secretary announced that Sarah's Law was under consideration. However, following a meeting of stakeholders, including police and probation representatives who advocated caution, a more measured and balanced set of objectives was agreed. The measures, which were enshrined in the 2000 Criminal Justice and Court Services Act, were hailed as a partial success by campaigners. Despite this, lobbying continued, and in 2007 a change of Home Secretary brought with it the announcement of a package of measures that were hailed as 'Sarah's Law proposals'. While the previous Home Secretary had been unwilling to undermine profession discretion about the disclosure of information about offenders, a hardening of the government's approach to crime control resulted in the creation in 2010 of a series of pilot schemes that granted parents and carers the right to access information about adults with whom their children were coming into contact. The *News of the World*, never slow to gain credit for the campaign's achievements, published headlines proclaiming: 'we have won the battle to protect our children from paedophiles'.

The combination of a grieving mother and a high-profile media campaign seemed to have delivered serious policy changes. But how was this possible?

Expressive justice and the power of the victims' voices

Some (Farmer, 2006) argue that the contemporary power to punish is increasingly organised around the figure of the victim, with particular individuals or groups being used as the focus to mobilise crime control initiatives. Victimhood touches deep, visceral public sentiments that engender attitudes and beliefs supportive of retributive punishment. In contemporary criminal justice policy-making, emotive sentiments, previously held in check, have acquired a new significance; governments increasingly adopt crime solutions that incorporate public anger and resentment. Expressive justice is most apparent in policies aimed at criminals whose behaviour is deemed to be the most dangerous and is particularly evident in relation to abhorrent sexual predators (Pratt, 2005). The culture of anxiety and fear that the dangerous 'other' engenders provides 'a rich scope for media and political campaigns that are graphically emotive, and charged with vicarious victimization, anxiety and resentment' (Sparks, 2006: 34).

The use of emotion in campaigning, while not new, is a powerful device. The 'moral authority of grief', encapsulated in the iconic figure of the mother mourning the loss of an innocent child, provides an imperative to action. Consequently, in the politics of the victim, mothers find themselves in a 'unique position as symbols of those suffering loss when that loss is transferred to protest' (Savage and Charman, 2010: 448). The power of the mother (as was the case with Sara Payne) is enhanced when there is public 'identity attachment', and individualised, private sentiments can be transformed into the shared, the public and the collective (Spalek, 2006). Identity attachment relies heavily upon the victim conforming to the demographic requirements of the 'ideal victim': white, young, female and photogenic (Greer, 2007).

New social movements and the media

In the case of the Sarah's Law campaign, media coverage was pivotal to its being kept in the public eye. While pressure groups traditionally use techniques of lobbying, education, information dissemination, conference speeches, etc. to advance their cause, what was noteworthy about the Sarah's Law campaign was the way in which tactics associated with protest movements with direct appeals to the public were employed. Differentiating the tactics of 'outsider' and 'insider' pressure groups, Savage and Charman argue:

> new social movements operate in very different ways from traditional insider groups, which focused upon the close, consultative relationships with ministers and government departments. Instead, we witness groups with fluid memberships who adopt the more traditional lobbying tactics of outsider groups. This centres on the mobilisation of public support and a high profile media presence.
>
> (Savage and Charman, 2010: 446)

The mobilisation of public support was achieved and maintained through the targeting of sympathetic audiences. Having secured the backing of the most widely read national tabloid paper, campaigners had a ready conduit for the promotion of an easily understood, simplified message. In the politics of public protection policy, public fear and anxiety are commodities to be exploited. The *News of the World* campaign proved that readers, already sensitised to the issue by previous decades of media coverage, needed little persuading that it would be dangerous to do nothing. The adoption of a front cover of the murdered child provided compelling evidence to readers that inactivity was not an option (Savage and Chapman, 2010). As Mitchell (1979, as cited in Maloney *et al.*, 2007) points out, people are more likely to respond to a collective threat than to a collective good.

But how did the News of the World *mobilise public sentiments around the campaign?*

Savage and Charman (2010) have identified a number of ways in which this was achieved. These overlap with categories of 'newsworthiness' – factors that determine whether or not a story receives press coverage – identified by Jewkes (2010).

Proximity: spatial proximity is the geographical 'nearness' of an event, whereas cultural proximity refers to the 'relevance' of the story to the audience.

Spatial proximity: the problem was portrayed as being very close in the *News of the World* campaign. The *News of the World* campaign ran a headline about everyone in Britain living within one mile of a paedophile.

Cultural proximity: the problem was portrayed as an issue that was relevant to all parents.

Use of emotion: highly personalised accounts that revolve around emotions of grief are favoured by the tabloid press. A mother's loss was a powerful weapon in the justice campaign.

Ethnicity and gender: the fact that the victim was white, young and female ensured that the victim achieved victim attribution status. 'If the victim is male, working class, of African Caribbean or Asian descent . . . reporters perceive that their audience is less likely to relate to, or empathize, the victim, and the case gets commensurately lower publicity' (Jewkes, 2010: 57).

Sources: Jewkes (2010), Savage and Charman (2010)

Key points summary

This chapter covers the key debates about the role that the public play in shaping criminal justice policy, and in particular the degree to which public concerns about law and disorder are mediated by a sensationalist mass media. It argues the following:

- The penal welfare state that was the dominant political, economic and social configuration in the post-war period was characterised by a bi-partisan consensus on law and order. Law and order was not a party political issue, and was left in the hands of a liberal elite. This elite had oversight of policy-making and managed dissenting public voices. The public were effectively excluded from the policy-making process.
- The election of Margaret Thatcher in 1979 signalled the decline of the prevailing political hegemony and ushered in a new period of criminal justice policy-making in which the appeal was directly to the public. Although Thatcher maintained a top-down authoritarianism, the changing political landscape that her administration heralded shifted the penal axis away from elite, expert-driven bureaucratic rationalism. This created new opportunities for public participation that some criminologists argue constitutes a new phase of democratisation. As successive governments sought to galvanise the public, politicians have become increasingly media-savvy, employing spin doctors and adopting new technologies of communication.
- The last 30 years have seen a dramatic increase in the prison population, and the implementation of a raft of new measures to punish the offender. With only a brief respite, successive governments have sought to 'out-tough' each other on law and order. Despite this, the view that this new punitiveness is attributable to the increasingly punitive sensibilities of the public (generated in part by tabloid representations of crime), and the emergence of a system in which the media orchestrated public anxieties, public expectations and public emotions, have become matters to be responded to by politicians (rather than deflected by bureaucrats) is contested.
- Over the last 30 years, the victim and those who claim legitimacy for their views on the basis that they speak for the victim have become primary stake-holders in the criminal justice system. While this has improved the way in which the victim is treated in the criminal justice process, the victim agenda has been hijacked by the politicians and the populist press, who have used it to promote their own particular variant of law and order policy-making.

Critical thinking discussion topics

1   To what extent has the changed political landscape transformed the relation-ship between governments and the public?
2   Governments seek legitimacy for their actions on the basis that they are enacting the 'will of the people'. What are the arguments for and against the claim that public opinion has driven the new punitiveness?

3   If Dean is correct that the government manipulates the press, does this mean that the government constitutes an 'interested party', as some pluralists argue?

4   How helpful is Weber's variant of elite policy-making theory in providing a critique of the Platonic guardians? Are criminologists such as Loader in danger of adopting an overly nostalgic view of their role in policy-making?

5   Which interest groups have benefited most from the diminution of the Platonic guardian's domination of the policy-making process?

6   How far does the network model of policy-making explain the collaborative power of the different groups involved in the Sarah's Law campaign? Was the existence of this coalition of interested parties helpful or a hindrance to the government policy-making process?

Seminar task

Identify a recent single-issue law and order campaign (e.g. Stephen Lawrence, Sarah's Law, Ben Kinsella and knife crime) and explore the role played by the media in promoting 'justice' for the victim. Consider why these cases attracted press attention, and how the campaigns impacted on policy-making. What are the implications of press involvement in law and order campaigns, and what problems can arise from policy-making that favours the 'loudest' voices? Do you agree or disagree with the view that the press has acquired the 'power to punish'?

Recommended further reading

Garland, D. (2001) *Culture of Control*. Oxford: Oxford University Press.

Loader, I. (2006) 'Fall of the "Platonic guardians": liberalism, criminology and political responses to crime in England and Wales'. *British Journal of Criminology*, 46(4): 561–86.

Matthews, R. (2005) 'The myth of punitiveness'. *Theoretical Criminology*, 9(2): 175–201.

Pratt, J. (2007) *Penal Populism*. London: Routledge.

Spalek, B. (2006) *Crime Victims: Theory, Policy and Practice*. Cullompton: Willan.

References

Armstrong, S.C. and McAra, L. (2006) 'Audience, borders and architecture: the contours of control'. In S. Armstrong and L. McAra (eds) *Perspectives on Punishment: The Contours of Control*. Oxford: Oxford University Press.

Bandalli, S. (1998) 'Abolition of the presumption of *doli incapax* and the criminalisation of children'. *Howard Journal of Criminal Justice*, 37: 114–23.

BBC News (1988) Child Killer Living in Fear. Retrieved from http://news.bbc.co.uk/1/hi/uk/90976.stm (accessed November 2013).

Beckett, K. and Sasson, T. (2000) *The Politics of Injustice: Crime and Punishment in America*. Thousand Oaks, CA: Pine Forge Press.

Bell, E. (2007) 'A new direction for penal politics? Putting the popular back into populism'. In R. Roberts and W. McMahon (eds) *Social Justice and Criminal Justice*. London: Centre for Criminal Justice Studies.

Berry, M., Tiripelli, G., Docherty, S. and Macpherson, C. (2012) 'Media coverage and public understanding of sentencing policy in relation to crimes against children'. *Criminology and Criminal Justice*, 12(5): 567–91.

Bottoms, A. (1995) 'The politics of sentencing reform'. In C. Clarkson and R. Morgan (eds) *The Philosophy and Politics of Punishment and Sentencing*. Oxford: Oxford University Press.

Bowcott, O. (2013, August 6) 'Owners of dogs that kill could face life in prison'. *Guardian*.

Cobley, C. (2000) *Sex Offenders: Law, Policy and Practice*. Bristol: Jordans.

Cullen, F., Fisher, B. and Applegate, B. (2000) 'Public opinion about punishment and corrections'. In M. Tonry (ed.) *Crime and Justice: A Review of Research*, Vol. 27. Chicago: University of Chicago Press.

Dean, M. (2012) *Democracy Under Attack: How the Media Distort Policy and Politics*. Bristol: Policy Press.

Elias, R. (2011) *The Politics of Victimization: Victims, Victimology, and Human Rights*. Oxford: Oxford University Press.

Farmer, L. (2006) 'Tony Martin and the nightbreakers: criminal law, victims, and the power to punish'. In S. Armstrong and L. McAra (eds) *Perspectives on Punishment: The Contours of Control*. Oxford: Oxford University Press.

Garland, D. (2000) 'The culture of high crime societies'. *British Journal of Criminology*, 40(3): 347–75.

Garland, D. (2001) *Culture of Control*. Oxford: Oxford University Press.

Garside, R. (2007) '"Punitiveness" and "populism" in political economic perspective'. In R. Roberts and W. McMahon (eds) *Social Justice and Criminal Justice*. London: Centre for Criminal Justice Studies.

Greer, C. (2007) 'News media, victims and crime'. In P. Davis, P. Francis and C. Greer (eds) *Victims, Crime and Society*. London: Sage.

Hall, S. (1980) 'Popular-democratic vs authoritarian populism: two ways of "taking democracy seriously"'. In S. Hall (ed.) *The Hard Road to Renewal: Thatcherism and the Crisis of the Left*. London: Verso.

Hough, M. and Roberts, J.V. (1995) *Understanding Public Attitudes to Criminal Justice*. Milton Keynes: Open University Press.

Hough, M. and Roberts, J.V. (1999) 'Sentencing trends in Britain: public knowledge and public opinion'. *Punishment and Society*, 1(1): 11–26.

Iyengar, S. (1991) *Is Anyone Responsible? How Television Frames Political Issues*. Chicago: University of Chicago Press.

Jewkes, Y. (2010) *Crime and Media*. London: Sage.

Kemshall, H. (2003) *Understanding Risk in Criminal Justice*. Maidenhead: Open University Press.

Kitzinger, J. (1999) 'The ultimate neighbour from hell? Stranger danger and the media framing of the paedophiles'. Reprinted in C. Critcher (ed.) (2006) *Critical Readings: Moral Panics and the Media*. Maidenhead: Open University Press.

Loader, I. (2006) '"Fall of the 'Platonic guardians'": liberalism, criminology and political responses to crime in England and Wales'. *British Journal of Criminology*, 46(4): 561–86.

Luhmann, N. (1989) *Ecological Communication*. Cambridge: Polity Press.

Luhmann, N. (1990) *Political Theory in the Welfare State*. New York: Walter de Gruyter.

Maloney, W., Jordan, G. and Clarence, E. (2007) *Democracy and Interest Groups: Enhancing participation?* Basingstoke: Palgrave Macmillan.

Maruna, S. and King, A. (2004) 'Public opinion and community penalties'. In A. Bottoms, S. Rex and G. Robinson (eds) *Alternatives to Prison*. Cullompton: Willan.

Mathiesen, T. (2004) *Silently Silenced. Essays on the Creation of Acquiescence in Modern Society*. Winchester: Waterside Press.

Matthews, R. (2005) 'The myth of punitiveness'. *Theoretical Criminology*, 9(2): 175–201.

Moeller, H.G. (2006) *Luhmann Explained: From Souls to Systems*. Chicago: Open Court.

Peelo, M. (2006) 'Framing homicide narratives in newspapers: mediated witness and the construction of virtual victimhood'. *Crime, Media, Culture*, 2(2): 159–75.

Pratt, J. (2005) 'Elias, punishment and decivilisation'. In J. Pratt, D. Brown, M. Brown, S. Hallsworth and W. Morrison (eds) *The New Punitiveness: Trends, Theories, Perspectives*. Cullompton: Willan.

Pratt, J. (2007) *Penal Populism*. London: Routledge.

Roberts, J., Stalans, L., Indermaur, D. and Hough, M. (2003) *Penal Populism and Public Opinion: Lessons from Five Countries*. Oxford: Oxford University Press.

Ryan, M. (2003) *Penal Policy and Political Culture in England and Wales*. Winchester: Waterside Press.

Ryan, M. (2005) 'Engaging with punitive attitudes towards crime and punishment. Some strategic lessons from England and Wales'. In J. Pratt, D. Brown, M. Brown, S. Wallsworth and W. Morrison (eds) *The New Punitiveness: Trends, Theories, Perspectives*. Cullompton: Willan.

Savage, S. and Charman, S. (2010) 'Public protectionism and "Sarah's Law": exerting pressure through single issue campaigns'. In M. Nash and A. Williams (eds) *Handbook of Public Protection*. Cullompton: Willan.

Solomon, E. (2006) 'Crime soundbites'. In P. Mason (ed.) *Captured by the Media: Prison Discourse in Popular Culture*. Cullompton: Willan.

Spalek, B. (2006) *Crime Victims: Theory, Policy and Practice*. Cullompton: Willan.

Sparks, R. (2006) 'Ordinary anxieties and states of emergency: statecraft and spectatorship in the new politics of insecurity'. In S. Armstrong and L. McAra (eds) *Perspectives on Punishment: The Contours of Control*. Oxford: Oxford University Press.

Thomas, T. (2008) 'The sex offender "register": a case study in function creep'. *Howard Journal*, 47(3): 227–37.

Topping, A. (2013, January 10) 'Nick Clegg launches LBC radio show – and admits to owning a onesie'. *Guardian*. Retrieved from http://www.guardian.co.uk/politics/2013/jan/10/nick-clegg-lbc-radio-show (accessed 8 May 2013).

Wacquant, L. (2001) 'The penalisation of poverty and the rise of neo-liberalism'. *European Journal on Criminal Policy and Research*, 9(4): 401–12.

Winnett, R. (2009, January 25) 'Sara Payne to become Government's first Victims' Champion'. *Telegraph*.

Young, J. (2003) 'Winning the fight against crime? New Labour, populism and lost opportunities'. In R. Mattthews and J. Young (eds) *The New Politics of Crime and Punishment*. Cullompton: Willan.

Zander, M. (2005) *Police and Criminal Evidence Act* (5th edn). London: Sweet & Maxwell.

7 International influences on criminal justice policy-making

Chapter summary

In recent years, increasing attention has been given to the similarities between penal policies that operate in different jurisdictions in advanced, industrial western states. Linked to the notions of globalisation and the spread of neoliberalism, public policy writers have sought to explore the interaction between macro-level economic and social changes that characterise 'late modern' capitalist societies, and the micro-level decision-making of individual political actors in nation states. With this in mind, this chapter is designed to help you to critically evaluate the international influences on British penal policy, in particular the importance of the USA as an exporter of ideas about crime control and punishment to England and Wales.

The focus of the chapter is recent specific policy developments that reflect the degree to which the importer state moulds the policy that it transfers in to domestic sensibilities and professional and organisational procedures and practices. When reading this chapter, you will be introduced to key aspects of penal policy, namely privatisation and 'three strikes and you're out' mandatory sentences, and will be encouraged to distinguish between the symbolic politics of the rhetorical and the real.

This chapter looks at:

- the key features of the divergence and convergence debate;
- the 'structuralist' and 'agency-led' perspectives on policy convergence;
- the spread of 'new punitiveness' as an example of policy convergence;
- the commodification of crime control and punishment as an example of policy convergence among neoliberal states;
- competing explanations for policy transfer, emulation and lesson learning;
- the impact of international agreements and directives on penal policy with a particular focus on the European Court of Human Rights' directive on prisoners' right to vote;
- the Americanisation of penal policy in England and Wales;
- the impact of international influences on specific aspects of British penal policy.

Case study: UK Privatisation

In the case study, you will be introduced to key debates about an aspect of policy transfer from the USA to the UK. The case study explores the degree to which privatisation (a policy that has parallels with the USA) has gained momentum in recent years in the UK. It highlights the current Coalition government's policy of the diversification of criminal justice delivery that has seen privatisation encroach upon an ever-widening range of criminal justice services, and has raised concerns that services such as the probation service are under threat. When reading the case study, you should consider the moral issues raised by the expansion of the private sector into the field of criminal justice. In particular, you should identify the implications for the offender, the victim and the public of 'making profit from punishment'.

Policy convergence and divergence

Over the last two decades, criminologists have increasingly turned their attention to the study of 'the extent to which, and the ways in which, criminal justice and penal policy ideas and innovations travel across national boundaries' (Jones and Newburn, 2006: 782). From this field of inquiry, a body of work has emerged that can be divided into two broad perspectives: policy convergence and policy divergence.

What is policy convergence?

Although the concept of policy convergence is relatively new (Bennett, 1991), the notion that there is 'remarkable correspondence' in the penal policies of different countries, and that this suggests a *homogenization* of penal policy (Muncie, 2005), occupies a prominent position within comparative penology literature. In defining policy convergence, Bennett (1991) seeks to differentiate between 'being' and 'becoming' alike: convergence is the process by which different jurisdictions move 'from different positions towards a common point'. He states:

> To know that countries are alike tells us nothing about convergence. There must be a movement over time toward some identified common point.
> (Kerr 1983: 3, as cited by Bennett, 1991: 219)

In seeking to elaborate upon this definition, Bennett, posing the question 'what is policy convergence?', argues that there are five key aspects, outlined in the following box.

Policy goals: a coming together of intent to deal with common policy problems.

Policy content: a coming together of the formal manifestations of government policy – statutes, administrative rules, regulations, court decisions, etc.

Policy instruments: a coming together of instrumental tools available to administer policy, whether regulatory, administrative or judicial.

Policy outcomes: a coming together of impacts and consequences – the results (positive, negative, effective or ineffective).

Policy style: a more diffuse notion signifying the process by which policies are formulated, e.g. consensual or conflictual.

Source: Bennett (1991: 218)

What is policy divergence?

Although the notion of policy convergence has gained prominence within contemporary comparative penology, it is not without its critiques. Indeed, a growing number of empirical studies attest to the contrasts and differences (the divergences) between penal policies in different jurisdictions (Jones and Newburn, 2007). Muncie's (2005) analysis of youth justice policy is illustrative of this approach. While recognising the influence of global economic pressures and universal legal conventions, he demonstrates how nation states seek to retain sovereignty over their penal policies as a 'powerful symbolic display' of independent statehood.

One example of policy divergence is the capacity of nation states to resist the prevailing trend towards 'new punitiveness' (see below). Pratt *et al.*'s (2005) international study of penal strategies provides several examples of countries whose national sensibilities, juridical systems and inclusive welfare state politics have resulted in their not embarking on 'such trajectories of development'. This resonates with Downes' earlier study of imprisonment in Europe, in which he identifies countries that have 'resisted the trend' towards ever higher rates of imprisonment. He explains that:

> the Scandinavian countries have maintained very high welfare spending with low, and in the case of Finland, strikingly falling imprisonment rates. France and Germany have maintained a steady rate despite rising crime rates.
>
> (Downes, 2001: 62–3)

Explanations of policy convergence

Explanations for policy convergence can broadly be divided between those that emphasise the importance of macro-structural changes at an economic and social level, in particular neoliberal globalisation, and those that place emphasis on the autonomous actions of politicians.

The structuralist perspective: globalisation and the onward march of neoliberal punitiveness

The structuralist perspective is closely associated with the political economy approach, which attributes changes in social organisation to changes in economic conditions. From this perspective, convergence can be explained as being the result of a 'tendency of societies to grow more alike' economically, and in so doing to develop similarities in structures, processes and performances. As Bennett claims:

> The general convergence argument suggests that, as societies adopt a progressively more industrial infrastructure, certain determinate processes are set in motion which tend over time to shape social structures, political processes and public policies in the same mould.
>
> (Bennett, 1991: 216)

For many writers, the driving force of policy convergence is the phenomenon of globalisation, and the 'burgeoning of international commerce' driven by the spread of neoliberal free trade practices and free market ideology from the USA. While there is no one overarching definition of globalisation, a number of themes are present in the literature. Fundamentally, globalisation is an economic phenomenon of the expansion of capital that can be traced back to the 1990s. It is predicated on the principles of the free market, and has been facilitated by technological changes that have made it possible to speedily move large amounts of money around the globe. This primarily economic phenomenon has had considerable political impact. The establishment of a free market in capital (and products) has resulted in a growing interconnectedness between nation states as they seek to adapt their economic and political systems to attract international capital (Muncie, 2005). As Harris states:

> globalisation is currently dominated by Neo-liberalism with its emphasis on free markets and the associated economic rights of the individual. As a consequence, there is a broadly similar trend, regardless of the political persuasion of the national governments, of global capitalist developments moving social welfare regimes in a neo-liberal direction.
>
> (Harris, 2005: 81–2)

The globalising spread of neoliberalism (e.g. to the UK) has transformed international penal systems. Cavadino and Dignan (2006a, 2006b) argue that there is a causal relationship between the individual penal systems of nation states and the underlying economic conditions and social structure. They state that countries which are generally similar in their economies, culture, language, ideology and politics are likely to resemble each other in terms of both the welfare and the penal systems that they adopt. In their study, nation states are assigned to four archetypal 'family groups': the neoliberal welfare state (the USA, England and Wales, Australia and New Zealand), the conservative corporatist welfare state (France, Germany,

Italy and the Netherlands), the social democratic welfare state (Sweden and Norway) and the oriental corporatist state (Japan) (Cavadino and Dignan, 2006b).

Nation states, in particular the Scandinavian states (as noted by Downes above), that have retained their social democratic welfare state have comparatively low rates of imprisonment, maintain predominantly inclusive welfare systems and adopt 'left-wing' rights-oriented penal systems. By contrast, nation states that have adopted a neoliberal welfare state are characterised by high imprisonment rates, the privatisation of penal services, exclusive welfare systems and a preference for 'law and order' criminal justice policies (Cavadino and Dignan, 2006a, 2006b). Rose's intra-state analysis of family resemblances in public policy-making within jurisdictions (see Chapter 3) has applicability to Cavadino and Dignan's family groups. By combining these two analytical perspectives, we can understand why countries that share similar political economies (such as the USA and the UK) adopt a similar social ethos and social belief system, share similar beliefs about the 'model of the person to be governed', and embrace similar causation models of crime. It is this convergence of penal ideology and philosophy, underpinned by shared economic and political structural arrangements, that accounts for the similarities that can be identified in terms of penal modes and forms – policies, practices and procedures (Rose, 2000).

Globalisation and glocalisation

For Muncie, however, globalisation is both a 'seductive and [a] flawed' analytical concept. While its appeal rests with its seeming ability to provide a mode of explanation for the emerging similarities in penal systems and policies (e.g. the diminution of state welfarism and the concomitant rise of retributive authoritarianism, actuarial justice, 'responsibilisation' and penal expansion), its flaw lies with its tendency towards overgeneralisation. The argument that 'criminal justice is becoming a standardised global product can be sustained only at the highest level of generalisation'. Globalising international pressures are subject to resistance; their effects are neither uniform nor consistent, and are always 'mediated by distinctive national and sub-national cultures and socio-economic cultural norms' (Muncie, 2005: 57). From this perspective, penal policy should be viewed as 'glocal' (the merging of the global and local): nation states always adapt penal policy from the outside to local sensibilities, local identities and local cultures. As Tonry argues:

> The world increasingly may be a global community, have a global economy and be moving towards the adoption of English as a global language, but explanations of penal policy remain curiously local or . . . 'contingent'.
>
> (Tonry, 2001: 518)

The spread of 'new' punitiveness: an example of policy convergence?

As stated earlier, central to the convergence perspective is the argument that the spread of neoliberalism has been characterised by 'new punitiveness' (the expansion of the prison population and more draconian sentences), which has its origins in the USA. As Muncie points out:

> Numerous authors have remarked upon ... a growing homogenization of criminal justice across western societies, driven in particular by the spread of punitive policies from the USA.
>
> (Muncie, 2005: 38)

Garland (2000) argues that a US-inspired 'culture of control' has emerged in the UK. The culture of control manifests itself in a public appetite for harsher punishment and expressive justice, linked to the politicised figure of the 'sanctified victim' (see Chapter 6) whose feelings and sentiments are 'routinely invoked in support of measures of punitive segregation' (Garland, 2000: 251). This development has its origins in a growing sense of public insecurity that is a key feature of late modern, neoliberal, 'high-crime' societies. Garland attributes the rise of the 'high-crime society' to economic and social transformations. These transformations include: demographic changes (e.g. new patterns of the middle-class family household, work and living arrangements); the post-war boom in consumer goods; a greater spatial mobility (as a result of the spread of private car ownership) that brought crime to middle-class suburbs; the reduction of traditional forms of informal social controls; and changing patterns of criminal activity and social disorder that rendered them more visible, raising public fears of random acts of violence and resulting in a search for new ways to control 'risk' (Christie, 2000; Garland, 2000, 2001).

In high-crime societies, such as the UK and USA, crime is seen as the norm. Crime consciousness becomes institutionalised into the media, popular culture and the built environment. Traditional approaches to crime control are reconsidered, resulting in the emergence of a two-pronged strategy: (a) *the adoption of adaptive strategies*, in particular the creation of new partnerships between the state and non-state agencies that seek to coordinate preventive strategies that will reduce crime opportunities; and (b) *the emergence of more punitive and expressive forms of crime control and punishment* that are responsive to populist sentiments. The first part of the strategy is characterised by the dispersal of the responsibility for crime control provision to new providers (e.g. the private sector) and the 'responsibilisation' of non-criminal justice agencies (e.g. commercial interests, private citizens and the providers of non-criminal justice welfare services). The second part of the strategy is characterised by the adoption on both sides of the Atlantic of US-inspired punitive measures, including zero tolerance policing, sex offender registration, mandatory sentences, 'three strikes and you're out' and the greater use of imprisonment (Garland, 2000, 2001).

The agency-led perspective

While globalisation and the concomitant spread of neoliberalism are key aspects of the structuralist perspective, authors adopting an agency-led perspective reject economic determinism, and direct our attention instead to the conscious, purposive actions of groups and individuals. In the agency-led perspective, the central role of elected officials as the primary agents in the policy-making process is highlighted. From this perspective, it is the values of politicians that shape the decisions made about public policy: it is 'their endorsement [that] is needed to legitimate the adoption of programmes' (Rose, 1993: 52, cited in Dolowitz, 2000: 17). Politicians operate choice over policy direction, setting the boundaries of influence of policy entrepreneurs (pressure groups such as think tanks, corporations, single-issue interest groups and trade unions) who seek to set their stamp on policy formulation (Dolowitz, 2000). Policy-making is essentially a conscious and deliberate political act: autonomous politicians select the policies that conform to their political imperatives and predilections. Ultimately, it is people not structures that determine policy outcomes. They 'lobby for penal innovations, frame legislation [or] pass sentences' (Hudson, 1996, cited in Jones and Newburn, 2002: 178).

A false dichotomy?

Writers on each side of the structuralist and agency debate tend to occupy polarised positions, leading some (Garland, 2001) to argue that a false dichotomy has been created, and that any analysis of international penal policy transformations must take account of the interplay between 'structural and cultural shifts associated with globalisation' and the 'intentional actions of political actors' (Jones and Newburn, 2007: 33–4). Bennett is among those who argue that any causal analysis of policy convergence must embrace a multidimensional approach that recognises both 'macro level' theories associated with the range of 'social economic forces produced by industrialism', as well as those that highlight the 'autonomous preferences of policy makers to fashion convergent policies' (1991: 215). He makes the point that the convergence of public policy occurs through a number of distinct processes. Consequently, 'it is not enough to say that comparable conditions produce comparable problems which produce comparable policies' (1991: 217).

Dolowitz (2000), who identifies three determinants of policy convergence (changes to the structural or systemic determinants of policy-making, changes to the dominant ideological discourse of the political system, and the desire to learn about policy or policy-making in another political system), agrees with Bennett that any analysis of policy convergence must acknowledge the contribution of both 'structuralist' and ' agency-led' perspectives. Similarly, Garland argues that political agency does not take place in a vacuum; rather, it is contingent upon 'shifts in social practice and cultural sensibilities' that are shaped by economic conditions. Prevailing social and economic structures place limits upon the political decision-making process and provide the context within which it operates. Garland states:

> [Although] politics and policies always involve choice and decision making, and the possibility of acting otherwise . . . certain conditions of possibility

and the presence of these background conditions substantially increase the probability that these policies will occur.

(Garland, 2001: 348)

What is meant by policy transfer?

A key feature of the convergence perspective is the concept of policy transfer. Dolowitz and Marsh define policy transfer as the 'process in which knowledge about policies, administrative arrangements, institutions etc. in one time and/or at one place is used in the development of policies, administrative arrangements and institutions in another time and/or place' (1996: 344). Tonry acknowledges that while 'transfers of policies and practices are not simple' and the processes of adoption and adaption are neither straightforward nor easy, this does not invalidate the contention that they happen. He points out that advances in modern communication, and the widespread use of English, mean that 'little goes on that cannot be learnt about elsewhere' (Tonry, 2001: 527). In his analysis of penal policy, politicians purposively seek out innovations that seem to satisfy important crime control and punishment needs better than previous practice. As Dolowitz and Marsh point out:

> If governments are searching for policy solutions to new or changing problems, then they are increasingly likely to look for 'solutions' abroad. This is much easier than it was in the past because of the growth in all forms of communication; politicians and civil servants from different countries now meet more frequently, in bilateral as well as multi-lateral meetings. At the same time, policy entrepreneurs 'sell' policies around the world. International policy networks, advocacy coalitions or epistemic communities develop and promote ideas. As such, there is no doubt that there is a great deal of transfer and that this transfer has shaped policies.
>
> (Dolowitz and Marsh, 2000: 21)

Variants of policy transfer

Bennett (1991) explains that there are different types of policy transfer. He provides a framework for analysing policy convergence that involves four processes: *emulation, elite networking, harmonisation* and *penetration*, as outlined in the following box.

Emulation: this indicates voluntary policy transfer through the utilization of evidence about a programme or programmes from overseas and active lesson-drawing from the experience. The process involves explicit borrowing, copying or imitation.

Emulation can explain a convergence of 'policy goals, of policy content, or of policy instruments', but cannot account for 'outcome or style'. 'In the

---

emulation of policy goals, the policy of another country is employed as an exemplar or model' (p. 221) that is adapted to local conditions.

Elite networking: this results from the 'existence of shared ideas' and a shared concern for policy problem resolution among a 'relatively coherent and enduring network of elites' (p. 224) engaging in regular collaborative interactions at the transnational level. This international policy community, comprising an informal elite of professionals from different spheres, is bound by knowledge and expertise about a shared problem, and engages in a shared experience of active lesson-learning. Policy convergence occurs as a consequence of the 'emergence of consensus of motivation and concern' (p. 225) about a common problem that arises among the participants, and the spread of policy solutions emanating from the group at a supranational level to their respective domestic 'societies and governments' (p. 225).

Harmonisation: this process requires both a 'coherent group (of regularly interacting) transnational actors' with a 'broad consonance of motivation and concern' (p. 225), and authoritative action by formal, responsible inter-governmental organisations and structures. The process is driven by the recognition of the transnational nature of problems, and the reliance of nation states on each other to avoid inconsistencies and discrepancies. The aim of harmonising policy is to ensure that there is a 'common response to common problems' (p. 225), and to avoid inconsistencies and discrepancies. It occurs when there is a shared and enduring commitment to a set of pre-existing governing arrangements (e.g. the Council of Europe), and a commitment to cooperative action for the good of the community.

Penetration: this process, which 'contrasts with the seemingly cooperative relations under harmonisation' (p. 227), involves coerced conformity. It occurs when nation states are forced by the actions of others (e.g. other nations, external organisations or multinational business) to bring their domestic law, policy or practices into conformity, under threat of exclusion from the benefits of membership of a transnational organisation or inter-national regime.

Source: Bennett (1991)

Dolowitz, building upon Bennett's typology, argues that there are four variants of policy transfer: *copying*, which constitutes the full and total transfer; *emulation*, which involves the partial transfer of ideas, but not policy or programme details; *combinations*, which involve 'the mixture of several different policies or programmes'; and finally *inspiration*, where the final version of the policy adopted is at significant variance to the original, but has been inspired by it (Dolowitz, 2000: 5). He also distinguishes between two ideal types. These are the perfectly rational and purely voluntary, and the imposed and coercive, which Dolowitz places on a continuum.

Voluntary transfer

Dolowitz (2000) argues that there are different variants of voluntary transfer.

Lesson learning: actors willingly and actively search for 'new' ideas from elsewhere as a 'cheap' means of problem-solving. As Rose (1991) argues, this involves the scanning for programmes in operation elsewhere and evaluating their applicability to a local problem.

Perceptual policy transfer: actors in one policy-making system seek out policies from another policy-making system on the basis of what is deemed to be best practice by competitor nation state regardless of its effectiveness or applicability. This may be driven by the desire to obtain international recognition or acceptability.

Source: Dolowitz (2000)

Coercive transfer

Dolowitz (2000) argues that there are also different variants of coercive transfer.

Coercion by transnational organisations: actors in one policy-making system are coerced by transnational organisations and other international agencies to adopt a specific policy direction as a condition of presence or aid.

Policy harmonisation and international treaties: actors in one policy-making system are coerced to implement policy in response to directives from international conventions that they have signed up to, e.g. the United Nations, Council of Europe or European Council on Human Rights.

Source: Dolowitz (2000)

Policy harmonisation and international treaties

An aspect of coerced policy transfer is policy harmonisation, which is brought about by the imposition on nation states of directives from international conventions. While there is evidence to support the claim that European Union (EU) directives have had an impact on determining the policy-making of succession states (e.g. states seeking to join the EU must abolish the death penalty), evidence of the influence that is exerted over UK penal policy by international treaties remains contradictory. Despite claims that the domestic drug policy, and related policing and security responses to 'organised crime', are determined by international agreements, there are numerous examples of the UK adopting a stance of procrastination, delay or only partial compliance with international directives.

While Hobbs (2013), in his ethnographic study of organised crime, argues that a key determinant of domestic policy on drugs was the UK's signing up to the 1988 United Nations (UN) Convention Against Illicit Traffic in Narcotic Drugs and Psychotropic Substances, which internationalized America's drug prohibition and 'war on drugs' stance, Muncie (2005), by contrast, in his analysis of international youth justice policy, cites several examples of the UK's failure to adopt UN conventions. This is particularly the case in relation to the protection of children's and young people's rights. Examples include: the UK's exercising of its right to opt out of using children for military service (and targeting them for recruitment); and its abolition of the principle of '*doli incapax*' that established the age of criminal responsibility as 10 years (when it had previously been 14 years), which flew in the face of the UN's advice to raise the age of criminal responsibility. Muncie also highlights the UN's 2002 censure of the UK's increasing use of imprisonment for juveniles, its failure to ban corporal punishment in the home, and the conditions in the youth estate that fail to protect children from abuse, bullying and self-harm.

A current example of the UK's failure to comply with international conventions in relation to adult prisoners is successive governments' adoption of delaying tactics in respect of the European Council of Human Rights' (ECHR) judgment on prisoners' rights to vote. Despite the judgement handed down in the 2005 Hirst case (Travis, 2005), which established that the UK's refusal to grant serving prisoners the right to vote contravened Article 3 of Protocol No. 1 of the European Convention of Human Rights, successive UK governments have adopted a range of strategies to forestall their implementation of the ruling. On 6 September 2011, the UK government was granted a delay to the deadline by which it would be required to introduce legislation until after the *Scoppola v Italy* judgment (White, 2011). However, on 22 May 2012, the ECHR upheld the principle established in the Hirst case that a blanket ban on voting contravenes the ECHR.

> The ruling in the case of *Scoppola v Italy* (No 3) makes clear that most sentenced prisoners in the UK have the right to vote. It upholds the principles set out in the original *Hirst* (No 2) judgment, in particular that the disenfranchisement of 'a group of people generally, automatically and indiscriminately, based solely on the fact that they were serving a prison sentence, irrespective of the length of the sentence and irrespective of the nature or gravity of their offence and their individual circumstances, is not compatible with Article 3 of the Protocol No 1'.
>
> (Prison Reform Trust, 2012)

Despite this ruling and extensive lobbying for change by penal reform groups, two public consultations and an expression of regret by the Council of Europe's Committee of Members at the lack of progress (in 2010), the legislation that would enshrine the right into UK penal policy remains elusive (White, 2011; Prison Reform Trust, 2012). The ECHR judgment continues to be resisted by the government as it is not in its political interests to pursue it. The judgment has received considerable negative coverage by the tabloid press, is perceived by ministers to be generally unpopular with an electorate that has little sympathy for prisoners, and runs counter to the Prime Minister's political commitments and ideological preferences.

In 2010, the Prime Minister, David Cameron, made his opposition to the *Hirst* judgment clear when he stated, 'it makes me physically ill to contemplate giving the vote to prisoners. They should lose some rights including the right to vote'. What is more, the Master of the Rolls indicated that the domestic courts would not interfere if parliament chose to reject the controversial decision. Any outcome, he claimed, was a 'political decision', and if the government chose to ignore a Strasbourg ruling, there would be 'nothing objectionable' in British law (Whitehead, 2011).

Direction of policy transfer: American expansionism

While the direction of policy transfer is neither 'one dimensional [nor] one directional' (Muncie, 2005: 42), much of the literature on the direction of policy transfer focuses upon the USA as the 'penal workshop of the world' (Downes and Howard, 1996). From this perspective, it is argued that 'neoliberal penality', characterised by social welfare retrenchment and the growing use of the penal system as an instrument for managing social insecurity and containing the social disorders created at the bottom of the class structure by neoliberal economic policies of labour deregulation, first established in the USA, has been disseminated throughout the world (Wacquant, 2001).

There is evidence of importation to the UK of penal policies that do not have their origins in the USA (e.g. restorative justice ideas from New Zealand and Australia, which feature predominantly in youth offending strategies) (Muncie, 2005). However, Dolowitz, in his analysis of the direction of penal policy transfer, argues that in the lender–borrower relationship, the USA features frequently as the lender, exporting its variants of crime control and punishment, whereas Britain is invariably (but not exclusively) the borrower (Dolowitz, 2000). Jones and Newburn (2002), summing up the view, argue that this process is frequently referred to as *Americanisation:*

> There is a view, not always framed explicitly, that the field of British social policy in general (including crime control policy) has become increasingly 'Americanized' in recent years. Such arguments often suggest a rather straightforward exertion of American influence, which manifests itself via deliberate policy transfers from the USA, and the conscious emulation of US policy innovation by UK policy-makers.
>
> (Jones and Newburn, 2002: 177)

A number of explanations have been offered for the willingness of successive British governments to embrace penal ideas and policy formulations that have originated from the USA. While Nellis attributes this development to a shared language, similarities in the legal system and 'common ideological outlooks' (2000: 5), Dolowitz (2000) maintains that the exportation of ideas, practices and policies from the USA to Britain has its origins in the structural similarity of their political economies, the rise of the New Right in the USA in the 1970s, and the forging of the 'special relationship' with the USA during the Thatcher/Regan administrations. A similar point is made by Savage and Atkinson (2001), who argue that the special relationship with the USA, established in the Republican era by Thatcher, continued under Blair's New Labour administration, with Clinton's (New) Democrats providing the source of policy inspiration (2001: 15). This point is further developed by Newburn (2002), who claims that the New Democrats provided New Labour with a template for electability after nearly 20 years in opposition. He provides a detailed analysis of the attractiveness of US penal policies to New Labour, identifying six key determinants, described in the following box.

Ideological proximity: a shared neoliberal agenda; a shared language and terminology within which to define the problem; shared models of the offender; and close ideological ties and a close relationship.

Electoral success: a shared search for electoral success in the face of right-wing party domination; lesson-learning from the Clinton electoral breakthrough, in particular the rebranding of the party to appeal to middle England, and the rapid rebuttal of accusations of 'soft on crime' policies.

The language of politics: the emulation of the New Democrats in the adoption of elements of New Right discourse, key terms and phrases that have 'mesmeric appeal', such as the 'war' metaphor.

Symbolic politics: the formulation of electorally popular law and order policies, or postures that are intended to communicate concern about an issue, to distinguish between 'good and bad', but are not necessarily believed to be instrumentally effective or implemented or, if implemented, are assumed to be met by adaptive, nullifying responses by practitioners, e.g. judges.

Penal industrial complex: the influence of corporations that profit from the building and running of prisons, and the provision of other associated services.

Neoliberal penal policy complex: the influence of neoliberal 'policy networks', 'advocacy coalitions' and think tanks with interchangeable personnel and interest groups that make a profit from the privatisation of penal provision and services. These policy networks exert power to encourage government to adopt punitive policies. These networks operate beyond national borders and export their ideas to the UK.

Source: Newburn (2002)

Examples of the Americanisation of penal policy

Examples of penal policy initiatives that feature most frequently in academic, media and political discourse on policy transfer from the USA include the

privatisation of punishment, the 'three strikes and you're out' approach, mandatory sentences, zero tolerance policing, sex offenders' registration, electronic
monitoring and drug Czars (Garland, 2000; Nellis, 2000; Jones and Newburn,
2002, 2007). Acknowledging 'the simultaneous existence of elements of
convergence and divergence between nations and regions, and [accepting]
that policy outcomes arise from a complex interplay between local, national
and international forces' (Jones and Newburn, 2006: 782), Jones and Newburn
argue that the timescales, the language used and the 'similarities in policy ideas,
content and instruments . . . support the contention that cross-national transfer
was involved in some way' (2007: 144). As stated above, this is for some the
manifestation of the 'Americanisation' of penal policy (Jones and Newburn,
2002).

However, while there are identifiable similarities, policy transfer is rarely
'total'. At both the design stage and the implementation stage, policy is resisted by
pressure groups and reworked by professionals in the context of local sensibilities
and culture. As Muncie states:

> Policy transfer [is] . . . piecemeal and reconfigured in local contexts. What-
> ever the rhetoric of government intention, the history of youth justice (e.g. in
> England and Wales) is also a history of active and passive resistance from
> pressure groups and from the magistracy, the police and from youth justice
> workers through which such reform is to be effected.
>
> (Muncie, 2005: 275)

Soft policy and hard policy transfer

When discussing policy transfer, an important distinction needs to be made
between 'soft policy transfer' (the symbolic element of rhetoric and policy
ideas) and 'hard policy transfer' (the policy content and legislative and administrative instruments). Not infrequently when analysing the details of policy
content in both jurisdictions, it is penal rhetoric and the language of tough-
sounding crime policies (such as 'three strikes and you're out' and zero
tolerance) that appear to be a more successful import than the specific penal
policy itself. That said, it is important to recognise that, in 'race to the bottom',
in which political parties seek to 'out-tough' each other on law and order,
rhetoric is a potent electoral device that signals a political party's policy mood
and intentions. Furthermore, even when the direct impact of US-style policy
appears to be largely symbolic, this does not mean that the measures can
be dismissed as 'all talk and no action' (Jones and Newburn, 2006). As Garland
argues:

> political rhetoric and official representations of crime and criminals have a
> symbolic significance and a practical efficacy that have real social conse-
> quences. Sometimes 'talk' is 'action'.
>
> (Garland, 2001: 22)

Indeed, it would be wrong to underplay the long-term practical significance of the political rhetoric of punitiveness. The rhetoric of punitiveness is important because it sensitises the courts to the political will, and signals to the judiciary that the public looks to it to pass longer sentences. It also contributes to the creation of a climate that is favourable to further draconian legislation. The notion of a dichotomy between the symbolic and the real obscures the impact that interaction between the two has. When commenting on the importation of the US 'three strikes and you're out' policy, Newburn and Jones state:

> Although ... the legislation was primarily symbolic, ... such symbolism may have some negative practical effects: first, in contributing to a punitive culture in which there is a pressure on sentencers to increase the use of custody; and secondly, in setting the precedence for the introduction of further mandatory minimum sentences.
>
> (Newburn and Jones, 2006: 799)

Privatisation

One of the central tenets of neoliberalism is the promotion of corporate and private interests through the dismantling of state ownership and control. In terms of penal policy, this has taken the form of the creation of a mixed economy of crime control and punishment, distinguished by the privatisation of a range of penal provisions and services. For some (Christie, 2000), this amounts to the *commodification of punishment*, with punishment reduced to a profit-making commodity that can be sold to the lowest bidder.

In Lilly and Deflem's analysis, among the exemplars of the influence of the US on UK penal policy is the exportation of privatised penal services, products and 'know-how'. They state that American multinationals, which seek to profit from the sale of their penal products and 'know-how' to like-minded countries (such as the UK), are major players in international penal policy-making. In the USA, free market enterprise and privatisation ideology go hand in hand, creating a highly lucrative punishment industry that has sought to take advantage of the profit-making opportunities afforded by globalised liberalism (Lilly and Deflem, 1996). The combination of American economic power and American cultural dominance ensures that America has 'a substantial balance of payments surplus in penal ideas and products' (Cavadino and Dignan, 2006b: 11).

The recognition of commercial potential of the punishment industry in the USA has its origins in the 1980s. The rapid rise in the prison population in USA coincided with the emergence of a number of key private providers that sought to profit from the provision of services to the expanding prison system. These services ranged from providing catering and training to publicly run prisons, through to the design, management and construction of new prisons. During this period, an alliance was forged between private profit and penal policy-makers within the USA. This constituted the 'corrections–commercial complex': the symbiotic relationship between the state and commercial interests. The key participants formed part of a massive self-serving policy-making alliance that remains 'low profile' and operates 'without public scrutiny' (Lilly and Knepper, 1992). Participants in this increasingly global policy network, who share the same policy goals, vision and objectives, seek to exert power over the policy-making process in order to ensure that the allocation of government resources (e.g. service delivery contracts) meets their interests. They are:

1   'Private corporations that are devoted to profiting from imprisonment';
2   'Government agencies anxious to maintain their existence';
3   'Professional organisations that sew together an otherwise fragmented group into a powerful alliance' (Lilly and Knepper, 1992: 154).

These themes are illustrated in the case study at the end of the chapter.

Three strikes and you're out

While privatisation can be understood as an example of both *elite networking* and *emulation*, the importation of the US-style 'three strikes and you're out' policy provides an interesting example of both the operation of 'local contingencies and resistance' (Muncie, 2005), and the primacy of soft policy transfer (Jones and Newburn, 2002). It also highlights the way in which policy transfer is neither straight-forward nor total, but rather reflects the 'complex relationship between political actors at the local, national and global level' (Jones and Newburn, 2007: 73).

In their study of the 'three strikes and you're out' mandatory minimum sentencing policy for repeat offenders that originated in the USA and later appeared in a muted form in the UK, Jones and Newburn (2006) differentiate between the symbolic and the substantive. Through an analysis of the development of the policy in both the US and the UK, the authors explain how differences in political structures, cultures and sensibilities – in particular the greater degree of judicial independence (USA judges are elected), the absence of an American tradition of policy-making via voter initiative, and the reduced range of opportunities for direct lobbying by single-issue interest groups – shaped the policy transfer process and militated against direct emulation of the policy's more draconian US features.

They argue that the passage of the Crime (Sentences) Act in 1997, which owed much to the desire of the Conservative Home Secretary of the day (Michael Howard) to go beyond the expressive/symbolic and to implement a policy that would have the operational effect of binding sentencers to his political intent of offender incapacitation, faced significant resistance from backbenchers in the lower House, peers in the upper House and the judiciary when it was introduced in 1996. It was only passed after significant amendments were imposed by the House of Lords, driving 'a coach and horses through the provisions of the bill' (Jones and Newburn, 2006: 795). Furthermore, once passed, the policy faced further resistance from professional practitioners as the original intentions of the legislation were thwarted by judges who, seeking to mould the policy to fit with pre-established cultural norms of judicial independence from political interference, invoked the discretion provided by the amended legislation to limit the practical impact on sentencing outcomes. Consequently, only a small number of offenders received sentences that could be directly attributed to the legislation.

In summarising their findings, the authors argue that, despite the similarities between the USA and the UK in terms of 'hard policy' content (both adopting statutory instruments to provide for the enhanced sentencing of repeat offenders, and imposing mandatory sentences to reduce judicial discretion), there is 'limited evidence of direct policy transfer' (Jones and Newburn, 2006: 798). Rather they argue that it was 'soft policy transfer' in the form of policy ideas, as indicated by Howard's attraction to US conservative thinking on crime control, that provided the political imperative. Despite this, in terms of a direct contribution to changes to sentencing policy, it is generally agreed that although the statistics prove that the Act itself was primarily symbolic, its long-term contribution to the more punitive sentencing environment was real in its consequences.

Case study: UK privatisation

This case study illustrates the way in which privatisation, an exemplar of US policy, has become a driving force of contemporary penal policy. It also shows how powerful commercial interests combine with politicians to shape policy-making.

The return of the private prison

The (re)introduction of private prisons into England and Wales from the 1990s and the expansion of the private sector into an increasing range of penal services appears to be one of the more straightforward examples of the UK actively looking to the US for policy solutions, and commercial interests in the UK and US joining forces to take advantage of the profit-making opportunities offered by the UK's adoption of US inspired neoliberal principles of the free market. While opinions remain divided, this is for some illustrative of American expansionism (Jones and Newburn, 2007).

The privately run prison is not a new phenomenon. The 'fee system', whereby private jail keepers provided food, bedding and fuel to their captives and received a payment from them, operated from the middle ages and was finally abolished in 1815. The system that was highly criticised by penal reformers of the day exposed a number of defects. These were the exploitation and maltreatment of inmates, the lack of oversight and accountability, and the corruption of operators and officials (Cavadino and Dignan, 2007). By the late nineteenth century, a state-run, centrally managed prison system – the creation of du Cane – had emerged (Morris and Morris, 1963).

Despite its ignominious history, the involvement of private contractors in the detention business re-emerged in 1970 when the government awarded the private security firm Securicor Ltd the contract to operate a detention centre for suspected illegal immigrants at Heathrow and Manchester airports. This development attracted little attention, and it was not until the late 1980s, under the Thatcher administration, that the move towards privatising UK prisons really gained momentum. Underpinned by the political ideology of neoliberalism, with the 'rolling back' of the welfare state and the concomitant reduction of role of the state in delivering public services, the privatisation initative was promoted by a network of key policy entrepreneurs, including the right-wing think tank the Adam Smith Institute, a small group of vocal Conservative backbench MPs and peers, and lobbyists for potential commercial providers.

In 1987, the parliamentary Home Affairs Select Committee, which had been set up to investiagte the rising prison population and prison overcrowding, published a report that called for contracting out of the construction and management of prison to the private sector. The report was published in the wake of a series of ministerial fact-finding visits to private prison facilities in the USA, operated by the Corrections Corporation of America (CCA). Shortly after the report's publication, its chairman was appointed as the chairman of a company whose remit was to exploit the new opportunities (Cavadino and Dignan, 2007). In the same year, the CCA formed a British company, UK Detention Services Ltd (UKDS), as a joint venture with two long-established British construction companies, Sir Robert McAlpine & Sons Ltd and John Mowlem & Co., whose owners were regular contributors to the then ruling Conservative Party. One of UKDS's stated aims was the lobbying of the government to implement prison privatisation.

In 1988, a Green Paper was published, recommending an assessment of the potential of privatising the management of remand centres. In September, the private prison network came together at a dinner given by the Conservative Carlton Club's political committee. The dinner was attended by representatives of the Adam Smith Institute and other right-wing policy units, civil servants, architects and people from the consortia. In 1991, the Criminal Justice Act was passed, which provided the statutory instruments for the privatisation agenda. The Act set in motion the contracting out of the prison to any agency that the Home Secretary considered appropriate. In the same year, following a tendering process in which the public sector was barred from participating, Group 4 was awarded the first ever UK private prison contract to manage HMP Wolds.

Despite opposition from trade unions, professional organisations and penal reform groups, and a series of damning reports by the inspectorate that have highlighted problems of security and safety created by high staff turnover (Prison Reform Trust, 2011), the privatisation of prison continues to expand. In November 1992, the Private Finance Initiative (PFI), a financial mechanism to obtain private finance for the prison building programme without affecting public borrowing, was launched. Although the privatisation of prisons was initially condemned by New Labour, who promised to abolish it while in opposition, they made a U turn when they were elected and embraced the PFI scheme as a means of fulfilling their tough on crime vision through the expansion of the prison estate (Nathan, 2003; Cavadino and Dignan, 2007).

The contracting out of prison management to the private sector shows no signs of abatement. The UK currently has the most privatised prison system in Europe, with nearly 10,000 prisoners held in private prisons: there is a higher proportion of prisoners in private prisons in the UK than in the USA (Carter, 2003). Through a series of name changes and buy-outs, US/UK business partnerships and government awards of preferred bidder status, the UK has acquired its own commercial industrial complex of global providers. As Nathan states: 'The prison contracts are shared by the same companies that are marketing their services across the world: Group 4 Falk, Wackenhut Corrections Corporation/Serco, Sodexho and Securicor'(2003: 167).

Privatisation and the Coalition government: new horizons

Since the establishment of the mixed economy of punishment, the pace and depth of the private sector's immersion into the punishment business have escalated as successive governments have sought to offer the private sector an increasingly diversified range of service provision opportunities. While the private sector has tended to 'cherry pick' the 'shallow end', less risky aspects of service delivery where it is comparatively easy to achieve the contracted performance results, the range and scope of potential private sector provision have been given a considerable boost by a series of Coalition government penal policy initiatives that have aimed to transform the model of service delivery (Cavadino and Dignan, 2007; Ministry of Justice, 2010; Prison Reform Trust, 2011) by opening up the 'range of providers competing to offer a better service to private companies, community and voluntary sector organi-sations, and to Public Service Mutuals' (House of Commons, 2012). A key feature of this policy is the highly controversial contracting out of 70 per cent of probations work (*NAPO News*, 2013) on the grounds of efficiency, effec-tiveness and economy (Ministry of Justice, 2013). Publicly owned and managed probation trusts seeking to bid for contracts are either barred from doing so (*NAPO News*, 2013), or can only do so by forming partnerships with the private sector (House of Commons, 2012).

Payment by results

Pivotal to the Coalition government's marketisation strategy is the introduc-tion of a 'payment by results' scheme under which funding is provided on the basis of achievement and outcomes, rather than the inputs, outputs or proc-esses of a service (Cabinet Office, 2011). Promoted as the centre right solu-tion to reducing re-offending at a time of austerity, payment by results is underpinned by a series of financially driven checks and balances that reward those who achieve contracted outcomes, and penalise those who fail (Dominey, 2012). Under the scheme, service providers receive a basic tariff to cover their costs, as well as additional payments for meeting contracted targets to reduce re-offending (Fox and Albertson, 2012).

The policy strategy, which represents the latest manifestation of the erosion of the boundary between the public and private sectors in criminal justice systems, remains highly controversial. While initially cautiously welcomed by the not for profit sector and charities as a potential new source of revenue, the high cost of the competitive tendering process and the financial risks associated with the service level contracts have favoured a limited number of large multinational business-focused organisations, which already dominate other realms of social provision (e.g. work and pensions, as well as security and criminal justice). In the bidding process, not for profit organisations are increasingly used as 'bid candy' for large corporations to demonstrate a sense of social responsibility. The charities, which are effectively the poor relations in the private sector–not for profit marriage, often secede from the deal later on, either because they do not get any referrals or because they are only given the 'hard to reach' cases (Taylor, 2012; Williams, 2012). As Fox and Albertson explain:

> The underlying difficulty . . . is that payment by results, rather than leading to a greater diversification of providers and new opportunities for voluntary sector providers and Small and Medium sized Enterprises (SMEs) actually might lead to the opposite and exclude smaller organisations and voluntary and public sector organizations from the provision of services.
>
> (Fox and Albertson, 2012: 365)

The story so far . . .

To date, several publicly owned prisons and community justice services have been put out to tender, and lucrative contracts have been awarded to the private sector (aided and abetted by former senior staff from the prison and probation service public sector) either as single entities or as part of joint ventures with social enterprises and public service mutuals (Fletcher, 2011; Ledger, 2011). In 2011, Sodexo (North America's largest provider of facility management contracting) became part of a tripartite criminal justice consortium with the not for profit sector working alongside the public sector Essex Probation Trust to bid for community justice contracts (Sodexo, 2011). In October 2011, HMP Birmingham became the first prison in the UK to move from public to private control following a highly controversial bidding process that saw the contract, worth £468.3 million over 15 years, awarded to G4S. Their bid was headed up by Phil Wheatley, who had previously been Director of the Prison Service (Fletcher, 2011). In July 2011, eight publicly owned prisons were put out to competitive tender, and a year later the first contract to provide community offender services was awarded to a joint public and private sector enterprise, made up of London Probation Trust and Serco, which won a contract to deliver Community Payback in London (Ministry of Justice, 2012). The four-year contract, under which 15,000 offenders are expected to carry out 1.3 million hours of unpaid work, is worth £37 million (Travis, 2012). In the year following the award of the contract, Serco announced its intention to make 99 of the 300 London Probation Trust staff who had been transferred to the new providers redundant (Waterman, 2013).

Graham, who has been studying the development of privatisation in the UK, summed up recent developments with this cautionary observation:

> With virtually no public debate or democratic scrutiny, crucial pieces of our criminal justice and public security systems are being taken over by private security corporations. The long-term implications for public justice, accountability, transparency and equality are likely to be very grave indeed.
>
> (Graham, cited in Taylor, 2012)

The tagging scandal

There can be little doubt that the punishment business is a highly lucrative one. It is estimated that, in 2010, companies involved in the full range of outsourcing received £80 billion from the Treasury. In their rush to expand privatisation, governments have repeated mistakes of the past. Light touch oversight and scrutiny of private providers means that outsourcing offers considerable opportunities for poor service (as in the case of G4S, which, despite its failure to fulfil its contractual obligations to provide sufficient security staff at the Olympics, has won contracts worth £30 million a year since the Games, including the management of two prisons (Neate, 2013), and less than scrupulous auditing arrangements. Private providers of electronic monitoring have recently been accused of 'overcharging' for services. In 2013, the Serious Fraud Squad was asked to investigate allegations that G4S and Serco had overcharged the Treasury by tens of million of pounds for the provision of electronic monitoring services for offenders whose period of 'tagging' had ceased, in some cases because the offender had died, left the country or been returned to prison. As Travis states in explaining the scandal to the House of Commons:

> Grayling told MPs that G4S and a second major supplier, Serco, had been overcharging on the existing £700m contract, with the Ministry of Justice being billed for non-existent services that dated back to at least 2005 and possibly as long ago as 1999.
>
> Grayling added that it included charging for monitoring people who were back in prison and had had their tags removed, people who had left the country, and those who had never been tagged in the first place.

'There are a small number of cases where charging continued for a period when the subject was known to have died,' he told the Commons.

'In some instances, charging continued for a period of many months and indeed years after active monitoring ceased. This is a wholly indefensible and unacceptable state of affairs. The house will share my astonishment that two of the government's biggest suppliers would seek to charge in this way.'

(Travis, 2013)

Key points summary

This chapter has explored the degree to which policy transfer has shaped developments in penal policy in England and Wales. It argues that:

- Despite evidence of similarities between countries' penal policies, the question of whether or not the seeming convergence of penal policy constitutes a globalisation of penal policy is the subject of considerable debate. These debates can be broadly divided into two conflicting perspectives of structuralism and agency that are explored in detail.
- Although there is a burgeoning literature on the influence of American penal policy on UK penal policies, empirical evidence of policy transfer indicates that local sensibilities, local actors and local culture provide important modifying influences.
- International conventions and directives are only partially successful in harmonising penal policies. The UK is one of a number of countries that adopt a 'pick and choose' approach to attempts by international governing bodies to determine domestic policy. As the example of prisoners' right to vote demonstrates, resistance and procrastination are strategies adopted when policies run contrary to populist notions of punishment.
- Since the 1990s, the UK has embarked upon a policy of eroding the public sector monopoly of the provision of punishment that has parallels with developments in the USA. However, while there is a case to be made that private companies in the USA have made an impact on the privatisation of prisons in the UK, the ever-widening range of criminal justice services that have been earmarked for privatisation can be attributed as much to the political ideology and pragmatism of political agents as it can to American expansionism.

Critical thinking discussion topics

1 What are the distinctive features of the policy convergence and divergence debate?
2 What are the different types of policy transfer, and what distinguishes coercive from voluntary policy transfer?

3   Why and to what extent has the USA influenced UK penal policy?
4   How and why has privatisation increased under the Coalition government? In your view, is the development primarily ideological or fiscal?
5   What does the case study tell us about the strategies that interested parties adopt to exert pressure on the policy-making process?
6   How far does the Marxist version of the elite policy-making process model help us to explain this policy development?

Seminar task

Identify a contemporary aspect of penal policy (e.g. sex offenders registration, privatisation, 'three strikes and you're out' or prisoners' voting rights) and consider the following:

1   Where does your chosen aspect of policy fit within Bennett's typology of policy transfer? How useful is Bennett's typology as a framework for analysis?
2   Does your chosen example support or contest Tonry's claim that:

> the world increasingly may be a global community, have a global economy and be moving towards the adoption of English as a global language, but explanations of penal policy remain curiously local or as Zimring and Hawkins . . . called them 'contingent'.

Recommended further reading

Cavadino, M. and Dignan, J. (2006) *Penal Systems: A Comparative Approach*. London: Sage.

Jones, T. and Newburn, T. (2007) *Policy Transfer and Criminal Justice*. Maidenhead: Open University Press.

Lilly, J.R. and Deflem, M. (1996) 'Profit and penality: an analysis of the corrections-commercial complex'. *Crime and Delinquency*, 42(1): 3–20.

Muncie, J. (2005) 'Globalisation of crime control: the case of youth and juvenile justice'. *Theoretical Criminology*, 9(1): 35–64.

Nathan, S. (2003) 'Prison privatisation in the United Kingdom'. In A. Coyle, A. Campbell and R. Neufeld (eds) *Capitalist Punishment: Prison Privatisation and Human Rights*. London: Clarity Press.

References

Bennett, C. (1991) 'What is policy convergence and what causes it?' *British Journal of Political Science*, 21: 215–33.

Cabinet Office (2011) *Open Public Services*. London: Cabinet Office.

Carter, P. (2003) *Managing Offenders, Reducing Crime*. London: Home Office.

Cavadino, M. and Dignan, J. (2006a) 'Penal policy and political economy'. *Criminology and Criminal Justice*, 6(4): 435–45.

Cavadino, M. and Dignan, J. (2006b) *Penal Systems: A Comparative Approach*. London: Sage.

Cavadino, M. and Dignan, J. (2007) *The Penal System: An Introduction* (4th edn). London: Sage.

Christie, N. (2000) *Crime Control as Industry* (3rd edn). London: Routledge.

Dolowitz, D.P. (2000) 'Policy transfer: a framework for analysis'. In D.P. Dolowitz with R. Hume, M. Nellis and F. O'Neil (eds) *Policy Transfer and British Social Policy*. Maidenhead: Open University Press.

Dolowitz, D.P. and Marsh, D. (1996) 'Who learns from whom? A review of policy transfer literature'. *Political Studies*, 44: 343–57.

Dolowitz, D.P. and Marsh, D. (2000) 'Learning from abroad: the role of policy transfer in contemporary policy making'. *Governance*, 13(1): 5–24.

Dominey, J. (2012) 'A mixed market of probation services: can lessons from the recent past shape the near future?' *Probation Journal*, 59(4): 339–54.

Downes, D. and Howard, M. (1996) 'Law and order futures'. *Criminal Justice Matters*, 26(1): 3–5.

Downes, D. (2001) 'The "macho" penal economy: mass incarceration in the United States – a European perspective'. *Punishment and Society*, 3(1): 61–80.

Fletcher, H. (2011) 'Top prison staff join private sector rivals'. *NAPO News* (226): 3. Retrieved from http://www.napo.org.uk/publications/napo_news.cfm (accessed 28 November 2013).

Fox, C. and Albertson, K. (2012) 'Is payment by results the most efficient way to address the challenges faced by the criminal justice sector?' *Probation Journal*, 59(40): 355–75.

Garland, D. (2000) 'The culture of high crime societies'. *British Journal of Criminology*, 40(3): 347–75.

Garland, D. (2001) *Culture of Control*. Oxford: Oxford University Press.

Harris, J. (2005) 'Globalisation, neo-liberal mangerialism in UK social work'. In I. Ferguson, M. Lavette and E. Whitemore (eds) *Globalisation, Global Justice and Social Work*. London: Routledge.

Hobbs, D. (2013) *Lush Life*. Oxford: Oxford University Press.

House of Commons (2012) Chris Grayling announcement of transforming rehabilitation. *Parliament UK TV Live*.

Jones, T. and Newburn, T. (2002) 'Policy convergence and crime control in the USA and UK'. *Criminal Justice*, 2(2): 173–203.

Jones, T. and Newburn, T. (2006) 'Three strikes and you're out: exploring symbol and substance in America and British crime control politics'. *British Journal of Criminology*, 46(5): 781–802.

Jones, T. and Newburn, T. (2007) *Policy Transfer and Criminal Justice*. Maidenhead: Open University Press.

Ledger, J. (2011) 'Jonathan Ledger writes'. *NAPO News* (228): 4. Retrieved from http://www.napo.org.uk/publications/napo_news.cfm (accessed 28 November 2013).

Lilly, J.R. and Deflem, M. (1996) 'Profit and penality: an analysis of the corrections-commercial complex'. *Crime and Delinquency*, 42(1): 3–20.

Lilly, J.R. and Knepper, P. (1992) 'An international perspective of corrections'. *Howard Journal*, 31(3): 174–91.

Ministry of Justice (2010) *Breaking the Cycle: Effective Punishment, Rehabilitation and Sentencing of Offenders*. London: MOJ.

Ministry of Justice (2012) *Punishment and Reform: Effective Probation Services*. London: MOJ.

Ministry of Justice (2013) *Transforming Rehabilitation: A Revolution in the Way We Manage Offenders*. London: MOJ.

Morris, T. and Morris, P. (1963) *Pentonville: A Sociological Study of a Prison*. London: Routledge & Kegan Paul.

Muncie, J. (2005) 'Globalisation of crime control: the case of youth and juvenile justice'. *Theoretical Criminology*, 9(1): 35–64.

NAPO News (2013) 'Justice not for sale: time for action'. *NAPO News* (248): 2–3. Retrieved from http://www.napo.org.uk/publications/napo_news.cfm (accessed 28 November 2013).

Nathan, S. (2003) 'Prison privatisation in the United Kingdom'. In A. Coyle, A. Campbell and R. Neufeld (eds) *Capitalist Punishment: Prison Privatisation and Human Rights*. London: Clarity Press.

Neate, R. (2013, 14 March) 'G4S profits tumble on Olympics failing'. *Guardian*.

Nellis, M. (2000) 'Law and order: the electronic monitoring of offenders'. In D.P. Dolowitz with R. Hume, M. Nellis and F. O'Neill (eds) *Policy Transfer and Social Policy*. Maidenhead: Open University Press.

Newburn, T. (2002) 'Atlantic crossings: policy transfer and crime control in USA and Britain'. *Punishment and Society*, 4(2): 165–94.

Pratt, J., Brown, D., Brown, M., Hallsworth, S. and Morrison, W. (eds) (2005) *The New Punitiveness: Trends, Theories, Perspectives*. Cullompton: Willan.

Prison Reform Trust (2011) Private Prisons – Way Forward or Costly Mistake? Retrieved from http://www.prisonreformtrust.org.uk/PressPolicy/News/vw/1/ItemID/124 (accessed 6 November 2012).

Prison Reform Trust (2012) Government Has Six Months to Overturn Prisoners' Voting Ban. Retrieved from http://www.prisonreformtrust.org.uk/ProjectsResearch/Citizenship/BarredfromVoting (accessed 20 January 2013).

Rose, R. (1991) 'What is lesson-drawing?' *Journal of Public Policy*, 11 (1): 3–30.

Rose, N. (2000) 'Government and control'. In D. Garland and R. Sparks (eds) *Criminology and Social Theory*. Oxford: Oxford University Press.

Savage, S. and Atkinson, R. (2011) 'Introduction: new Labour and Blairism'. In S. Savage and R. Atkinson (eds) *Public Policy Under Blair*. London: Macmillan.

Sodexo (2011) New Three Sector Consortium to Help Deliver Community Justice Services. Retrieved from http://www.cjp.org.uk/news/non-governmental-organisations/third-sector/new-three-sector-consortium-to-help-deliver-criminal-justice-services-21-06-2011/ (accessed November 2013).

Taylor, M. (2012, June 20) 'How G4S is securing your world'. *Guardian*.

Tonry, M. (2001) 'Symbol, substance and severity in western penal policies'. *Punishment and Society*, 3(4): 517–36.

Travis, A. (2005, October 7) 'Worst criminals will not get vote in jail despite European court ruling'. *Guardian*.

Travis, A. (2012, July 13) 'Serco wins first private probation contract'. *Guardian*.

Travis, A. (2013, July 12) 'G4s faces fraud investigation over tagging contracts'. *Guardian*.

Wacquant, L. (2001) 'The penalisation of poverty and the rise of neo-liberalism'. *European Journal on Criminal Policy and Research*, 9(4): 401–12.

Waterman, P. (2013) 'Lessons from part privatisation of London Community Payback'. *NAPO News* (248): 6. Retrieved from http://www.napo.org.uk/publications/napo_news. cfm (accessed 28 November 2013).

White, I. (2011) Prisoners' voting rights: House of Commons standard Note. London: House of Commons' Library. Retrieved from http://www.parliament.uk/documents/commons/lib/research/briefings/snpc-01764.pdf (accessed 20 February 2013).

Whitehead, T. (2011, 13 April) 'European court gives Cameron ultimatum on prisoner votes'. *Telegraph*.

Williams, Z. (2012, 20 June) 'Public sector outsourcing: finally, an unfairness we can do something about'. *Guardian*. Retrieved from http://www.guardian.co.uk/commentisfree/2012/jun/20/public-sector-outsourcing-fairness (accessed 10 June 2013).

Glossary of key terms

Bipartisan consensus This term indicates that there is a close agreement in some area of public policy between the main political parties. In criminology, the term tends to be used to describe aspects of the period prior to the mid to late 1970s; a period in which there was a generalised political consensus around issues of crime and punishment. With the gradual politicisation of law and order, this consensus was fractured and disappeared. However, some would argue that the period since the mid-1990s has seen the emergence of a new bipartisan consensus, this time around populist punitivism.

Bureaucracy *Bureaucracy* is the term given to a system of administration, frequently hierarchical governmental administration, staffed by officials (civil servants) and founded in division of labour (departments). Modern bureaucracies often contain a high degree of technical knowledge and specialisation, with the distribution of tasks and goals linked to the concept of official duty. The term is frequently connected to the work of Max Weber, who saw bureaucracy as the most efficient and appropriate administrative system for the modern nation state to pursue its organisational goals.

Globalisation Some argue that neoliberalism is the driving force behind *globalisation*: the creation of a global free market. The term is used to describe growing international economic, political, legal and cultural interconnectedness based on advances in technology and communications, and the removal of trade barriers underpinned by neoliberal economics and politics. It is overwhelmingly capitalist and commercial in nature and is linked to the *transnationalisation* of capitalism: capital mobility across the globe, and the burgeoning of international commerce and capital accumulation. It involves a massive increase in the international flow of information and information exchange, and has implications for crime, crime control and punishment. For criminologists, globalisation is closely associated with the spread of ideas, policies and practices in law and order across nation states, and the *internationalisation* of penal policy.

Governance *Governance* is a term from the political science and sociological literature that focuses on the systems of regulation and ordering (governing) of contemporary societies. Where this might once have focused on the agencies and institutions of the state, the term is now generally taken to refer to strategies of governing both within and beyond the state. Some argue that, with the spread of neoliberalism, new networks of *pluralized governance* have emerged in which the government 'operates at a distance' and provides regulation through performance management measures that are imposed upon non-state service providers.

Moral panic   *Moral panic* is the term used to describe a disproportionate social reaction to perceived individual or collective deviant or criminal activity. When such activity is discovered, the resultant public hysteria (moral panic) is harnessed by the media as a signifier of moral or social decline, and followed by calls from community leaders to man cultural and moral barricades. The initial reaction on the part of the media, police and politicians can often be identified as exaggerated, and the moral panic is quickly forgotten. However, when moral panic occurs during times of significant social change, particularly when society has not had time to adapt to such change, the hostile reaction becomes galvanised and can influence both policy and law.

Neoliberalism   This is a term from political science that focuses on an economic system based on a reassertion of the nineteenth-century liberal principles of the free market, namely a free movement of labour and capital, market competition and enterprise. Associated with the Thatcher and Reagan administrations of the 1980s and 1990s, it is a reversal of penal welfarism. The politics of neoliberalism is characterised by the passing of laws aiming to curtail the power of trade unions, reduce labour costs, deregulate finance, privatise welfare service provision, extend market competition and curb welfare benefits.

Outsourcing   This term refers to the payment of public money by the state for the delivery of services, which it has previously provided, to non-public institutions – private businesses, charities and not for profit organisations. This forms part of the *mixed economy of welfare* in which the state no longer holds the monopoly of welfare provision. See also *privatisation*.

Penal populism   The term (and its near neighbour *populist punitiveness*) refers to the rise of a new politics of crime from the early 1990s onwards. In particular, it refers to the growing politicisation of crime control and to the apparent increasing desire of politicians to defer to public opinion (or certain segments of public opinion) when making decisions on crime policy. Populist policy making has as its objective obtaining electoral advantage, rather than providing policy that is informed by evidence of effectiveness. Such populism has coincided with a growing 'punitiveness' (the creation of new criminal laws, a greater use of custody and longer prison sentences) in penal policy, captured in such phrases as 'prison works' and 'tough on crime'.

Penal welfarism   *Penal welfarism* refers to the field of crime control that dominated until the 1970s, and was based on a casual explanation of crime as a presenting symptom of social problems that a combination of a welfare state provision of basic social needs, and positivist treatment programmes aimed at rehabilitating the individual, could resolve. The penal welfare state refers to the complex of state institutions that operated within this framework of understanding (e.g. the police, courts, prisons and probation).

Penality   This term refers to ideas and philosophy about punishment, as well as to actual modes of penal practices.

Penology   *Penology* is the study of punishment that takes account of different modes of punishment. The *penal system* is the system that a state adopts to punish those who have been convicted of a criminal offence. In the UK, punishment is administered by public institutions (e.g. the probation and prison services), as well as a growing number of private organisations (e.g. Serco and G4S).

Political economy   This is a term taken from political science that focuses on the interdependence of economic and political institutions. It encompasses the ability of politics and markets to supply goods and services, and to solve social problems. Cavadino and Dignan (see Chapter 7) have devised a typology of political economies that links the underlying economic and political system to the model of the penal system adopted in a particular nation state. In their analysis, there are four ideal types: neoliberalism, social democratic corporatism, conservative corporatism and oriental corporatism. See also *neoliberalism*.

Privatisation   At its simplest, this is the shift of the ownership and control of penal services (e.g. prison escorts, prison building and management) from the public to the private sector. In practice, privatisation can cover a range of policies including civilisation, 'contracting out', the increasing use of sponsorship and private finance, and the establishment of public–private partnerships. The term is closely linked to the concept of *contestability,* whereby private and not for profits organisations are invited to compete with publicly owned organisations, such as the probation service, for the management and/ or provision of discrete aspects of service delivery, for example unpaid work, also known as Community Payback. Under the Coalition government, the austerity agenda has seen the expansion of privatisation with plans to *contract out* or *outsource* 70 per cent of probation service delivery. For critics of privatisation, the creation of a market in punishment that introduces the profit motive into the provision of services constitutes the *commodification of punishment*: the reduction of punishment to a commodity that can be purchased by the cheapest supplier.

Problematisation   This is the social process by which a behaviour or activity becomes defined as a problem that requires a public policy response. The concept differentiates between 'private troubles' – problems that stay within the private realm of the family – and troubles that become 'public issues' and enter the public realm. The degree to which a problem is perceived as a threat to social values or public order is a factor that triggers the process.

Responsibilisation   *Responsibilisation* is a term referring to a set of strategies adopted by governments in which the aim is to redistribute the crime control, crime prevention and management of crime risk activities beyond the state to the individual and the community. It is associated with terms such as *partnership, multi-agency* and *interagency cooperation, active citizenship* and *active communities.* In terms of direct work with offenders, it refers to remoralising and re-educating treatment modes that emphasise accepting responsibility for one's own criminal activities and the self-management of one's own crime risks.

Social change   Social change theory seeks to examine both how society is constructed and how it evolves. Each human society is reliant on a number of social institutions, ranging from basic institutions, such as family or kinship, through to highly complex institutions, such as religious, political or legal systems. Societies are seen to develop and change over time, becoming more complex and requiring more sophisticated means of administration and social control, a process known as 'differentiation'. Much modern sociology, particularly functionalist sociology, has concerned itself with the concept of social change as progress, and the tools that allow change to be instigated and crafted by way of social norm, social policy and legislation.

Social contract   The concept of the *social contract* is attributable to the works of the Enlightenment philosophers Hobbes (1588–1679), Locke (1632–1704) and Rousseau (1712–18), who sought to define the relationship between the emerging state and civil society. It is a term that refers to the invisible agreement entered into between the government and the public about social rights or entitlements and social obligations.

The social contract is not fixed; rather, it is historically contingent and the subject of renegotiations that reflect the political ideology of the government in power. With the development of the post-war welfare state, it encompassed social rights such as entitlements to welfare state service and provisions, for example out of work benefits and health and education. However, with New Labour's adoption of the citizenship agenda, the social contract was reconfigured: social entitlements became conditional on acceptable behaviour. Those who failed to meet their behavioural responsibilities to look for work were subject to benefit sanctions. In addition, individuals or families that displayed behaviour deemed to be anti-social were subject to new forms of regulation that blurred the boundaries between civil and criminal law.

Social control   When society undergoes a period of social change, or detects social problems, there is a perceived need for 'social control'. Social control theory examines what it is that makes individuals conform within society or rebel against it. The default position is that human nature itself is anti-social, and that it is the institutions within society, such as family, education and law, that provide impetus, opportunity and coercion for compliance. Our social lives in contemporary society are subject to a number of ever-increasing controls, both formal and informal.

Index

.